RV Camping in Corps of Engineers Parks

Guide to over 600 Corps-managed campgrounds
on nearly 200 lakes around the country

Published by:

Roundabout Publications
PO Box 19235
Lenexa, KS 66285

800-455-2207

www.TravelBooksUSA.com

Published by:

Roundabout Publications
PO Box 19235
Lenexa, KS 66285

Phone: 800-455-2207
Internet: www.TravelBooksUSA.com

Library of Congress Control Number: 2015939614

ISBN-10: 1-885464-60-6
ISBN-13: 978-1-885464-60-6

Contents

Introduction

Huge portions of public lands, managed by a variety of government agencies, are available to the general public for recreational use. The U.S. Army Corps of Engineers provides over 30 percent of the recreational opportunities found on these public lands. This book will guide you to more than 600 Corps-managed campgrounds around the country.

Guide For RVers

Included are only those projects and locations that have campgrounds with developed sites that are suitable for RVs. Walk-in or boat-in primitive camping areas that are not vehicle accessible are not included. Similarly excluded are areas that offer primitive sites for tent, pop-up camper or tiny trailer camping.

Project Listings

The U.S. Army Corps of Engineers projects are listed alphabetically by state – Alabama through Wisconsin. Each Corps of Engineers project area typically covers thousands of land and water acres and, in many cases, projects cross over state lines. Project listings may appear in both state sections or will be cross-referenced.

Each project's section begins with the name, address, phone number and managing district, followed by a general description of the size and/or scope of the project. Directions are provided to the project office and visitor center, if applicable. Visitors will find it helpful to stop at the office or visitor center to obtain maps and information on the recreational facilities at the project.

The *Activities* chart summarizes the major recreational opportunities at each project, but it is not all-inclusive. Types of recreation offered in and around Corps lakes are many and tend to vary from project to project, depending on locale, equipment, facilities and local needs. Also included in the text before campground listings will be general information about points of interest in the area and other unique features of the project.

Campground Listings

Corps-operated campgrounds at each project are listed in alphabetical order. Each listing includes the following features where available:

1) *Season*: The campground's season of operation.
2) *Total number and types of sites*: Types of sites include basic and developed. Basic sites provide a pad (gravel or paved) but no hookups. Developed sites include a pad, picnic table, lantern post, and usually electric and/or water hookups.
3) *Pull thrus*: Where available.
4) *Hookups*: Includes electric, water, and/or sewer.
5) *Non-reservable*: Where applicable, this indicates that some or all sites at the campground are available on a first-come, first-serve basis and cannot be reserved through recreation.gov. Note that many campgrounds also have non-reservable sites available off-season.
6) *Daily Fee*: Range of daily fee for an individual, single RV-occupancy site.
7) *Basic Amenities*: drinking water, dump station, restrooms, showers, laundry – listed where available. Other amenities and features will also be noted.
8) *RV length limit*: Rare. Most Corps of Engineers campgrounds can accommodate big rigs, although at some locations the number of big rig sites is limited.
9) *Directions*: Directions from a nearby town; generally the directions supplied by recreation.gov.
10) *Address*: Physical or street address of campground where available.
11) *Phone*: Direct line to the campground where available, or the direct line to the project office.

Camping Reservations

You can check availability and make reservations online anytime at www.recreation.gov or call toll free 1-877-444-6777 to check availability and to make reservations over the phone: Mar 31 to Oct 31, 10am to midnight EST and Nov 1 to Feb 28, 10am to 10pm EST. The Call Center is closed on Thanksgiving, Christmas and New Years Day.

More information about camping reservations can be found in Appendix B.

Alabama

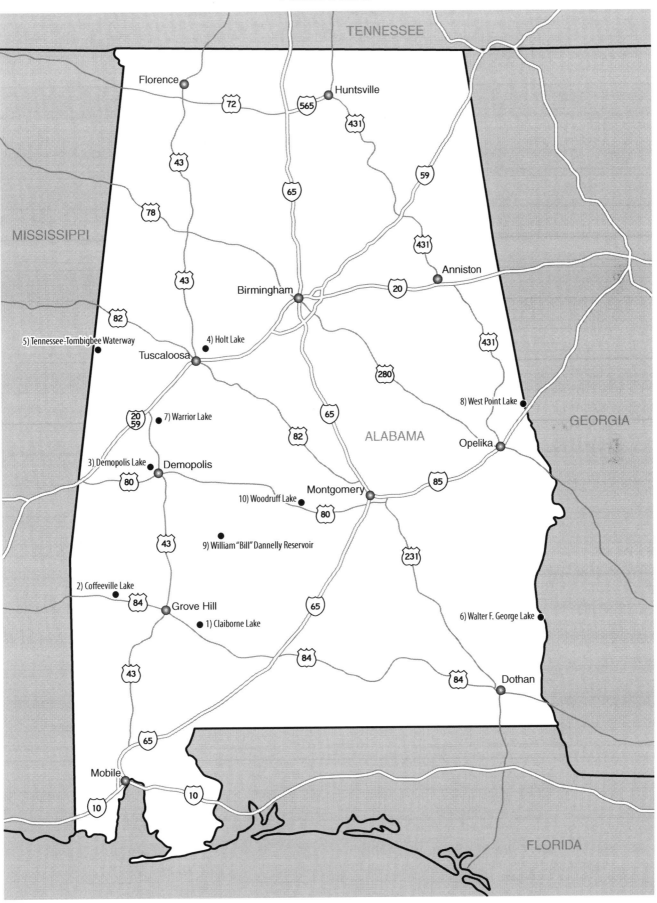

Activities

	Auto Touring	Biking	Boating	Climbing	Cultural/Historic Sites	Educational Programs	Fishing	Groceries/Supplies	Hiking	Horseback Riding	Hunting	Lodging	Off Highway Vehicles	Visitor Center
1) Claiborne Lake		♦	♦				♦	♦	♦		♦			
2) Coffeeville Lake			♦				♦				♦			
3) Demopolis Lake		♦	♦				♦	♦	♦		♦			♦
4) Holt Lake	♦	♦	♦		♦		♦	♦	♦		♦			
5) Tennessee-Tombigbee Waterway	♦	♦	♦		♦	♦	♦	♦	♦		♦			♦
6) Walter F. George Lake	♦		♦				♦		♦		♦	♦		♦
7) Warrior Lake			♦				♦		♦		♦			
8) West Point Lake			♦			♦	♦		♦		♦			♦
9) William "Bill" Dannelly Reservoir		♦	♦		♦		♦	♦	♦		♦			♦
10) Woodruff Lake		♦	♦				♦		♦		♦			♦

Alabama Projects

1) Claiborne Lake

U.S. Army Corps of Engineers
1226 Powerhouse Rd
Camden, AL 36726-9109
Phone: 334-682-4244
District: Mobile

Claiborne Lake is located north of Mobile in southwestern Alabama. From the junction of US-43 & US-84 in Grove Hill, go east on US-84 to SR-41, north to CR-17, west to the dam. Nestled in the state's southwest hill country, the lake encompasses over 60 miles of the Alabama River. The project includes 2,743 land acres, 5,850 water acres and 204 shoreline miles. Much of the lake's surrounding park land is being allowed to revert to its natural state, providing habitation for abundant wildlife. Claiborne is noted for being the most pristine of the Alabama River lakes. It has great appeal to sportsmen, bird-watchers and naturalists.

RV Camping

Isaac creek: All year, 47 sites with electric (50amp) and water hookups, $18–$20. **Amenities**: Dump station, restrooms, showers, laundry, playground, boat ramp, fishing pier, fish cleaning station and a convenience store nearby. **Directions**: From Monroeville, Alabama, travel 8 miles north on SR-41 to CR-17 west and follow signs. 5030 Lock and Dam Rd, Unit 4, Franklin, AL 36444 / 251-282-4254. **GPS**: 31.62222, -87.55028

2) Coffeeville Lake

U.S. Army Corps of Engineers
384 Resource Mgmt Dr
Demopolis, AL 36732
Phone: 334-289-3540
District: Mobile

Coffeeville Lake is located 60 miles south of Demopolis on US-84. It is the third largest lake in the Black Warrior-Tombigbee chain of lakes in western Alabama. It has a surface area of 8,800 acres and a length of 97 miles. The 4,000-acre Choctaw National Wildlife Refuge at Coffeeville Lake is managed by the U.S. Fish & Wildlife Service primarily for migratory waterfowl.

RV Camping

Service Park: All year, 32 sites with electric (50amp) & water hookups, some pull thrus, two tent-only sites $14, others $18–$20. All spacious campsites are near the water. Campground gates close at 10pm. **Amenities**: Dump station, restrooms, showers, laundry, boat ramp, fishing, playground. **Directions**: From Coffeeville, Alabama, 4 miles west on US-84 to the campground. 451 Service Park Rd, Silas, AL 36919 / 251-754-9338. **GPS**: 31.745, -88.14306

3) Demopolis Lake

U.S. Army Corps of Engineers
384 Resource Mgmt Dr
Demopolis, AL 36732
Phone: 334-289-3540
District: Mobile

Demopolis is the largest of the Black Warrior-Tombigbee chain of six lakes. Located at the confluence of the two rivers, Demopolis Lake covers 10,000 acres and extends 48 miles upriver on the Black Warrior and 53 miles up the Tombigbee. The lake is situated 50 miles south of Tuscaloosa. From the town of Demopolis, take US-80 west for 2 miles to Lock & Dam Road to the Black Warrior & Tombigbee Resource Center where maps and directions to various lake areas are available.

Fishing is the most popular activity on the lake. Whether by boat or along the banks, anglers will find bass, crappie, bream and catfish. Biking, hiking and wildlife viewing are popular activities at the two Corps-managed campgrounds. A highlight of the year at Demopolis Lake is the week-long "Christmas on the River" celebration featuring a night time parade on the river viewed by huge crowds from the white bluff above the Tombigbee River.

RV Camping

Forkland: All year, 42 sites with electric & water hookups, $18-$20. Campground gates close at 10pm. *Amenities*: Dump station, restrooms, showers, boat ramp, courtesy dock, laundry, playground, group shelter. *Directions*: From Demopolis, go 9 miles north on US-43, follow signs, turn left on the county road (unpaved) for one mile. 1365 Forkland Park Rd, Forkland, AL 36740 / 334-289-5530. *GPS*: 32.62222, -87.88056

Foscue Creek: All year, 48 full hookup sites, 5 sites with electric & water hookups, (50amp throughout), $22. Campground gates close at 10pm. *Amenities*: Dump station, restrooms, showers, laundry, boat ramp, courtesy dock. *Directions*: From Demopolis, go west for 3 miles on US-80; turn right, follow signs. Lock Dam Rd, Demopolis AL 36732 / 334-289-5535. *GPS*: 32.51556, -87.86944

4) Holt Lake

U.S. Army Corps of Engineers
Box 295
Peterson, AL 35478
Phone: 205-553-9373
District: Mobile

Holt Lake is 6 miles northeast of Tuscaloosa and just northwest of the town of Peterson. From Tuscaloosa, go 10 miles east on AL-216 to the Resource Office. The lake is a narrow, winding body of water that stretches for 18 miles and encompasses 3,200 surface acres. It is part of the Black Warrior-Tombigbee chain of lakes. Water skiing is a popular activity on the lake. There are two privately managed marinas.

RV Camping

Burchfield Branch: All year, 37 sites with electric (50amp) and water hookups, $18-$20. The campground is situated among the forested shores of the lake. Scenic foliage and wildlife viewing are excellent. *Amenities*: Dump station, restrooms, showers, laundry, boat ramp, fishing pier, swimming beach, group shelter. *Directions*: From Tuscaloosa take I-59 Exit 86 to CR-59 toward Brookwood. Right at the traffic light in Brookwood to Hwy-216, then left (NE) on to CR-59. Left at the stop sign on to Lock 17 Road. Turn left at Lock 17 Grocery and follow Lock 17 Road (approximately 23 miles from Brookwood). 15036 Bankhead Rd, Adger, AL 35006 / 205-497-9828 or 205-553-9373. *GPS*: 33.44778, -87.36583

Deerlick Creek: Mar-Nov, 40 sites with electric (50amp) & water hookups, some pull thrus, 6 tent sites, $14–$20. *Amenities*: Dump station, restrooms, showers, boat ramp, fishing pier, laundry, swimming beach, hiking and bicycle trails. *Directions*: From I-59 Exit 73, take Hwy-82 (McFarland Blvd) west for 4.2 miles then right on CR-30 (Rice Mine Rd) for 3.4 miles. Right at the stop sign to CR-42 (Lake Nicol Rd) for 3.4 miles to CR-89 (Deerlick Rd) Right for 3.2 miles. 12421 Deerlick Rd, Tuscaloosa, AL 35406 / 205-759-1591. *GPS*: 33.25944, -87.43028

5) Tennessee–Tombigbee Waterway

Tom Bevill Visitor Center
1382 Lock & Dam Rd
Pickensville, AL 35447
Phone: 205-373-8705
District: Mobile

The 234-mile long Tenn-Tom Waterway stretches through western Mississippi and, for a short distance, into Alabama. The 1820-1850 era antebellum-style Tom Bevill Visitor Center welcomes visitors to the Alabama portion of the waterway. From Tuscaloosa, go west on US-82 for 18 miles, turn left (southwest) on SR-86 for 24.4 miles, then left on SR-14 for .4 mile, then right on Lock & Dam Road. The U.S. Snagboat Montgomery (National Historical Landmark) is located at the Center.

RV CAMPING

Two Tenn-Tom recreation areas with RV camping are in Alabama (near the MS state line). Pickensville Campground at Aliceville Lake is just north of the Visitor Center and Cochrane Campground at Gainesville Lake is about 15 miles to the south. Swimming, playgrounds, multi-use courts and fish cleaning stations are available. Campground gates are open 6am-10pm.

Cochrane: All year, 60 shaded sites with electric and water hookups, some sites have sewer, some pull thrus, $16–$20. *Amenities*: Dump station, restrooms, showers, drinking water, laundry, boat ramp, fishing. *Directions*: From Pickensville, south on SR-14 to the town of Aliceville, then SR-17 south for 10 miles. Approximately 2 miles from the Huyck Bridge, turn right at the sign for Cochrane area and travel about 2 miles, entrance on left. 707 Tenntom Park Rd, Aliceville, AL 35442 / 205-373-8806. *GPS*: 33.0842, -88.2697

Pickensville: All year, 176 sites with electric (some 50amp) and water hookups, 29 sewer hookups, $16–$20. *Amenities*: Dump station, restrooms, showers, drinking water, laundry, boat ramp, fishing. *Directions*: From Tuscaloosa, take US-82 west to SR-86, turn left, travel west on SR-86 west to Pickensville. The entrance road to the campground is 2.5 miles from the yellow caution light. 61 Camping Rd, Carrollton, AL 35447 / 205-373-6328. *GPS*: 33.22639, -88.27667

6) Walter F. George Lake

U.S. Army Corps of Engineers
427 Eufala Rd
Ft. Gaines, GA 39851
Phone: 229-768-2516
District: Mobile

W.F. George Lake, sometimes referred to as Lake Eufala, extends 85 miles along the Chatahoochee River and borders Alabama and Georgia. From Fort Gaines, Georgia, take Hwy-39 north for 2 miles; the W.F. George Resource Building is on the left. With 640 miles of shoreline the lake has plenty of room for water-related activities. The project consists of 34,853 land acres and 45,181 water acres. Gracious antebellum mansions are located in nearby historic towns, including Eufala. Lakepoint State Park, 7 miles north of Eufala, has camping, cabin rentals and restaurants.

RV CAMPING

The quiet campgrounds are ideal for enjoying the natural beauty of the lake and the Chatahoochee River. Boating, swimming, fishing and wildlife viewing are popular activities. Campground gates are open 7am-10pm.

Bluff Creek: Mar-Dec, 71 sites with electric (50amp) and water hookups, some non-reservables, $22. *Amenities*: Dump station, restrooms, showers, laundry, boat ramp, fishing pier, playground. *Directions*: From Eufala, north on US-431, then right on SR-165 for 18 miles, follow signs. 144 Bluff Creek Rd, Pittsview, AL 36871 / 334-855-2746. *GPS*: 32.17972, -85.01333

Hardridge Creek: Mar-Nov, 74 sites (55 with electric & water hookups and 19 sites with full hookups), some pull thrus, some non-reservables, $22. *Amenities*: Dump station, restrooms, showers, laundry, swimming, boat ramp, fishing pier, playground. *Directions*: From Eufala, US-431 south, then east on SR-95, then left on CR-97, follow signs. 592 U.S. Government Rd, Abbeville, AL 36310 / 334-585-5945. *GPS*: 31.64056, -85.10222

White Oak Creek: All year, 130 sites with electric & water hookups, some non-reservables, $22. *Amenities*: Dump station, restrooms, showers, laundry, swimming, boat ramp, fish cleaning station, fishing pier, playground. *Directions*: From Eufala, US-431 south, then east on SR-95 for 2 miles, follow signs. 395 Hwy 95, Eufala, AL 36027 / 334-687-3101. *GPS*: 31.77612, -85.15416

7) Warrior Lake

U.S. Army Corps of Engineers
384 Resource Mgmt Dr
Demopolis, AL 36732
Phone: 334-289-3540
District: Mobile

Located on the Black Warrior River, just outside of Eutaw, Warrior Lake is 36 miles south of Tuscaloosa, Alabama. Activities include river fishing, swimming, hiking trails (difficult) and wildlife viewing.

Mound State Monument is located on the lake at mile 303.4. Forty Indian temple mounds rise from a bluff overlooking the Black Warrior. The area is maintained by the State of Alabama and features a village site, burial grounds and museum.

RV CAMPING

The Corps-managed campground, Jennings Ferry, is also known as Roebuck Landing.

Jennings Ferry: All year, 52 sites with electric (50amp) and water hookups, some pull thrus, $18-$20. Gates open at 6am and close at 10pm. *Amenities*: Dump station, showers, laundry, boat ramp, fish cleaning station, playground. *Directions*: From I-29/59 take Exit 40 (Eutaw/Aliceville, Hwy-14) toward Eutaw. Follow Hwy-14 for about 9 miles. 1001 Jennings Ferry Rd, Akron, AL 35441 / 205-372-1217. *GPS*: 32.84944, -87.72194

8) West Point Lake

U.S. Army Corps of Engineers
500 Resource Management Dr
West Point, GA 31833
Phone: 706–645–2937
District: Mobile

West Point Lake straddles the AL/GA border, just north of I-85. From I-85 Exit 2 in Georgia follow US-29 north 5 miles to the Visitor Center on the left. Information and maps are available. The project includes 32,282 land acres, 25,864 water acres and 539 shoreline miles. Surrounded by deep forests and rolling hills, West Point Lake extends along the Chattahoochee River. A wildlife management area of 10,000 acres is located at the upper end of the lake, providing a habitat for many kinds of game and non-game wildlife.

Fishing is the most popular activity at the lake. A dozen creeks and more than 40 square miles of lake provide plenty of good fishing spots. The lake abounds with bass, catfish, crappie and bream. Bank fishing is excellent at most locations. Personal watercraft and water safety courses are offered from February to September in the Visitor Center.

RV CAMPING

Three other West Point Lake campgrounds are listed in the Georgia section of this guide.

Amity: Mar-Sep, 93 sites with electric & water hookups, 3 tent only sites, $16–$22. Campground gates are open 7am-10pm. *Amenities*: Drinking water, dump station, restrooms, showers, laundry, boat ramp, basketball, tennis and volleyball courts, playground, hiking trails, wildlife viewing. *Directions*: From Lanett, Alabama, go 7 miles north on CR-212 and follow signs. 1001 Country Road 393, Lanett, AL 36863 / 334-499-2404. *GPS*: 32.97083, -85.22222

9) William "Bill" Dannelly Reservoir

Millers Ferry Resource Office
1226 Powerhouse Rd
Camden, AL 36726
Phone: 334-682-4244
District: Mobile

From I-65 Exit 128, take SR-10 west for 40 miles to Camden then Hwy-28 west 9 miles to the dam. Maps and directions to various camping and recreational areas are available at the Resource Office. Bisecting Alabama's Black Prairie Belt, the William "Bill" Dannelly Reservoir includes 105 miles of the Alabama River, a reservoir of 27 square miles and a shoreline of more than 500 miles. Boating, fishing, hunting and hiking are the most popular activities. Numerous fishing tournaments are held during the year. Annual festivals and Civil War enactments are also held in the area.

RV CAMPING

In addition to the three Corps-managed areas, camping is also available at Roland Cooper State Park.

Chilatchee Creek: All year, 33 sites with electric & water hookups, drinking water, $18–$20. *Amenities*: Dump station, restrooms, showers, laundry, boat ramp, courtesy dock. *Directions*: From Alberta (west of the reservoir) CR-29 southeast for 11 miles. Turn left on Chilatchee Creek Rd for 2 miles. 2267 Chilatchee Creek Rd, Alberta, AL 36720 / 334-573-2562. *GPS*: 32.14139, -87.27417

Millers Ferry: All year, 42 sites with electric and water hookups, 9 basic, one pull thru, $18–$20. *Amenities*: Dump station, drinking water, restrooms, showers, laundry, boat ramp, swimming beach, playground, fishing dock and fish cleaning station. *Directions*: From Camden (south of the reservoir) 12 miles northwest on SR-28. Turn right before the Lee Long Bridge, follow signs. 111 East Bank Park, Camden, AL 36726 / 334-682-4191. *GPS*: 32.11583, -87.38972

Six Mile Creek: All year, 31 sites with electric (50amp) & water hookups (most waterfront), $18–$20. *Amenities*: Dump station, restrooms, showers, laundry, boat ramp, courtesy dock, multi-purpose courts. *Directions*: From Selma (north of the reservoir) follow Hwy-41 south for 9 miles and turn right on CR-139, follow signs. 6485 County Rd 77, Selma, AL 36701 / 334-875-6228. *GPS*: 32.32417, -87.01583

10) Woodruff Lake

U.S. Army Corps of Engineers
8493 U.S. Hwy-80 West
Hayneville, AL 36040
Phone: 334-872-9554
District: Mobile

Woodruff Lake is just 30 miles west of Montgomery; the Project Office is located along US-80. The project includes 21,814 land acres, 12,300 water acres and 372 shoreline miles.

RV Camping

Gunter Hill: All year, 50 sites with electric (50amp) & water hookups, some non-reservable sites available, $18. Offers a peaceful setting of trees on the backwaters of the river. *Amenities*: Dump station, restrooms, showers, laundry, boat ramp, fishing, playground. Good bow hunting opportunities for whitetail deer. *Directions*: From I-65 Exit 167, go 9 miles west on SR–80, then 4 miles north on CR-7, follow signs. 561 Booth Rd, Montgomery, AL 36108 / 334-269-1053. *GPS*:32.36667, -86.46667

Prairie Creek: All year, 42 sites with electric (50amp) & water hookups, some non-reservable sites available, 4 tent-only sites, $16–$20. On the banks of the Alabama River beneath moss-draped oaks. Many sites are waterfront. *Amenities*: Drinking water, dump station, restrooms, showers, laundry, boat ramp, fishing, playground, swimming, canoeing and water skiing. *Directions*: From Montgomery, west on US-80 for 25 miles, then 5 miles north on CR-23, and 3 miles west on CR-40, follow signs. From Selma follow US-80 east for 25 miles then left on CR-23, follow signs. 582 Prairie Creek Rd, Lowndesboro, AL 36752 / 334-418-4919. *GPS*: 32.3375, -86.76944

Arkansas

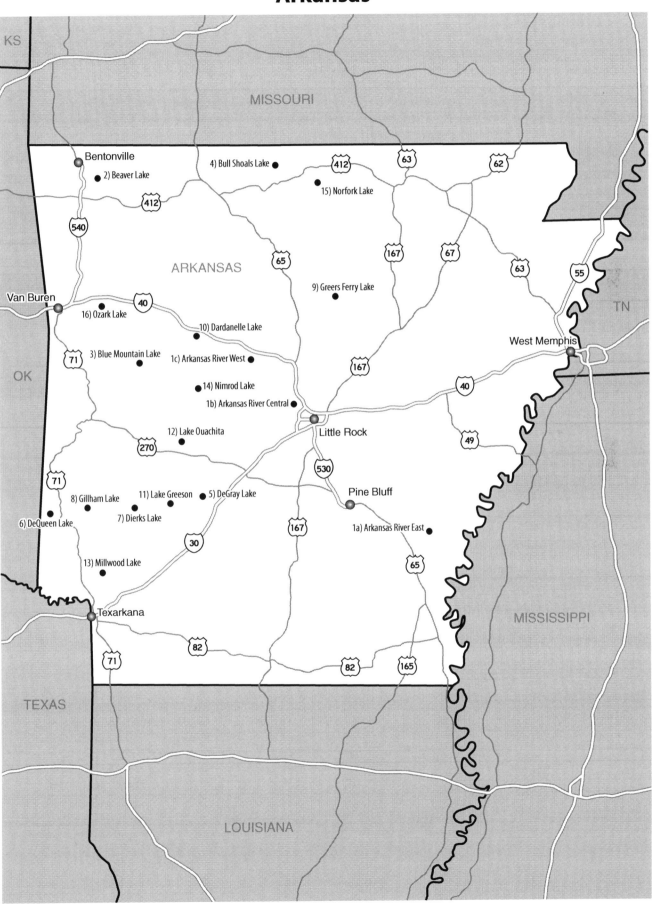

Activities

	Auto Touring	Biking	Boating	Climbing	Cultural / Historic Sites	Educational Programs	Fishing	Groceries / Supplies	Hiking	Horseback Riding	Hunting	Lodging	Off Highway Vehicles	Visitor Center
1) Arkansas River	♦		♦				♦		♦					
2) Beaver Lake	♦		♦	♦	♦		♦	♦	♦		♦			♦
3) Blue Mountain Lake			♦				♦		♦		♦	♦		
4) Bull Shoals Lake			♦				♦		♦		♦			
5) Dardanelle Lake	♦	♦	♦	♦		♦	♦	♦	♦		♦	♦		♦
6) DeGray Lake	♦		♦		♦		♦		♦	♦	♦	♦		♦
7) DeQueen Lake	♦		♦				♦	♦	♦		♦			
8) Dierks Lake	♦		♦		♦		♦	♦	♦		♦			
9) Gillham Lake			♦				♦		♦		♦			
10) Greers Ferry Lake			♦				♦		♦		♦			♦
11) Lake Greeson		♦	♦		♦	♦	♦		♦		♦			
12) Lake Ouachita	♦		♦		♦		♦		♦	♦	♦	♦		
13) Millwood Lake			♦				♦		♦	♦	♦			
14) Nimrod Lake			♦		♦		♦	♦	♦		♦			
15) Norfork Lake			♦				♦	♦	♦		♦			♦
16) Ozark Lake			♦				♦		♦		♦			

Arkansas Projects

1) Arkansas River Camping Areas

 a) East (AR/MS state line to Pine Bluff)
 b) Central (near Little Rock)
 c) West (along I-40)

Project offices include:
Pine Bluff Project Office at 870-534-0451
Toad Suck Ferry Resource Office at 501-329-2986
Greers Ferry Office at 501-362-2416.
All campgrounds are within the Little Rock District.

The Arkansas River, the state's namesake, flows through Arkansas from Fort Smith southeast to where it meets the Mighty Mississippi at the eastern border of the state. It's easy to catch the big one when fishing in Arkansas. The entire stretch of the Arkansas River is popular among anglers seeking largemouth bass.

RV Camping

Camping areas along the river are listed below, east to west: five campgrounds are between the MS/AR line and Pine Bluff, three are near Little Rock and three are west of Little Rock (accessible from I-40).

1a) East (AR/MS state line to Pine Bluff)

Merrisach Lake: All year, 69 sites with electric (some 50amp) & water hookups and 6 basic, $16–$19. *Amenities*: Dump station, drinking water, restrooms, showers, boat ramp, fishing, hunting, 2-mile interpretive trail, playground. *Directions*: From DeWitt, Arkansas, south on US-165 for 8.1 miles, then east on SR-44 for 5.3 miles to Tichnor Blacktop Rd, 8.2 miles south to Merrisach Ln, follow signs. Near the Wilbur D. Mills Lock. PFO 35 Wild Goose Ln, Tichnor, AR 72166 / 870-548-2712. *GPS*: 34.03028, -91.26639

Notrebes Bend Park: Mar-Oct, 30 sites with electric (50amp) and water hookups, $19. *Amenities*: Dump station, restrooms, showers, laundry, boat ramp, fishing, bait shop, hunting. *Directions*: Located on the river. From DeWitt, Arkansas, south on US-165 for 8.1 miles, then east on SR-44 for 5.3 miles to Tichnor Blacktop Rd, 8.4 miles to W.D. Mills Rd, 7 miles to the campground on the east side of the dam. 870-548-2291. *GPS*: 33.98806, -91.30917

Pendleton Bend: All year, 31 sites with electric (some 50amp) & water hookups, $16–$19. *Amenities*: Dump station, restrooms, showers, boat ramp, fishing, hunting, playground. *Directions*: From Dumas, Arkansas, US-165 north 9 miles, then SR-212 east for 2 miles, follow signs. 870-534-0451. *GPS*:33.98694, -91.36083

Wilbur D. Mills: Mar-Oct, 21 sites with electric & water hookups, $16. *Amenities*: Dump station, restrooms, showers, boat ramp, fishing, hunting. *Directions*: Follow directions to Pendeleton (above) drive through & continue 2 miles to W.D. Mills. 870-534-0451. *GPS*: 33.97889, -91.30861

Rising Star: Mar-Oct, 25 sites with electric (50amp) and water hookups, $19. *Amenities*: Dump station, restrooms, showers, boat ramp, fishing, hunting, playground, wildlife viewing. *Directions*: From Pine Bluff, US-65 southeast for 7.8 miles to Linwood, then north 3.5 miles on Blankenship Rd. 870-534-0451. *GPS*: 34.16889, -91.73667

1b) Central (near Little Rock)

Maumelle: All year, 95 sites with electric (some 50amp) and water hookups, some pull thrus, $22–$26. *Amenities*: Dump station, restrooms, showers, dock, boat ramp, fishing, playground, group shelter, hiking on the Nuttail Trail. *Directions*: From I-430 Exit 9, northwest 4 miles on SR-10, then 4 miles north on Pinnacle Valley Rd, follow signs. 9009 Pinnacle, Little Rock, AR 72223 / 501-868-9477. *GPS*: 34.82944, -92.43194

Tar Camp: All year, 55 sites (39 with electric (some 50amp) and water hookups), $19. *Amenities*: Dump station, drinking water, restrooms, showers, boat ramp, hunting, playground, rock climbing wall, basketball courts, group shelter, nature trails. *Directions*: From I-530 Exit 20, to Redfield, Arkansas, junction US-65/SR-46, east to SR-46 to SR-365, north 1 block, then 4 miles east to campground, follow signs. (On the river at Pool 5 Lock & Dam.) 4600 River Rd, Redfield, AR 72132 / 501-397-5101. *GPS*: 34.44972, -92.1125

Willow Beach: All year, 23 sites with electric (50amp) and water hookups, some non-reservable, $19. *Amenities*: Dump station, restrooms, showers, dock, boat ramp, fishing, playground, ball field. *Directions*: From I-440 Exit 7, east on US-165 for 2.5 miles, then south for 3 miles on Colonel Maynard Rd, then west 1 mile on Blue Heron, follow signs. 11690 Willow Beach Park Dr, Scott, AR 72142 / 501-961-1332. *GPS*: 34.69917, -92.13722

1c) West (along I-40)

Cherokee: Mar-Oct, 33 sites with electric (some 50amp) & water hookups, all non-reservable, $18-$20. *Amenities*: Dump station, restrooms, showers, boat ramp, playground, ball field, shady sites. *Directions*: From I-40 Exit 108, Hwy-9 south to Hwy-64 to Morrilton, then .7 mile south on Cherokee Street, then .8 mile south on Quincy, follow signs. (At Lock & Dam #9.) 501-354-9155. *GPS*: 35.131439, -92.782459

Toad Suck Ferry: All year, 48 sites with electric (some 50amp) & water hookups, $18-$20. *Amenities*: Dump station, restrooms, showers, boat ramp, fishing, playground, group picnic shelter. Cadron Settlement, popular tourist attraction, is nearby. *Directions*: From I-40 Exit 129, go 7 miles west on SR-60, follow signs. 3298 State Hwy 60 West, Conway, AR 72032 / 501-759-2005. *GPS*: 35.07389, -92.54472

2) Beaver Lake

U.S. Army Corps of Engineers
2260 North 2nd St
Rogers, AR 72756
Phone: 479-636-1210
District: Little Rock

Nestled in the Ozark Mountains of northwest Arkansas, birthplace of the White River, the project covers 28,000 acres and has 487 miles of natural shoreline. From I-540, take the US-62/SR-102 exit east to the Project Office (listed above) where you can obtain maps and information on the recreational opportunities available, special events, craft fairs and fishing tournaments.

RV Camping

There are 11 Corps-managed camping areas, as well as Beaver State Park and several private campgrounds around the large lake.

Dam Site Lake Park: Apr-Oct, 48 sites with electric (50amp) hookups, some pull-thrus, non-reservable, $19. *Amenities*: Dump station, drinking water, restrooms, showers, dock, boat ramp, fishing, swimming, biking, playground, trails, volleyball. *Directions*: From Eureka Springs, 9 miles west on US-62, then 3 miles south on SR-187, follow signs. 479-253-5828. *GPS*: 36.4203, -93.85541

Dam Site River Park: Apr-Oct, 59 sites with electric (some 50amp) and water hookups, $18-$20. *Amenities*: Dump station, drinking water, restrooms, showers, boat ramp, fishing, swimming, scuba diving, canoeing, playground, trails. River rafting trips are available. Caves, museums and historic sites are nearby. *Directions*: From Eureka Springs, 9 miles west on US-62, then 2.5 miles south on Hwy-187. 479-253-9865. *GPS*: 36.42194, -93.84583

Hickory Creek: Apr-Oct, 61 sites with electric (50amp) hookups, $19. *Amenities*: Dump station, drinking water, restrooms, showers, boat ramp, fishing, swimming, scuba diving, water skiing, sightseeing, marina nearby. *Directions*: From I-540 exit at Hwy-264 for 4.5 miles, then right on Cow Face Rd, left on Hickory Creek Rd. Note: Do NOT exit from I-540 on Wagon Wheel Rd as there is an almost impossible turn to Hwy-71B. 12618 Hickory Creek Rd, Lowell, AR 72745 / 479-750-2943. *GPS*: 36.24278, -94.0375

Horseshoe Bend: Apr-Oct, 63 sites with electric hookups and 3 tent sites in the East loop; 125 sites with electric (some 50amp) hookups in the West loop, some pull thrus, $18-$20. *Amenities*: Dump station, drinking water, boat ramp, courtesy dock, fishing, water skiing, swimming, marina, nature trail. *Directions*: From Rogers, take the New Hope Rd/Hwy-94 East exit, then east for about 2 miles, continue across 71B/8th Street on New Hope Rd/Hwy-94 east for 4 miles. Turn left on Hwy-94 at junction of Hwy-94 spur & Hwy-94 east. Road dead ends at the park. 16165 E Hwy 94, Rogers, AR 72758 / 479-925-2561. *GPS*: 36.28667, -94.01944

Indian Creek: May-Sep, 33 sites with electric (some with water) hookups, non-reservables, $18. *Amenities*: Dump station, drinking water, restrooms, showers, boat ramp, playground, trails, volleyball. *Directions*: From Garfield, 3 miles east on Hwy-62, then right on Indian Creek Rd (CR-89) for 4 miles south. 479-656-3145. *GPS*: 36.41862, -93.8882

Lost Bridge North: Apr-Sep, 42 sites with electric hookups, $18. *Amenities*: Dump station, drinking water, restrooms, showers, boat ramp, marina, playground, swimming, water skiing, trails. *Directions*: From Rogers, Hwy-62 east for 13 miles to Garfield. Right on Hwy-127 for 6 miles, turn on 127 spur, then left on Marina Rd. Marina Rd, Garfield AR 72732 / 479-359-3312. *GPS*: 36.41083, -93.89333

Lost Bridge South: May-Sep, 36 sites with electric (some 50amp) hookups, non-reservables, $19–$20. *Amenities*: Dump station, drinking water, restrooms, showers, boat ramp, marina, swimming, playground, trails. *Directions*: From Garfield, Arkansas, turn off Hwy-62 and take Hwy-127 for 6 miles, follow signs. 12001 Buckhorn Circle, Garfield, AR 72732 / 479-359-3755. *GPS*: 36.39714, -93.90411

Prairie Creek: Apr-Oct, 112 sites with electric (some 50amp) hookups, $18–$25. Some seasonal sites. *Amenities*: Dump station, drinking water, restrooms, showers, laundry, boat ramp, fishing, marina, interpretive trail, swimming, water skiing, playground. *Directions*: From Rogers, turn east at the intersection of 2nd and Locust. Travel east on Hwy-12 for 4 miles, then left on North Park Rd. 9300 North Park Rd, Rogers, AR 72756 / 479-925-3957. *GPS*: 36.35472, -94.05056

Rocky Branch: Apr-Oct, 43 sites with electric hookups (some 50amp), non-reservable, $18. *Amenities*: Dump station, drinking water, restrooms, showers, boat ramp, dock, fishing, laundry, beach access, wildlife viewing. *Directions*: From Rogers, take SR-12 east 11 miles to SR-303 for 4.5 miles, turn left, follow signs (15 minutes from Rogers). 479-925-2526. *GPS*: 36.3343, -93.93357

Starkey: May-Sep, 23 shady sites with electric hookups (some full hookup), non-reservable, $21. *Amenities*: Dump station, drinking water, restrooms, showers, marina, beach access, boat ramp. *Directions*: From Eureka Springs, 2.5 miles on Hwy-62, then left on Hwy-187 for 4.2 miles. Turn right on Carroll County Rd 2176 (Mudel Road) for 4.3 miles. 479-253-5866. *GPS*: 36.39, -93.87693

War Eagle: May-Sep, 26 sites with electric hookups, non-reservable, $18. Campsites are not adjacent to the water. *Amenities*: Dump station, drinking water, restrooms, showers, boat ramp, fishing, playground, beach access. *Directions*: From Springdale, Arkansas, go 14 miles east on Hwy-412, left on Knob Hill Loop (CR-389), then take Washington CR-95 for 2.1 miles, entrance on left. 479-750-4722. *GPS*: 36.21842, -94.01591

3) Blue Mountain Lake

U.S. Army Corps of Engineers
Route 1 Box 173AA
Waveland, AR 72842
Phone: 479-947-2372
District: Little Rock

Blue Mountain Lake is 50 miles southeast of Fort Smith in west-central Arkansas. Located between two national forests, the area boasts of much natural beauty. From I-540 Exit 12, take US-71 south to SR-10 west to Booneville; continue for 17 miles to Waveland, then south on CR-309. The Blue Mountain project contains 14,119 land acres, 2,910 water acres and 50 shoreline miles.

RV CAMPING

Outlet Area: Mar-Oct, 26 sites with electric hookups, $16–$18. *Amenities*: Dump station, drinking water, restrooms, showers, boat ramp, playground, swimming, hiking, hunting, overlook area – beautiful scenery. *Directions*: From Booneville, Arkansas, take SR-10 for 7 miles east to Waveland, then south on Hwy-309 for 1 mile, then west on Waveland Park Rd, 1 mile to Blue Mountain Dam, follow signs. 479-947-2101. *GPS*: 35.10056, -93.6525

Waveland Park: Mar-Oct, 39 shaded sites with electric & water, non-reservables, $16–$18. *Amenities*: Dump station, restrooms, showers, boat ramp, fishing, hunting, off-road vehicle trails, playground. *Directions*: From Booneville, Arkansas, go 17 miles east on SR-10, then south on Hwy-309 for 1 mile, then west on Waveland Park Rd for 1 mile to Blue Mountain Dam, follow signs. 479-947-2102. *GPS*: 35.1075, -93.65806

4) Bull Shoals Lake

U.S. Army Corps of Engineers
324 West 7th St
Mountain Home, AR 72653
Phone: 870-425-2700
District: Little Rock

Bull Shoals Lake is located 135 miles north of Little Rock in north-central Arkansas. Take US-65 north to junction US-62, then 50 miles east to Flippin and 4 miles north to the lake. Maps and information can be obtained at the Project Office. Bull Shoals has 62,326 land acres, 45,440 water acres and 740 shoreline miles. Its extensive area straddles the states of Arkansas and Missouri. In the beautiful Ozark Mountains, the lake is known for its exceptional water quality and outstanding fisheries. Bull Shoals has hundreds of miles of lake arms and coves, perfect for boating, water sports, swimming and fishing. In autumn, foliage in the area is known as the Flaming Fall Revue.

RV Camping

Of the 10 Corps-managed campgrounds, 5 are in Arkansas and 5 in Missouri. They are included in their respective state sections. The public marinas have rental boats, supplies and guides for hire.

Highway 125: Apr-Oct, 39 sites with electric hookups, non-reservables, $20. *Amenities*: Dump station, drinking water, restrooms, showers, boat ramp, swimming, marina. *Directions*: From Yellville, Arkansas, take SR-14 for 14 miles northwest, then north on SR-125 for 13 miles, follow signs. 32 Marina Dr, Peel, AR 72668 / 870-436-5711. *GPS*: 36.48972, -92.77278

Lakeview: All year, 80 sites with electric (some 50amp) hookups, $18. *Amenities*: Dump station, drinking water, restrooms, showers, laundry, swimming, hiking trails, marina, general store, fuel available, 1.5-mile nature trail. *Directions*: From Mountain Home, Arkansas, SR-5 north for 6 miles to Midway, then west on SR-178 for 7 miles; north on Boat Dock Rd, follow signs. 450 Boat Dock Rd, Lakeview, AR 72642 / 870-431-8116. *GPS*: 36.37667, -92.54694

Lead Hill: Apr-Oct, 75 sites with electric (some 50amp) hookups, non-reservables, $18. *Amenities*: Dump station, drinking water, restrooms, showers, swimming area, marina, playground. *Directions*: From Lead Hill, Arkansas, go 4 miles north on SR-7, follow signs. 1500 West Shoreline, Diamond City, AR 72630 / 870-422-7555. *GPS*: 36.47472, 92.92194

Oakland Park: Apr-Oct, 29 sites with electric hookups, $18. *Amenities*: Dump station, drinking water, restrooms, showers, boat ramp, laundry, playground, swimming, marina. *Directions*: From Mountain Home, 14 miles north on SR-5, then 10 miles west on SR-202, follow signs. 9867 Oakland Rd, Oakland, AR 72661 / 870-431-5744. *GPS*: 36.44389, -9.63028

Tucker Hollow: Apr-Oct, 28 sites with electric (most 50amp) hookups, $20. *Amenities*: Dump station, drinking water, restrooms, showers, swimming, playground, boat ramp, marina, 35-foot RV length limit. *Directions*: From Lead Hill, Arkansas, 7 miles northwest on SR-14, then north on SR-281 for 3 miles. 23054 Hwy 281 N., Lead Hill, AR 72644 / 870-436-5622. *GPS*: 36.47611, -93.00694

5) Dardanelle Lake

U.S. Army Corps of Engineers
1598 Lock & Dam Rd
Russellville, AR 72802
Phone: 479-968-5008
District: Little Rock

Dardanelle Lake offers 34,300 acres of boating and fishing waters rimmed by 315 shoreline miles featuring choice picnic and camping areas. From I-40 Exit 81, go south on Hwy-7 for 5 miles to Lock and Dam Rd (Hwy-7 spur), then 3 miles west on the spur to the Project Office and Visitor Center.

The lake is in the Arkansas River Valley, a favorite wintering area for the American bald eagle. From late fall through early spring, eagle are often seen perched in large trees and on snags along the river as they hunt for their favorite prey – fish. There is excellent fishing and abundant wildlife viewing year-round.

Bream, crappie and largemouth bass are stocked in the lake providing excellent sport fishing. Dardanelle and Russellville State Parks are also at the lake.

RV CAMPING

A marina is located at Spadra. A mountain biking trail is at Old Post Campground and Bridge Rock Nature Trail is at Shoal Bay.

Old Post Road: All year, 37 sites with electric (50amp) & water hookups, prime sites are along the riverbank, $20. **Amenities**: Dump station, restrooms, showers, boat ramp, fishing, tennis/basketball courts, softball/soccer/football fields. **Directions**: Located in Russellville, from SR-7 go 1 mile on Lock & Dam Rd, follow signs. 1063 Lock and Dam Rd, Russellville, AR 72802 / 479-968-7962. **GPS**: 35.24722, -93.1625

Piney Bay: Mar-Oct, 67 sites with electric hookups, $16–$18. **Amenities**: Dump station, drinking water, restrooms, showers, boat ramp, fishing, amphitheater with educational programs, swimming, playground, group shelter. **Directions**: From London, Arkansas, go west on US-64 for 3 miles, then north for 3.5 miles on SR-359, follow signs. 189 Private Rd 2720, London, AR 72847 / 479-885-3029. **GPS**: 35.39944, -93.31444

River View: Mar-Oct, 8 sites with electric & water hookups and 10 basic sites, all non-reservable first-come first-serve, $16. **Amenities**: No dump station at this location but campers may use the dump across the river at Old Post Road. **Directions**: From Russellville, south on SR-7 across the outlet. Located west of SR-7 in Dardanelle on 2nd St, immediately below the dam. 1022 Dam Rd, Dardanelle, AR 72834 / 479-968-5008.

Shoal Bay: All year, 55 sites most have electric hookups, $18. **Amenities**: Dump station, drinking water, restrooms, showers, boat ramp, fishing, swimming, amphitheater, interpretive trails. **Directions**: From New Blaine, Arkansas, take SR-197 north for 2 miles, follow signs. Shoal Bay Rd, New Blaine, AR 72859 / 479-938-7335. **GPS**: 35.31, -93.43056

Spadra: All year, 23 sites with electric & water hookups, 5 tent sites, all non-reservable first-come first-serve, $16–$18. Caution, campground is in a high cliff area on bluffs overlooking the scenic Arkansas River. **Amenities**: Dump station, drinking water, restrooms, showers, 2 boat ramps, marina with restaurant. **Directions**: From junction US-64 in Clarksville, go 2 miles south through Jamestown on SR-103. 800 Marina Dr, Clarksville, AR 72830 / 479-754-6438.

6) DeGray Lake

U.S. Army Corps of Engineers
729 Channel Rd
Arkadelphia, AR 71923

Phone: 870-246-5501
District: Vicksburg

DeGray Lake is 8 miles west of Arkadelphia and 67 miles southwest of Little Rock. From I-30 Exit 78, take SR-7 north for 2 miles to the Visitor Center. With 13,800 water areas and 207 miles of shoreline, DeGray is a popular fishing destination. The lake is stocked with a variety of game fish and is a world-class striped bass fishery. Other popular activities at the lake include swimming, scuba diving and boating. On the Caddo River, the lake is noted for its geological formations.

RV CAMPING

There are 6 Corps-managed campgrounds at the lake. The nearby DeGray Lake State Park also has camping and varied amenities including a swimming pool, tennis, 18-hole golf course, equestrian trail, marina, restaurant and lodge.

Alpine Ridge: All year, 49 sites with electric (50amp) hookups, drinking water, $12–$18. **Amenities**: Dump station, restrooms, showers, boat ramp, fishing, playground, swimming. **Directions**: From I-30 Exit 73, take SR-8 west for 19 miles to Alpine, then right onto Fendley Rd for 8.5 miles. 870-246-5501. **GPS**: 34.25861, -93.22833

Arlie Moore: All year, 87 sites with electric (50amp) hookups, $12–$18. **Amenities**: Dump station, drinking water, restrooms, showers, playground, swimming, nature trail, amphitheater. **Directions**: From I-30 Exit 78, SR-7 north for 9 miles then left on Arlie Moore Rd, 2 miles. Located about midway of the lake. 870-246-5501. **GPS**: 34.27167, -93.20417

Caddo Drive: Mar-Oct, 72 sites with electric (some 50amp) hookups, $12. **Amenities**: Dump station, drinking water, restrooms, showers, laundry, playground, swimming, boat launch, fishing, trails, wildlife viewing. **Directions**: From I-30 Exit 78, SR-7 north for 6 miles, then left on to Edgewood Rd, 3 miles. 870-246-5501. **GPS**: 34.26111, -93.1875

Edgewood: All year, 49 sites with electric (50amp) hookups, some pull thrus, non-reservables, $12–$16. **Amenities**: Dump station, drinking water, restrooms, showers, laundry, playground, swimming, fishing. Closest to the state park and about 25 miles from Hot Springs National Park. **Directions**: From I-30 Exit 78, SR-7 for 6 miles, then left on Edgewood Rd, then 2 miles to campground. 870-246-5501. **GPS**: 34.25556, -93.185

Iron Mountain: All year, 69 sites with electric (50amp) hookups, non-reservables, $12–$16. **Amenities**: Dump station, drinking water, restrooms, showers, playground, boat ramp, fishing, horseback riding trails, hiking trails. **Directions**: From I-30 Exit 78, take SR-7 north 2.5 miles, then left on Skyline Drive for 2.5 miles across the lake, then right on Iron Mountain Rd. 870-246-5501. **GPS**: 34.22694, -93.121778

Shouse Ford: All year, 100 sites with electric (50amp) hookups, non-reservables, $12–$18. **Amenities**: Dump station, drinking water, restrooms, showers, boat ramp, fishing, swimming, playground, horseback riding tails. **Directions**: From I-30 Exit 78, SR-7 north to Bismarck, left on SR-84 for 9 miles west to Point Cedar, left on Shouse Ford Rd 4 miles. 870-246-5501. **GPS**: 34.28944, -93.26778

7) DeQueen Lake

U.S. Army Corps of Engineers
706 DeQueen Lake Rd
DeQueen, AR 71832
Phone: 870-584-4161
District: Little Rock

DeQueen Lake is located just 8 miles east of the OK/AR border. From the town of DeQueen, take US-71 north for 8 miles, then one-half mile west to the lake. The project has 7,112 land acres, 1,680 water acres and 32 shoreline miles. Sportsmen enjoy outstanding fishing and hunting opportunities at the project.

RV Camping

There are three Corps-managed campgrounds. Convenience stores for food, bait and tackle are located at Oak Grove and Pine Ridge.

Bellah Mine: All year, 25 sites with electric & some water hookups, some pull thrus, non-reservables, $13–$15. **Amenities**: Dump station, restrooms, showers, boat ramp, fishing, fish cleaning station, canoeing. **Directions**: From DeQueen, go 7 miles north on US-71 to Bellah Mine Rd, then west for 5 miles. 870-386-7511. **GPS**: 34.14444, -94.39639

Oak Grove: All year, 36 sites with electric & water hookups, some pull thrus, non-reservables, $13–$15. **Amenities**: Dump station, restrooms, showers, boat ramp, fishing, fish cleaning station, canoeing, swimming. **Directions**: From DeQueen, go 3 miles north on US-71, then 5.5 miles west on DeQueen Lake Rd, then .3 mile north, follow signs. 870-642-6111. **GPS**: 34.09667, -94.39444

Pine Ridge: All year, 45 sites (17 with electric & water hookups), 3 pull thrus, non-reservables, $9–$15. **Amenities**: Dump station, restrooms, showers, boat ramp, fishing, fish cleaning station. **Directions**: From DeQueen, go 3 miles north on US-71, then 5.5 miles west on DeQueen Lake Rd, then 1.5 miles west on County Rd 226, follow signs. 870-642-6111. **GPS**: 34.09734, -94.41530

8) Dierks Lake

U.S. Army Corps of Engineers
952 Lake Road
P.O. Box 8
Dierks, AR 71833
Phone: 870-286-2346
District: Little Rock

The 1,360-acre lake is 72 miles southwest of Hot Springs, north of Texarkana, east of DeQueen and 5 miles northwest of Dierks in southwest Arkansas. From Texarkana, travel 46 miles north on US-71, then 11 miles east on US-70. The project includes 4,139 land acres, 1,360 water acres and 33 shoreline miles.

The lake is known for bass and crappie fishing. Interesting places for day trips in the area are Hot Springs National Park and the Diamond Mine at Murfreesboro. Shopping and sightseeing are available in the area.

RV Camping

Three campgrounds are suitable for RV camping and have beautiful swimming beaches.

Blue Ridge: All year, 22 sites with electric and water hookups, all sites are non-reservable, $13. **Amenities**: Dump station, drinking water, restrooms, showers, boat ramp, swimming. **Directions**: From Dierks, travel 3 miles east on US-70, then 4 miles north on SR-278, then 2.6 miles west on county road, follow signs. 870-286-3214.

Horseshoe Bend: All year, 11 sites, with electric & water hookups, $13, all sites are non-reservable. **Amenities**: Dump station, restrooms, showers, swimming, playground, wooded area, bank fishing access. **Directions**: From Dierks, follow US-70 west for 3 miles to the paved access road.

Jefferson Ridge: Mar-Oct, 85 sites with electric & water hookups, $14–$16. Numerous waterfront sites. **Amenities**:

Dump station, restrooms, showers, beach access, boat ramp, canoeing, fishing, marina, playground. *Directions*: From Dierks travel 5 miles west on US-70, then 5 miles north on Green Chapel Rd, follow signs. 870-286-3214. 34.10722, -94.05056

9) Gillham Lake

U.S. Army Corps of Engineers
706 DeQueen Lake Rd
DeQueen, AR 71832
Phone: 870-584-4161
District: Little Rock

Gillham Lake is located six miles northeast of Gillham, Arkansas, and 15 miles north of DeQueen. From DeQueen go 15 miles north on US-71, then 5 miles east to the lake, which is located near the Oklahoma state line. The Gilliam project has 7,216 land acres, 1,370 water acres and 37 shoreline miles.

RV Camping

There are two RV camping areas at the project: Big Coon is on the lake and Cossatot Reefs is on the river, a wild and scenic stream that attracts adventurous recreationists. The two-mile Coon Creek Walking Trail wends through the rolling hills next to the lake.

Big Coon Creek: All year, 31 sites with electric (50amp) & water hookups, non-reservables, $13–$15. *Amenities*: Dump station, restrooms, showers, boat ramp, walking trail, swimming, fishing, fish cleaning station, playground, amphitheater. *Directions*: From Gillham, travel 6 miles northeast via county roads, follow signs. 870-385-7126. *GPS*: 34.17333, -94.32

Cossatot Reefs: All year, 26 sites with electric & water hookups, $13–$15. *Amenities*: Dump station, restrooms, showers, boat ramp, fish cleaning station, playground, amphitheater, swimming, water skiing, canoeing, interpretive nature trails. *Directions*: From Gillham, go six miles northeast via county road, close to the dam, follow signs. 870-386-7261. *GPS*: 34.20674, -94.23132

10) Greers Ferry Lake

U.S. Army Corps of Engineers
P.O. Box 1088
700 Heber Springs Rd N
Heber Springs, AR 72543
Phone: 501-362-2416
District: Little Rock

Greers Ferry Lake is 65 miles north of Little Rock, just three miles northeast of Heber Springs. From Little Rock, go 15 miles north on US-67/167, then 50 miles north on SR-5. The dam stands at the foot of Round Mountain in the Ozark Mountains. The Garner Visitor Center is on Hwy-25/5 just west of the dam and features an information desk, exhibit area and auditorium where visitors can view an audio-visual presentation. Call the Visitor Center at 501-362-9067 for hours and days of operation.

RV Camping

Eleven Corps-managed areas are available for RV camping. Some have marinas that provide rental services, food and supplies. The Josh Park Memorial Trail, a multi-purpose trail for jogging and biking, is near the Dam Site Campground. The Mountain Island National Nature Trail (moderately difficult) is located at the Sugar Loaf campground.

Choctaw: Apr-Nov, 91 sites with electric (some 50amp) & water, 55 basic sites, non-reservables, $17–$20. *Amenities*: Dump station, drinking water, restrooms, showers, boat ramp, swimming, playground, boat rentals, marina. *Directions*: From Clinton, AR, take US-65 south 5 miles to AR-330, then 3.5 miles east, follow signs. 3850 Highway 330 E, Clinton, AR 72031 / 501-745-8320. *GPS*: 35.53556, -92.38111

Cove Creek: Apr-Oct, 31 sites with electric hookups, 34 basic sites, all sites are non-reservable, $14–$19. *Amenities*: Dump station, drinking water, restrooms, showers, swimming, boat ramp. *Directions*: From Heber Springs, Arkansas, go 6.3 miles southwest on SR-25, then 3 miles northwest on SR-16, then 1.25 miles northeast on access road, follow signs. 734 Cove Creek Rd, Quitman, AR 72131 / 501-362-2416. *GPS*: 35.461981, -92.159779

Dam Site: Apr-Oct, 148 sites with electric, 104 basic sites, some pull thrus, $14–$22. *Amenities*: Dump station, drinking water, restrooms, showers, boat ramp, swimming, playground, marina. *Directions*: From Heber Springs go 3 miles north on SR-25B, follow signs. 315 Heber Springs Rd N, Heber Springs, AR 72543 / 501-362-2416. *GPS*: 35.52194, -91.9975

Devils Fork: Apr-Nov, 55 sites with electric hookups, non-reservables, $17–$20. *Amenities*: Dump station, drinking water, restrooms, showers, boat ramp, swimming, playground. *Directions*: From Greers Ferry, Arkansas, go north on SR-16 for .25 miles, follow signs. 73 Devils Fork Rd, Greers Ferry, AR 72067 / 501-825-8618. *GPS*: 35.58806, -92.18528

Heber Springs: Apr-Oct, 101 sites with electric (some 50amp), 36 basic sites, $14–$20. *Amenities*: Dump station, drinking water, restrooms, showers, boat ramp, swimming, playground, convenience store, marina. *Directions*: From Heber Springs, go 2 miles west on SR-110, then .5 miles north on paved access road, follow signs. 89 Park Rd, Heber Springs, AR 72543 / 501-250-0485. *GPS*: 35.50389, -92.06639

Hill Creek: Apr-Sep, 30 sites with electric hookups, 10 basic sites, $14–$17. *Amenities*: Dump station, drinking water, restrooms, showers, swimming, boat ramp. *Directions*: From Drasco, Arkansas, take SR-92 west for 12 miles, then SR-225 northwest for 3 miles. Then south 2 miles on paved access road, follow signs. 474 Hill Creek Rd, Edgemont, AR 72044 / 870-948-2419. *GPS*: 35.61083, -92.14917

John F. Kennedy: All year, 61 sites with electric hookups and 13 sites with electric & water, non-reservables, $17–$20. *Amenities*: Dump station, drinking water, restrooms, showers, boat ramp, fishing dock, playground, good wildlife viewing. *Directions*: Located below the dam on Little Red River trout stream. From Heber Springs, go north on SR-25 for 4 miles, cross dam, turn right at second road, follow signs. 375 Hatchery Rd, Heber Springs, AR 72543 / 501-250-0481. *GPS*: 35.51594, -91.99647

Narrows: Apr-Oct, 59 sites with electric hookups, non-reservables, $14–$19. *Amenities*: Dump station, drinking water, restrooms, showers, boat ramp, marina. *Directions*: From Greers Ferry take SR-16 southwest for 2.5 miles, follow signs. 7699 Edgemont Rd, Greers Ferry, AR 72067 / 501-825-7602. *GPS*: 35.56389, -92.19806

Old Highway 25: Apr-Oct, 84 sites with electric, 36 basic sites, $14–$19. *Amenities*: Dump station, drinking water, restrooms, showers, boat ramp, swimming. *Directions*: From Heber Springs, go 6.25 miles north on SR-25, then west on SR-258 for 3 miles, follow signs. 1500 Old Hwy 25, Tumbling Shoals, AR 72581 / 501-250-0483. *GPS*: 35.53417, -92.02194

Shiloh: Apr-Nov, 60 sites with electric, 56 basic sites, $14–$19. *Amenities*: Dump station, drinking water, restrooms, showers, boat ramp, swimming, playground, marina. *Directions*: From Greers Ferry, go 3.5 miles southeast on SR-110, follow signs. 1350 Shiloh Rd, Greers Ferry, AR 72067 / 501-825-8619. *GPS*: 35.5375, 92.14583

Sugar Loaf: Apr-Nov, 57 sites with electric, 37 basic sites, $14–$19. *Amenities*: Dump station, drinking water, restrooms, showers, boat ramp, marina, playground, swimming, interpretive trails. *Directions*: Sugar Loaf is 12 miles northeast of Bee Branch on SR-92, then 1.5 miles west on SR-337. 1389

Resort Rd, Higden, AR 72067 / 501-654-2267. *GPS*: 35.54583, -92.27222

11) Lake Greeson / Narrows Dam

U.S. Army Corps of Engineers
155 Dynamite Hill Rd
Murfreesboro, AR 71958
Phone: 870-285-2151
District: Vicksburg

Lake Greeson on the Little Missouri River is located 69 miles northeast of Texarkana and 6 miles north of Murfreesboro. The project encompasses 8,799 land acres, 7,260 water acres and 134 shoreline miles. From I-30 Exit 46, go north on SR-19 for 30 miles to Murfreesboro, then 6 miles north on SR-27.

A nature trail allows visitors to reach the site of a cinnabar mine. A 31 mile long motor bike trail and the Chimney Rock geological formation are located at Lake Greeson. The lake is a wintering site for American bald eagles.

RV CAMPING

Cowhide Cove: May-Sep, 50 sites with electric hookups, non-reservables, $13–$16. *Amenities*: Dump station, drinking water, restrooms, showers, boat ramp, fishing, hunting, playground, swimming, interpretive trails. *Directions*: From Murfreesboro, take SR-27 north for 9 miles to Cowhide Access Rd, west to the campground. 239 New Cowhide Cove Rd, Murfreesboro, AR 71958 / 870-285-2151. *GPS*: 34.17444, -93.66861

Dam Area: Mar-Oct, 24 sites (18 with electric hookups), all non-reservable, $13–$18. *Amenities*: Dump station, drinking water, restrooms, showers, boat ramp, swimming. *Directions*: From Murfreesboro, go north on SR-19 for 6 miles to the dam area. 145 Dynamite Hill Rd, Murfreesboro, AR 71958 / 870-285-2151.

Kirby Landing: May-Sep, 87 sites with electric (50amp) hookups (10 full hookup), non-reservables, $18, some pull thrus. The Bear Creek Cycle Trail, within the campground, is a draw for off-road vehicle enthusiasts. *Amenities*: Dump station, drinking water, restrooms, showers, boat ramp, fishing, hunting, playground, interpretive nature trails. *Directions*: From Murfreesboro, take SR-27 north for 15 miles, then west on US-70 for 3 miles to Kirby Landing access road, then south to the campground. 224 Kirby Landing Rd, Kirby, AR 71950 / 870-285-2151. *GPS*: 34.23167, -93.69361

Parker Creek: Mar-Oct, 60 sites most with electric hookups, non-reservables, $13–$16. *Amenities*: Dump station, drinking water, restrooms, showers, swimming, boat ramp, playground. *Directions*: From Murfreesboro, go north on SR-19 for 6 miles to Narrows Dam, cross the Little Missouri River and continue for 3 miles to the campground. 129 Parker Creek Rd, Murfreesboro, AR 71958 / 870-285-2151. *GPS*: 34.14167, -93.74583

Self Creek: Mar-Oct, 76 sites (41 with electric hookups), all non-reservable first-come first-serve, $18. *Amenities*: Dump station, drinking water, restrooms, showers, playground, boat ramp, swimming. *Directions*: From Murfreesboro, take SR-27 north for 15 miles to Kirby, then west on US-70 for 6 miles to the campground. 4206 Highway 70 West, Daisy, AR 71950 / 870-285-2151.

12) Lake Ouachita

Lake Ouachita Field Office
1201 Blakely Dam Rd
Royal, AR 71968
Phone: 501-767-2101
District: Vicksburg

Lake Ouachita, the largest man-made lake in the state, is located 67 miles southwest of Little Rock. From Hot Springs, go 13 miles west on US-270, then north on SR-277. The lake's crystal-clear waters make it a popular site for scuba diving. The project includes 66,324 total acres of land and water. There are 975 miles of shoreline, ideal for fishing and water sports, and 20,000 acres of public land open for hunting in season. World class striper fishing is a popular activity.

There is a boating trail for viewing geological formations on the shoreline. Several marinas at the lake offer boat rentals and other services and supplies. Other activities nearby include horseback riding, sightseeing, miniature golf and numerous local shops and restaurants. Lake Ouachita State Park has a modern campground.

RV Camping

Corps-managed RV camping areas are all on the south side of the lake, north of US-270 between Hot Springs and Mount Ida.

Brady Mountain: May-Sep, 57 sites with electric (some 50amp), 17 tent only sites, non-reservables, $10–$18. *Amenities*: Dump station, drinking water, restrooms, showers, boat ramp, fishing, fish cleaning stations, swimming, playground, hiking trail, equestrian trails, amphitheater. *Directions*: From Hot Springs, 13 miles west on US-270, then 6.1 miles north on Brady Mountain Rd. 132 Brady Mountain Overlook, Royal, AR 71968 / 501-760-1146. *GPS*: 34.58806, -93.26472

Crystal Springs: May-Sep, 52 sites with electric (most 50amp) & water hookups, 11 tent sites, $10–$18. *Amenities*: Dump station, drinking water, restrooms, showers, boat ramp, swimming, playground, marina. *Directions*: From Hot Springs, 16.8 miles west on US-270, then 1.5 miles north on Crystal Springs Rd. 501-767-2108. *GPS*: 34.54694, -93.36111

Denby Point: May-Sep, 58 sites with electric (some 50amp), 3 tent sites, non-reservables, $14–$18. *Amenities*: Dump station, drinking water, restrooms, showers, boat ramp, amphitheater, swimming, interpretive trail, fish cleaning station. *Directions*: From Mount Ida, 9.5 miles east on US-270, then .3 mile north on Denby Rd. 501-767-2108. *GPS*: 34.55194, -93.49333

Joplin: May-Sep, 36 sites with electric hookups, 2 tent only sites, non-reservables, $10–$16. *Amenities*: Dump station, drinking water, restrooms, showers, boat ramp, swimming, horse trails nearby. *Directions*: From Hot Springs, approximately 24 miles west on US-270, then north on Mountain Harbor Rd. 303 Camp Road Rd, Ida, AR 71957 / 501-767-2108 or 870-867-4472. *GPS*: 34.57528, -93.44028

Little Fir: All year, 29 sites with electric, all non-reservable, some pull thrus, $12–$14. *Amenities*: Dump station, drinking water, restrooms, boat ramp, fish cleaning station, marina, group camping. *Directions*: From junction SR-27, through Rubie, 3 miles east on SR-188, then 2.2 miles north. Follow signs. 501-767-2108.

Tompkins Bend: May-Sep, 15 sites with electric (50amp) & water hookups and 58 sites with electric only, 13 tent sites, non-reservables, $18–$20. *Amenities*: Dump station, drinking water, restrooms, showers, boat ramp, marina. *Directions*: From Mount Ida, 10.7 miles east on US-270, then 2.1 miles north on Tompkins Bend Rd. 501-767-2108 or 870-867-4476. *GPS*: 34.57306, -93.46889

13) Millwood Lake

U.S. Army Corps of Engineers
1528 Highway 32 East
Ashdown, AR 71822
Phone: 870-898-3343
District: Little Rock

Millwood is located in the southwest corner of Arkansas on the Little River. The project includes 112,147 land acres, 29,500 water acres and 87 shoreline miles. From Texarkana, travel 16 miles north on US-59/71 to Ashdown, then 9 miles east on SR-32.

Millwood Lake provides some of the best fishing in the country, and birders come to Millwood to view the more than 309 bird species that appear throughout the year.

RV Camping

Beards Bluff: All year, 25 paved sites with electric & water hookups, 3 full hookup sites, $10–$15, non-reservable. Located in a wooded area on the lake near the dam. *Amenities*: Dump station, restrooms, showers, boat ramp, bank fishing access, swimming, overlook. *Directions*: From Saratoga, Arkansas, take SR-32 for 3 miles south, follow signs. 870-388-9556.

Beards Lake: All year, 5 paved sites with electric & water hookups, non-reservable, $9–$13. *Amenities*: Dump station, restrooms, fishing dock, boat ramp, bank fishing access, short hiking trail with boardwalk. *Directions*: From Saratoga, Arkansas, take SR-32 for 4 miles south, below dam. 870-388-9556.

Cottonshed: All year, 46 paved shoreline sites with electric & water hookups, 3 tent sites, non-reservable, $13–$15. Campground is in a secluded wooded area. *Amenities*: Dump station, restrooms, hiking, 2 boat ramps, bank fishing access, fishing pier. *Directions*: From Mineral Springs travel 7 miles south on SR-355, follow signs. 870-898-3343.

Paraloma Landing: All year, 34 paved sites with electric & water hookups in a secluded wooded area, some pull thrus, non-reservable, $8–$11. *Amenities*: Dump station, restrooms, 2 boat ramps, bank fishing access, fish cleaning station, playground. *Directions*: Located on SR-234, 1.5 miles south of Paraloma. 870-898-3343.

14) Nimrod Lake

U.S. Army Corps of Engineers
3 Highway 7 South
Plainview, AR 72857
Phone: 479-272-4324
District: Little Rock

Nimrod Lake is located in the west-central part of the state. From Hot Springs, travel 40 miles north on SR-7, a National Scenic Byway. The project consists of 21,640 land acres, 3,550 water acres and 77 shoreline miles.

Nimrod is the oldest Corps lake in the state and has been popular for fishing and hunting since it was completed in 1942. Anglers will find crappie, largemouth bass, bream, catfish and white bass tugging on their hooks. Supplies are available at local stores and bait shops along the lake. Nearby places of interest include Petit Jean State Park, Mount Nebo State Park and Hot Springs National Park.

RV Camping

Five parks nestled along the north side of the lake provide modern camping facilities and an opportunity to relax amid the groves of tall, sweet-scented pines. Entrances to the parks are from SR-60 on the east and north sides of the lake. Three campgrounds are directly on the lake: Quarry Cove, County Line and Carter Cove. Sunlight Bay is on Wilson Slough, located just off the Fourche La Fave River upstream of the lake. River Road Campground is just downstream of the Nimrod Dam.

Boat ramps, fish cleaning stations and playgrounds are conveniently located at the campgrounds. Swimming is available at Carter Cove and County Line areas.

Carter Cove: Mar-Oct, 34 sites with electric (some 50amp) hookups, non-reservables, $16-$18. *Amenities*: Dump station, restrooms, showers, boat ramp, fishing, fish cleaning station, playground, swimming, trails, wildlife viewing. *Directions*: From Plainview, east 3 miles on SR-60 to access road, then 1 mile, follow signs. 479-272-4983. *GPS*: 34.96111, -93.23861

County Line: Mar-Oct, 20 sites with electric (some 50amp) & water hookups, non-reservables, $14-$16. *Amenities*: Dump station, restrooms, showers, boat ramp, fishing, fish cleaning station, playground, swimming, hiking. *Directions*: From Plainview, east 6 miles on SR-60 to access road, follow signs. 479-272-4945. *GPS*: 34.9633, -93.18806

Quarry Cove: Mar-Oct, 31 sites with electric (some 50amp) & water hookups, $16–$18. *Amenities*: Dump station, restrooms, showers, boat ramp, fishing, fish cleaning station, amphitheater, playground, swimming. *Directions*: From Ola, go 9 miles south on SR-7, then west on SR-60 for .5 mile to the access road. 479-272-4233. *GPS*: 34.95611, -93.16556

River Road: All year, 15 sites with electric (some 50amp) &

water hookups, 6 electric-only sites, non-reservables, $15–$18. **Amenities**: Dump station, drinking water, restrooms, showers, boat ramp, fishing, fish cleaning station, hiking, playground. **Directions**: From Ola, south on SR-7 for 9 miles to the access road. 479-272-4835. **GPS**: 34.95028, -93.15611

Sunlight Bay: All year, 28 sites with electric & water hookups, non-reservables, $14–$16. **Amenities**: Dump station, restrooms, showers, boat ramp, fishing, fish cleaning station, playground, hiking, swimming. **Directions**: From Plainview, go west on SR-28 for .25 mile to access road, then 2 miles south. 479-272-4234. **GPS**: 34.95472, -93.30389

15) Norfork Lake

U.S. Army Corps of Engineers
324 West 7th St
Mountain Home, AR 72653
Phone: 870-425-2700
District: Little Rock

Norfork Lake is just east of the Bull Shoals project and shares its Project Office. From Little Rock, go 135 miles north on US-65, then 50 miles east on US-62 to the Project Office where maps and information are available. Norfork consists of 32,195 land acres, 22,000 water acres and 380 shoreline miles.

Norfork provides both open breezy stretches for sailing and quiet secluded coves, which are ideal for water sports. Undeveloped shoreline allows for ample room to enjoy the hills and hollows. The Robinson Point National Recreation Trail and the Norfork section of the Ozark Trail enable nature observers and photographers to view the Ozark Mountains through the change of seasons.

RV CAMPING

The Corps operates 7 camping areas, several marinas provide boat rentals and related services.

Bidwell Point: May-Sep, 46 sites with electric hookups, 2 basic sites, $18–$19. **Amenities**: Dump station, drinking water, restrooms, showers, boat ramp, playground, swimming, hiking. **Directions**: From Mountain Home, Arkansas, go 9 miles east on US-412/62, then 2 miles north on SR-101. Cross the lake on the 101 bridge and take the first access road to the right, follow signs. 870-467-5375. **GPS**: 36.38611, -92.2375

Cranfield: Apr-Oct, 67 sites with electric (some 50amp)

hookups, $20. 35-foot RV length limit. **Amenities**: Dump station, drinking water, restrooms, showers, boat ramp, playground, canoeing, swimming. **Directions**: From Mountain Home, Arkansas, east 5 miles on US-412/62, then left on Cranfield Rd (CR-34) for 3 miles, follow signs. 870-492-4191. GPS: 36.40472, -92.32083

Dam-Quarry: May-Sep, 24 sites with electric (50amp) and water hookups and 44 electric-only sites, $18–$20. **Amenities**: Dump station, drinking water, restrooms, showers, fishing dock, marina, playground, hiking trails, swimming. **Directions**: From Mountain Home, go 14 miles south on SR-5 to Salesville, then left on SR-177 for 2 miles. The campground is located below Norfork Dam, follow signs. 870-499-7216. **GPS**: 36.25833, -92.24056

Gamaliel: May-Sep, 64 sites with electric hookups, $18-$19. 35-foot RV length limit. **Amenities**: Dump station, drinking water, restrooms, showers, boat ramp, marina, playground, swimming. **Directions**: From Mountain Home, go 9 miles east on Hwy-412/62, then 5 miles north on SR-101, then 3 miles southeast on CR-42, follow signs. 870-467-5680. **GPS**: 36.4211, -92.22222

Henderson Park: Apr-Sep, 38 sites with electric hookups, all non-reservable first-come first-serve, $14. Scenic lake views. 30-foot RV length limit. **Amenities**: Dump station, drinking water, restrooms, showers, boat ramp, marina, convenience store. **Directions**: From Mountain Home, go 10 miles east on US-412/62, cross the bridge, turn left at first access road, follow signs. 870-488-5282.

Panther Bay: Apr-Sep, 15 sites with electric hookups, 13 basic sites, all non-reservables, $9–$18. **Amenities**: Dump station, drinking water, restrooms, boat ramp, swimming, playground, marina. **Directions**: From SR-201 in Mountain Home, go east on US-62 for 8.6 miles, then 1 mile north on SR-101, turn right at the first access road, follow signs. 870-492-4544.

Robinson Point: Apr-Oct, 102 sites with electric (some 50amp) hookups, $18–$20. 35-foot RV length limit. **Amenities**: Dump station, drinking water, restrooms, showers, boat ramp, fishing, playground, swimming hiking trails. **Directions**: From Mountain Home, travel east 9 miles on US-412/62, turn right on CR-279 for 3 miles, follow signs. 870-492-6853. **GPS**: 36.35278, -92.23944

16) Ozark Lake

U.S. Army Corps of Engineers
6042 Lock & Dam Rd
Ozark, AR 72949
Phone: 479-667-2129
District: Little Rock

Ozark Lake extends 36 miles along the Arkansas River. The project covers 10,600 acres of water and 6,349 land acres. The shoreline of the lake varies from steep bluffs and tree-lined banks to open farmlands and level fields. The lock and dam is on the Arkansas River, 1 mile southeast of Ozark (just south of I-40). The project office is immediately below the dam.

Recreation facilities are located on the shorelines of Ozark and Hammerschmidt Lakes. Fishing is abundant from boats or riverbanks and boat ramps are conveniently located. The lake is stocked with striped sea bass and walleyed pike. Year round fishing is good for catfish, bream, crappie, white and largemouth bass. A hiking trail begins high atop the bluffs overlooking Ozark Lake and winds through the forest floor.

RV CAMPING

Aux Arc: All year, 60 sites with electric (some 50amp) & water hookups, $10–$20. *Amenities*: Dump station, drinking water, restrooms, showers, boat ramp, fishing, hunting, playground. *Directions*: From Ozark, Arkansas, take SR-23 south for 1.5 mile to SR-309. Turn left and follow signs. 1314 Aux Arc Rd, Ozark, AR 72949 / 479-968-5008. *GPS*: 35.46827, -93.82101

Clear Creek: Mar-Oct, 25 RV/tent sites with electric hookups and 11 basic sites, $10–$16. *Amenities*: Dump station, drinking water, restrooms, showers, boat ramp. *Directions*: From Alma, Arkansas, take SR-162 for 5.2 miles south, then left on the paved road for 3.6 miles, follow signs. 3610 Clear Creek Rd, Alma, AR 72921 / 479-632-4882. *GPS*: 35.43777, -94.16819

Springhill: All year, 33 sites with electric (some 50amp) & water hookups, 9 electric-only sites and 3 basic sites, $10–$20. *Amenities*: Dump station, drinking water, restrooms, showers, 2 boat ramps. *Directions*: From Barling, AR, go 1.5 miles north on SR-59 to Lock & Dam Rd in Fort Smith. 1700 Lock & Dam Rd, Barling, AR 72923 / 479-452-4598. *GPS*: 35.34173, -94.29634

Vine Prairie: All year, 1 full hookup site, 12 electric-only and 7 basic sites, non-reservable, $10-$18. *Amenities*: Dump station, drinking water, restrooms, showers, boat ramp. *Directions*: From Mulberry, Arkansas, go 1.7 miles south on SR-917. 543 Vine Prairie Rd, Mulberry, AR 72947 / 479-997-8122. *GPS*: 35.47674, -94.06159

California

Activities

	Auto Touring	Biking	Boating	Climbing	Cultural / Historic Sites	Educational Programs	Fishing	Groceries / Supplies	Hiking	Horseback Riding	Hunting	Lodging	Off Highway Vehicles	Visitor Center
1) Black Butte Lake		♦	♦			♦	♦	♦	♦	♦	♦			♦
2) Eastman Lake		♦	♦				♦	♦	♦	♦	♦			♦
3) Hensley Lake		♦	♦		♦	♦	♦		♦	♦	♦			♦
4) Kaweah Lake			♦			♦	♦	♦	♦					♦
5) Lake Mendocino		♦	♦			♦	♦	♦	♦		♦			♦
6) Lake Sonoma		♦	♦				♦		♦		♦			♦
7) Martis Creek Lake		♦				♦	♦							♦
8) New Hogan Lake		♦	♦		♦	♦	♦		♦			♦	♦	♦
9) Pine Flat Lake		♦	♦				♦	♦	♦			♦		♦
10) Success Lake			♦			♦	♦	♦	♦	♦	♦			♦

California Projects

1) Black Butte Lake

U.S. Army Corps of Engineers
19225 Newville Rd
Orland, CA 95963
Phone: 530-865-4781
District: Sacramento

Black Butte Lake is located in the scenic foothills of north-central California about 100 miles north of Sacramento and 60 miles south of Redding. From I-5, take the Orland/Hwy-32 exit and go west 8 miles via CR-200/Newville Road, follow signs. The Black Butte project includes 6,199 land acres, 2,718 water acres and 28 shoreline miles. The quiet lake, surrounded by beautiful, dark volcanic buttes, is best known for its warm-water fishing and is a popular destination for power boats and sailboats.

RV CAMPING

Two Corps-managed campgrounds operate at the lake. Summer campfire programs are featured in the centrally located amphitheater.

Buckhorn: All year, 93 sites, no hookups, some pull thrus, $18. **Amenities**: Drinking water, dump station, restrooms, showers, boat ramp, playground, fishing, fish cleaning stations, swimming, hiking, group camping. **Directions**: From I-5 take the Black Butte exit at Orland, then CR–200 (Newville Rd) west for 14 miles, turn left at the campground. 530-865-4781. **GPS**: 39.8121, -122.36684

Orland Buttes: Apr-Sep, 35 sites, no hookups, $18. Limited access to the lake due to steep cliffs. **Amenities**: Drinking water, dump station, restrooms, showers, boat ramp, fishing, hunting, interpretive trails, swimming, disk golf, hiking, group area. **Directions**: From I-5 Black Butte Lake exit at Orland, take CR-200 west for 6 miles, then left on CR-206 for 4 miles. 530-865-4781. **GPS**: 39.7722, -122.35285

2) Eastman Lake

U.S. Army Corps of Engineers
32175 Road 29
Raymond, CA 93653
Phone: 559-689-3255
District: Sacramento

Located 50 miles north of Fresno, Eastman Lake is 25 miles east of Chowchilla. The project encompasses 2,249 land acres, 1,070 water acres and 14 shoreline miles. From SR-99 at Chowchilla, follow Avenue 26 east to Road 29 and go north to the park entrance.

Tall grasses and scattered oak trees cover the rolling hills surrounding the lake. Wildlife is abundant. Eastman is a designated bass trophy lake, with fishing generally good throughout the year. Other popular activities include canoeing, swimming, water skiing and wildlife viewing.

RV CAMPING

Codorniz: All year, 65 sites with water hookups, 6 full hookup sites and 9 sites with electric (some 50amp) and water hookups, equestrian sites, some pull thrus, $20–$30. **Amenities**: Dump station, restrooms, showers, boat ramp, fishing, birding, hiking, hunting, horseback riding trails, amphitheater, group camping. **Directions**: From SR-99 at Chowchilla, go east on Avenue 26 then north on Road 29 and follow signs into the campground. 559-689-3612. GPS: 37.21583, -119.96861

3) Hensley Lake

U.S. Army Corps of Engineers
P.O. Box 85
Raymond, CA 93653
Phone: 559-673-5151
District: Sacramento

Hensley Lake is 17 miles northeast of Madera on CR-400. It is less than an hour's drive northeast of Fresno in the foothills of the Sierra Nevada en route to Yosemite National Park. The area that was once home to the Minok and Yokut Native Americans, now offers many outdoor recreation opportunities. Hensley consists of 1,860 land acres, 1,300 water acres and 22 shoreline miles. Game fish abound at the lake; anglers can keep two bass over 15 inches in length.

RV CAMPING

Hidden View: All year, 55 sites (19 with 50amp electric hookups), some pull thrus, $20–$30. Campsites are located within walking distance to the lake. **Amenities**: Drinking water, dump station, restrooms, showers, boat ramp, horseback riding trails, swimming, interpretive trails, playground, amphitheater. **Directions**: From SR-99 in Fresno, take SR-41 north for 21 miles to SR-145, then west 8.4 miles to Road 33, north 1.1 miles to Road 400; northeast 7 miles to Road 603, west 1 mile to Road 407; turn right for 1.7 miles to the park. 25207 Road 407 Raymond, Raymond, CA 93653 / 559-673-5151. **GPS**: 37.12472, -119.89722

4) Kaweah Lake

U.S. Army Corps of Engineers
34443 Sierra Dr
Lemon Cove, CA 93244
Phone: 559-597-2301
District: Sacramento

Kaweah Lake is located on the Kaweah River 10 miles from Sequoia National Park. From Visalia take Hwy-198 for 20 miles east to the park entrance. The project encompasses 2,006 land acres, 1,065 water acres and 22 shoreline miles. It is situated one hour southeast of Fresno.

There is both lake and stream fishing; trout are abundant during the winter. Access to the shoreline may vary month to month. Visitors may call ahead to check on conditions. The marina has camping supplies, tackle, boat rentals and fuel. Campers can enjoy bird-watching and wildflowers on interpretive trails.

RV CAMPING

Every year from May-July the campground may be closed due to flooding. Ranger programs are presented at the campground on Saturday evenings from May to September. In peak season, gates close at 10pm and off season at 9pm.

Horse Creek: All year, 76 sites including a few equestrian sites, no hookups, some pull thrus, $20. **Amenities**: Drinking water, dump station, restrooms, showers. **Directions**: From Visalia, California, take Hwy-198 for 20 miles east, follow signs to the campground. 559-597-2301. **GPS**: 36.39056, -118.95472

5) Lake Mendocino

U.S. Army Corps of Engineers
1160 Lake Mendocino Dr
Ukiah, CA 95482
Phone: 707-462-7581
Visitor Center: 707-485-8285
District: San Francisco

Lake Mendocino is located in the northern coast range of California, 3 miles northeast of Ukiah, where redwood forests meet the wine country. The project encompasses 3,550 land acres, 1,785 water acres and 15 shoreline miles. From Ukiah, travel 3 miles north on US-101, then exit on Lake Mendocino Dr. The Visitor Center, modeled after a Pomo round house, is operated jointly by the Corps of Engineers and the Coyote Valley Band of Pomo Indians; displays include information on the Pomo Indians, the Corps and Coyote Valley wildlife.

A hiking and horseback riding trail runs along the eastern shore of the lake and through the wildlife area. A hiking and bicycling trail follows the western shore of the lake. Wildlife viewing is excellent; bald eagles often winter on the east side of the lake. Fishing is a popular activity; the lake has an abundance of bass, stripers, crappie, bluegill and catfish.

RV Camping

Weekend programs are offered at campground amphitheaters.

Bushay: May-Sep, 126 sites, no hookups, 3 group areas, $25. **Amenities**: Drinking water, dump station, restrooms, showers, playground, horseback riding trails, fishing, hiking. biking. **Directions**: From Ukiah, go 5 miles north on US-101, then Hwy-20 east for 2.75 miles. Cross Russian River Bridge, turn left, continue 1 mile to the top of the hill. 707-462-7581 or 707-467-4200. **GPS**: 39.23389, -123.1525

Chekaka: May-Sep, 19 sites, no hookups, $20. **Amenities**: Drinking water, restrooms, horse trail, boat ramp, fishing, hiking, playground, 18-hole disc golf course in walking distance. **Directions**: From Hwy-101, 3 miles north of Ukiah, take the Lake Mendocino Drive exit, turn left at the North State Street traffic light and turn right (east) on Lake Mendocino Dr and follow signs. The campground is at the top of the hill, 2 miles from Hwy-101. 707-462-7581 or 707-467-4200. **GPS**: 39.20306, -123.18639

Kyen: Apr-Sep, 93 sites, no hookups, some pull thrus, $25. Walking distance to the lake, swim beach. **Amenities**: Drinking water, dump station, restrooms, showers, boat ramp, fishing, hiking, hunting, playground. **Directions**: From Ukiah, US-101 north 5 miles, then Hwy-20 east, right on Marina Dr. Continue past the north boat ramp to the campground entrance. 707-462-7581 or 707-467-4200. **GPS**: 39.23667, -123.17778

6) Lake Sonoma

U.S. Army Corps of Engineers
3333 Skaggs Springs Rd
Geyserville, CA 95441
Phone: 707-431-4590
District: San Francisco

Lake Sonoma is 2 hours north of San Francisco and 3 miles west of Geyserville. It is surrounded by world famous vineyards and land that is rich in history.

Take US-101 to Heraldsburg and exit at Dry Creek Road. Travel west for 11 miles to the park entrance and Visitor Center that features exhibits on the cultural and natural history of the Dry Creek Valley. A fish hatchery is located behind the Center. The lake extends westward for nine miles on Dry Creek and four miles on Warm Springs Creek. It has 2,637 water acres and 53 shoreline miles. 14,441 land acres are included at the Sonoma project.

The lake is surrounded by 40 miles of trails for use by hikers, mountain bikers and horseback riders. A detailed brochure on the trail system is available at the visitor center.

RV Camping

Liberty Glen Campground sits on a ridge with views of the Warm Springs arm of the lake, but the campground does not have access to the shoreline. It is the only camping area accessible by road. Campground gates close at 10pm.

Liberty Glen: All year, 97 sites, no hookups, $16. **Amenities**: Restrooms, showers, potable water. Dump station is currently closed until further notice. **Directions**: From US-101 in the town of Heraldsburg exit at Dry Creek Rd, go 11 miles west to the park boundary, continue west another 4 miles, follow signs. 3333 Skaggs Springs Rd, Geyserville, CA 95441 / 707-431-4533. **GPS**: 38.71361, -123.05639

7) Martis Creek Lake

U.S. Army Corps of Engineers
P.O. Box 6
Smartville, CA 95977
Phone: 530-587-8113 (Apr-Nov)
District: Sacramento

Martis Creek Lake is set in the Sierra Nevada Mountains near Lake Tahoe in northeastern California. It has 1,820 land acres, 71 water acres and 3 shoreline miles. From I-80 at Truckee, take the Central Truckee exit and turn south on SR-267 for 6 miles. The area provides unique opportunities to spot wildlife on a recurring basis and is a great place for bird watching.

Anglers will find a variety of trout in the lake. A catch-and-release program is in effect. No fishing is allowed in the streams above the lake. No motorized (gas or electric) boats are allowed.

RV Camping

Alpine Meadows: May-Oct, 25 sites, no hookups, pull thrus, all sites non-reservable, $18. 30-foot RV length limit. Peaceful off-the-beaten-path campground. Weekend evening campfire programs in season. Closed during winter months due to weather conditions. **Amenities**: Drinking water, restrooms, hiking, biking, canoeing, kayaking. **Directions**: From I-80 at Truckee, take the Central Truckee exit and turn south on to SR-267 southeast for six miles.

8) New Hogan Lake

U.S. Army Corps of Engineers
2713 Hogan Dam Rd
Valley Springs, CA 95252
Phone: 209-772-1343
District: Sacramento

Located an hour east of Stockton, New Hogan Lake is set against the foothills of the Sierra Nevada on the Calaveras River. The project includes 3,054 acres of land, 3,099 water acres and 50 miles on the shoreline. From Stockton, take SR-26 for 30 miles to Valley Springs. A mile before reaching town, turn right onto Hogan Dam Road and follow for 1.5 miles to the park entrance.

Water skiing is excellent along the entire 50-mile shoreline. The lake provides year-round fishing and fish cleaning facilities are available. Weekend camping is popular; early reservations are suggested. Campfire programs are featured on weekends in season. The south shore is a designated wildlife viewing area. Bald eagles may be viewed in the vicinity. Historic sites are nearby. A golf course is also nearby.

RV Camping

Acorn Camp East: All year, 128 sites, no hookups, some pull thrus, $16-$18. **Amenities**: Drinking water, dump station, restrooms, showers, boat ramp, fishing, hiking, horseback riding trails, Frisbee golf course. **Directions**: From Stockton, take Hwy-26 east for 30 miles, turn right on Hogan Dam Rd for 1 mile, follow signs. **GPS**: 38.17626, -120.79972

Oak Knoll: May-Sep, 47 sites, no hookups, some pull thrus, $14. **Amenities**: Drinking water, dump station, restrooms,

showers, boat ramp, fishing, group camping facility, horseback riding trails, hiking, interpretive programs. **Directions**: From Stockton, take Hwy-26 east for 30 miles, turn right on Hogan Dam Rd (one-half mile before Valley Springs), go 1 mile, follow signs. 209-772-1343. **GPS**: 38.18265, -120.80306

9) Pine Flat Lake

U.S. Army Corps of Engineers
P.O. Box 117
27295 Pine Flat Rd
Piedra, CA 93649
Phone: 559-787-2589
District: Sacramento

Pine Flat Lake, within the Sierra and Sequoia National Forests, is 35 miles east of Fresno. The lake, with 4,422 water acres and 67 shoreline miles, is surrounded by 8,668 land acres. From Fresno, take Belmont Avenue east (becomes Trimmer Springs Rd). The lake is about 3 miles past the town of Piedra on Trimmer Springs Rd. To get to the Park Headquarters and the dam, turn right on Pine Flat Rd from Trimmer Springs Rd in Piedra.

The last two spotted bass world records came out of Pine Flat Lake. Two marinas have boat and slip rentals and fuel. The Blue Oak Nature Trail is located at Island Park.

RV Camping

Camping is also available at Fresno County Parks and at RV parks and resorts around the lake.

Island Park: All year, 97 sites including 3 full hookup; 18 electric hookup (50amp) & 76 basic, drinking water, $20-$30. Some campsites may be closed due to high water levels; call the Corps office for information. **Amenities**: Dump station, restrooms, showers (fee), boat ramp, fishing, group camping area. **Directions**: From Fresno, travel east on Belmont Ave (turns into Timmer Springs Rd) and follow signs to Island Park recreation area, turn right and follow signs to the campground. GPS: 36.86464, -119.31573

Trimmer: All year, 10 sites overlooking the lake (5 are tent only), no hookups, one 40 ft site; others are 30 & 20 ft lengths, $20. **Amenities**: Restrooms, showers, boat ramp, boating, fishing, hiking, hunting, jet skiing, swimming. **Directions**: From Fresno, travel east on Hwy-180/Kings Canyon Highway, to the Clovis Ave exit. Turn right onto North Clovis Ave and then immediately turn left on East Belmont Ave. After about

13 miles the road veers left and becomes East Trimmer Springs Rd. Continue traveling for approximately 20 miles, the entrance to Trimmer Recreation Area is on the right. 559-787-2589. *GPS*: 369044, -119.29361.

10) Success Lake

U.S. Army Corps of Engineers
29330 Highway 190
Porterville, CA 93258
Phone: 559-784-0215
District: Sacramento

Success Lake is located 8 miles east of Porterville at the southern end of the Central Valley. From Porterville, travel 5 miles east on Hwy-190 to the Project Office. There are 3,016 land acres, 1,142 water acres and 11 shoreline miles in the project.

The lake provides good habitat for bass, crappie, bluegill and catfish. In spring and summer months, high water covers shoreline vegetation creating superb shoreline angling. Success Marina offers fishing and boating supplies, boat rentals and fuel. There is a golf course nearby.

RV CAMPING

Campfire programs are presented on Saturdays from Memorial Day to Labor Day.

Tule: All year, 103 sites (20 have 50amp electric hookups), some pull thrus, $20–$30. **Amenities**: Drinking water, dump station, restrooms, showers, boat ramp, fishing, playground, kayaking. **Directions**: From Hwy-99 at Tipton, take Hwy-190 east for 8 miles past Porterville and follow signs to the campground. 559-784-0215. **GPS**: 36.08028, -118.90222

Connecticut

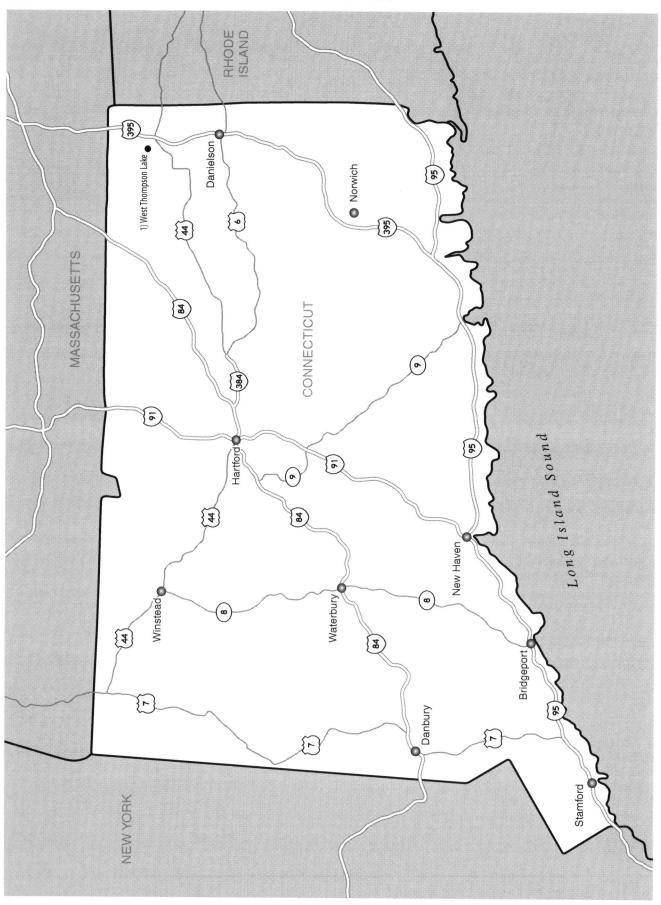

Activities

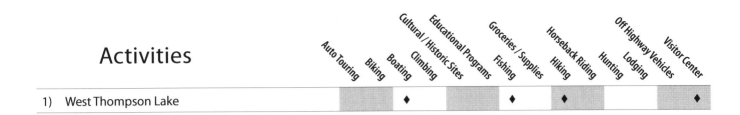

	Auto Touring	Biking	Boating	Climbing	Cultural / Historic Sites	Educational Programs	Fishing	Groceries / Supplies	Hiking	Horseback Riding	Hunting	Lodging	Off Highway Vehicles	Visitor Center
1) West Thompson Lake			♦				♦		♦					♦

Connecticut Projects

1) West Thompson Lake

U.S. Army Corps of Engineers
449 Readon St
Thompson, CT 06255
Phone: 860-923-2982
District: New England

The 200-acre lake, located in the northeast corner of the state, is popular with anglers of all ages. The West Thompson project encompasses 1,857 acres of natural resources where many wildlife viewing areas are available. From I-395 Exit 99, take SR-200 to SR-193, follow signs to the Visitor Center.

Swimming is available at a nearby state park and there is a convenience store in the area. There is an 18-hole golf course nearby.

RV Camping

West Thompson: May-Sep, 11 sites with electric hookups, 14 basic sites, $15–$30. The rustic campground offers wooded sites. **Amenities**: Drinking water, dump station, restrooms, showers, boat ramp, fishing, canoeing, playground, Frisbee golf, hiking, horseshoe pit, kayaking, basketball courts, amphitheater. **Directions**: From I-395 Exit 99, follow SR-200 to Thompson Center. Go 2 miles south on Rt-193. Cross Rt-12 at the traffic light. Turn right onto Reardon Rd. Travel one-half mile, turn left for .2 mile, then right. 860-923-3121. **GPS**: 41.945, -71.9

Florida

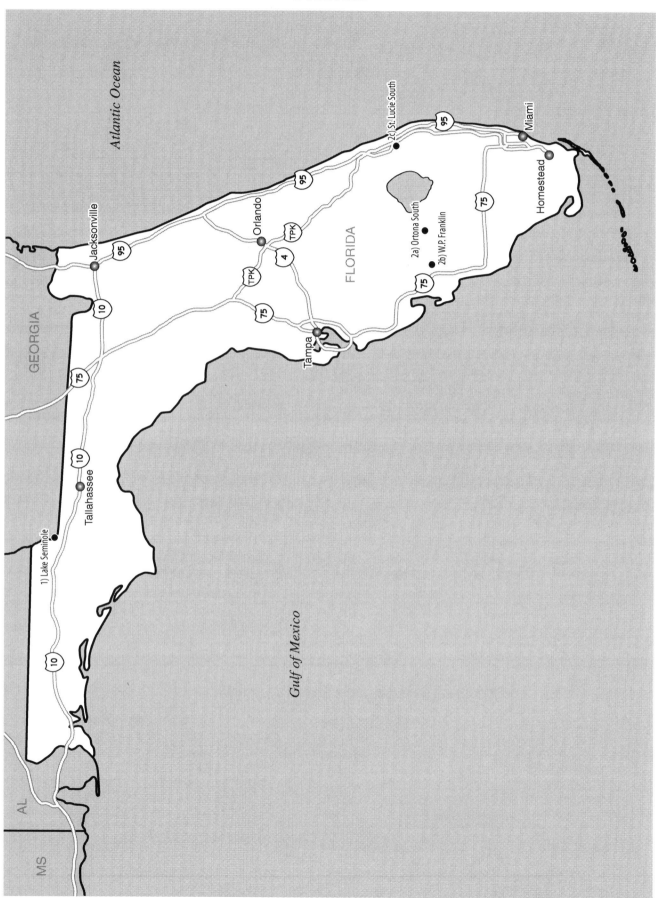

Activities

	Auto Touring	Biking	Boating	Climbing	Cultural/Historic Sites	Educational Programs	Fishing	Groceries/Supplies	Hiking	Horseback Riding	Hunting	Off Highway Vehicles	Lodging	Visitor Center
1) Lake Seminole			♦		♦		♦		♦				♦	♦
2) Okeechobee Waterway	♦		♦		♦		♦	♦	♦					♦

Florida Projects

1) Lake Seminole

U.S. Army Corps of Engineers
2382 Booster Club Road
P.O. Box 96
Chatahoochee, FL 32324
Phone: 229-662-2001
District: Mobile

Lake Seminole has 37,500 acres of water and over 18,000 acres of surrounding land. From Tallahassee, travel west on US-90 to Chatahoochee, then north on Decatur Street. Decatur becomes Booster Club Road. The dam and Visitor Center are on the left. Lake Seminole waters extend into Georgia. Historic Bainbridge, Georgia is nearby. The lake offers a variety of recreational opportunities; areas for wildlife viewing and bird-watching are abundant.

RV CAMPING

Eastbank: All year, 61 sites with electric (50amp) & water hookups, $22. *Amenities*: Drinking water, dump station, restrooms, showers, laundry, boat ramp with courtesy dock, biking, hiking, swimming, birding, water skiing. *Directions*: From I-10 Exit 166, north on Hwy-269, then left on US-90 to Bolivar St (Booster Club Rd). Turn right 1 mile, then left at East Bank Rd. 229-662-9273. *GPS*: 30.71806, -84.85111

Hales Landing: All year, 35 sites, with 50amp electric & water hookups, non-reservable, $18. *Amenities*: Drinking water, dump station, showers, boat ramp with courtesy dock, fishing. *Directions*: From US-84, southwest on SR-253 for 3.8 miles, then Ten Mile Still Rd 2 miles, follow signs. Located 12 miles south of Bainbridge, Georgia. 229-662-2001.

River Junction: All year, 11 sites, 50amp electric hookup, non-reservable, $18. *Amenities*: Drinking water, dump station, restrooms, showers, group camping area, boat ramp with courtesy dock. *Directions*: From I-10 Exit 166, north on Hwy-269, then left at US-90 (in Chatahoochee, FL) to Bolivar Street (Booster Club Rd). Turn right, 2 miles, then left at River Junction sign. 229-662-2001.

2) Okeechobee Waterway

    a) Ortona South
    b) W.P. Franklin
    c) St. Lucie South

U.S. Army Corps of Engineers
525 Ridgelawn Rd
Clewiston, FL 33440
Phone: 863-983-8101
District: Jacksonville

Okeechobee's lake, waterway and surrounding countryside has 26,377 land acres, 451,000 water acres and 402 shoreline miles. Lake Okeechobee is the largest lake in Florida and the second largest fresh water lake in the U.S. It is a popular fishing destination. Boat ramps are conveniently located throughout. Three marinas provide supplies and boating services. The Okeechobee Project Office is in Clewiston on the south side of the lake. It is about 65 miles west of West Palm Beach. From I-95 Exit 68, take US-98 west (becomes US-441 north). Take US-441 to SR-80 west (becomes US-27 north) into Clewiston.

RV CAMPING

The Corps manages recreation areas at the lake and along the adjacent waterways. RV camping is available on waterways leading into the lake. Ortona and Franklin campgrounds are west of the lake and St. Lucie campground is east of the lake. Manatees can be observed at all locations. Ortona, on the Caloosahatchee River section of the waterway, offers a tranquil, serene country setting. Franklin camping area is just 15 minutes from Fort Myers where visitors will find flea markets, malls and the historic Edison Home. Saint Lucie South is about 10 minutes from Stuart, Florida. Numerous state parks and private campgrounds are near Lake Okeechobee.

2a) Ortona South

Ortona South: All year, 45 sites with electric (50amp) & water hookups, $24, some pull thrus. **Amenities**: Dump station, restrooms, showers, laundry, fishing piers, golf nearby. **Directions**: From La Belle, Florida, east on SR-80 for 8 miles to Dalton Lane, follow signs. 4330 Dalton Lane SW, Moore Haven, FL 33471 / 863-675-8400. **GPS**: 26.78722, -81.30861

2b) W.P. Franklin

W.P. Franklin: All year, 30 RV/tent sites with electric (50amp) & water hookups, some pull thrus, 8 sleep-on-boat sites with electric & water, $24. **Amenities**: Drinking water, dump station, restrooms, showers, laundry, boat ramp, playground, fishing pier, waterfront sites. **Directions**: From I-75 Exit 141, follow SR-80 east 3 miles to SR-31 and go north 3 miles to River Rd then go east 5 miles to N Franklin Lock Rd, follow signs. 17801 North Franklin Lock Rd, Alva, FL 33920 / 239-694-8770. **GPS**: 26.72417, -81.69278

2c) Saint Lucie South

Saint Lucie South: All year, 9 sites with electric (50amp) and water hookups, 3 tent sites, 8 sleep-on-boat sites with electric, $20-$24. **Amenities**: Dump station, restrooms, showers, laundry, boat ramp, playground, group shelter. **Directions**: From I-95 Exit 101 (Stuart/Indiantown), SR-76 west for one-half mile to Locks Rd, then right, follow signs. 2170 SW Canal St, Stuart, FL 34997 / 772-287-1382. **GPS**: 27.11028, -80.285

Georgia

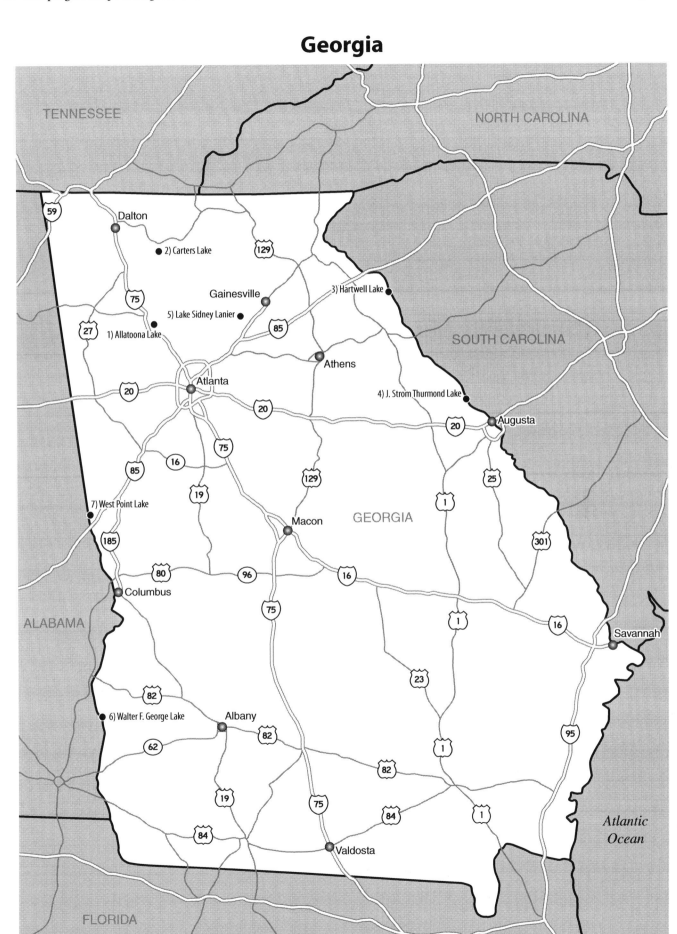

Activities

Activities	Auto Touring	Biking	Boating	Climbing	Cultural / Historic Sites	Educational Programs	Fishing	Groceries / Supplies	Hiking	Horseback Riding	Hunting	Off Highway Vehicles	Lodging	Visitor Center
1) Allatoona Lake	♦		♦		♦	♦	♦				♦		♦	♦
2) Carters Lake		♦	♦				♦	♦		♦	♦		♦	♦
3) Hartwell Lake			♦			♦	♦						♦	♦
4) J. Strom Thurmond Lake	♦	♦	♦		♦	♦	♦	♦	♦	♦	♦		♦	♦
5) Lake Sidney Lanier	♦		♦			♦	♦	♦	♦				♦	♦
6) Walter F. George Lake			♦			♦	♦		♦		♦		♦	♦
7) West Point Lake			♦			♦	♦		♦					♦

Georgia Projects

1) Allatoona Lake

U.S. Army Corps of Engineers
P.O. Box 487
1138 State Road Spur SE 20
Cartersville, GA 30120
Phone: 678-721-6700
District: Mobile

Allatoona Lake is located only 45 miles north of Atlanta, off I-75 and I-575 in the foothills of the Blue Ridge Mountains. From Atlanta, go 45 miles north on I-75 to Exit 290, east on GA-20 for 50 yards (to the first traffic light) then south onto the GA-20 spur for 4 miles to the Visitor Center. The Center features video exhibits and displays about the area's history ranging from the time of early Indians to the gold mining and iron making days, from Civil War up to the present. The Allatoona project encompasses 26,738 land acres, 12,010 water acres and 270 shoreline miles. More than 13 million visitors enjoy recreation at Allatoona each year. Wildlife viewing is abundant along the shores of the beautiful lake. Shopping, museums and historic sites are in the area.

RV Camping

There are eight Corps-managed campgrounds at Allatoona Lake with varied activities available. Other accommodations at the lake include Red Top Mountain State Park, private RV parks and cabin rentals.

Clark Creek North: Apr-Sep, 16 paved sites with electric (50amp) & water hookups, 8 sites with electric only, $28, some pull thrus, 40-foot RV length limit. **Amenities**: Dump station, restrooms, showers, laundry, boat ramp, fishing, swimming. **Directions**: From I-75 Exit 278, go north on Glade Rd for 2 miles, cross the bridge, follow signs. 6100 Glade Rd SE, Acworth, GA 30102 / 678-721-6700. **GPS**: 34.09722, -84.68056

McKaskey Creek: Mar-Sep, 35 sites with electric (most 50amp), 10 with electric & water hookups, 16 tent only sites, 30-foot RV length limit. $24–$28. **Amenities**: Drinking water, dump station, restrooms, showers, laundry, dock, boat ramp, swimming, playground. **Directions**: From I-75 Exit 290, go east 50 yards and turn right on GA Spur 20 for 2 miles then left onto McKasky Creek Rd for 1 mile, follow signs. McKaskey Creek Rd SE, Cartersville, GA / 678-721-6700. **GPS**: 34.19, -84.71806

McKinney: All year, 150 sites with electric (50amp), some sites with water hookups, some pull thrus, $24–$28. **Amenities**: Dump station, restrooms, showers, laundry, swimming, boat ramp, dock, fishing. **Directions**: From I-75 Exit 278, go east on Glade Rd for 3 miles, turn left at the second four-way stop at King's Camp Rd, go 1 mile to the road fork, take a left and follow signs. Kings Camp Rd SE, Acworth, GA 30102 / 678-721-6700.) **GPS**: 34.10694, -84.69556

Old Hwy 41 #3: Apr-Sep, 55 sites with electric (50amp) and some with water hookups, non reservables, $24–$28. Some waterfront sites. **Amenities**: Dump station, restrooms, showers, laundry, boat ramp, dock, fishing, playground, swimming, wildlife viewing. **Directions**: From I-75 Exit 278 (Glade Rd), go west .7 mile to stop light, then right onto GA-92 (Lake Acworth Dr) for .8 mile, crossing overpass, turn right and go to the bottom of the overpass, turn left, go 2.5 miles, follow signs. 678-721-6700. GPS: 34.08833, -84.71056

Payne: Mar-Sep, 43 sites with electric (50amp) & some with electric & water hookups, 2 full hookup sites and 12 tent sites, non-reservables, $24–$28. *Amenities*: Drinking water, dump station, restrooms, showers, laundry, boat ramp, fishing, swimming. *Directions*: From I-75 Exit 277, east on Hwy-92 about 2 miles, then left on Old Alabama Rd, then right on Kellogg Creek Rd for 1.5 miles, follow signs. 678-721-6700. *GPS*: 34.12083, -84.57917

Upper Stamp Creek: Apr-Sep, 18 sites with 50amp electric hookups, 2 tent sites, $28. 32-foot RV length limit. *Amenities*: Restrooms, dump station, showers, dock, boat ramp, fishing, swimming. *Directions*: From I-75 Exit 290, head east on Hwy 20 toward Canton/Rome; after 4 miles, turn right onto Wilderness Rd, then go left onto Chitwood Cemetery Rd. Follow signs. 678-721-6700. *GPS*: 34.30378, -84.67667

Victoria: Mar-Oct, 70 sites with electric (50amp) and 3 with electric & water hookups, 2 full hookup sites, non-reservables, $24. *Amenities*: Dump station, restrooms, showers, laundry, boat ramp, fishing, swimming, playground, dock. *Directions*: From I-575 Exit 11 (Sixes Rd) go west for 2.5 miles, then left on Bells Ferry Rd for 1.5 miles to Victoria Landing Dr, then right to the 3-way stop, then left to the 4-way stop, then right. 937 Victoria Landing Dr, Woodstock, GA 30189 / 678-721-6700. *GPS*: 34.15139, -84.61944

Sweetwater: Mar-Sep, 73 sites with electric (50amp) and 6 with electric & water hookups, 2 full hookup sites and 26 tent only sites, some pull thrus, $24–$28. *Amenities*: Drinking water, dump station, restrooms, showers, laundry, dock, fishing, boat ramp, playground, swimming. *Directions*: From I-75 Exit 290, go east on SR-20 for 12 miles, then right on Fields Chapel Rd for 2 miles, follow signs. 678-721-6700. *GPS*: 34.19444, -84.57889

2) Carters Lake

U.S. Army Corps of Engineers
1850 Carters Dam Rd
P.O. Box 96
Oakman, GA 30732
Phone: 706-334-2248
District: Mobile

Carters Lake is one of the most scenic lakes in the Southeast. It lies 70 miles north of Atlanta. From Atlanta take I-575 north to the Carters Lake exit and follow signs to the desired project location. Carters Lake has 4,250 surface acres and 76 miles of rugged, largely undeveloped shoreline.

The Amadahy Trail, a 3.5 mile loop with easy to moderately difficult terrain, is open to hikers and mountain bikers. The trailhead is at Woodring Branch Campground.

RV Camping

Doll Mountain: Apr-Oct, 35 sites with electric (some 50amp), 4 sites with full hookups, some pull thrus, 26 tent sites, $16–$24. *Amenities*: Drinking water, dump station, restrooms, showers, laundry, boat ramp, playground, fishing, boating, canoeing, sailing. *Directions*: From I-75 Exit 293, take Hwy-411 north, then right on Hwy-136, then left on Hwy-382, then right into the access road (across from fire station). Located on the south side of the lake. Caution: Park access road has a steep downhill grade going into the campground. 706-276-4413. *GPS*: 34.61333, -84.62389

Harris Branch: May-Sep, 10 sites, no hookups, non-reservable, $16. *Amenities*: Drinking water, restrooms, showers, laundry, playground, swimming, group camping. *Directions*: South side of the lake, three miles off Hwy-382. 706-276-4545.

Woodring Branch: Apr-Oct, 28 sites with electric (some 50amp), 11 tent sites, $16–$22. *Amenities*: Drinking water, dump station, restrooms, showers, laundry, swimming, playground, hiking trail, boat ramp, marina, canoeing, sailing. *Directions*: From I-75 Exit 293, follow Hwy-411 north, then right on Hwy-136, follow signs. North side of the lake. 706-276-6050. *GPS*: 34.67056, -84.55

3) Hartwell Lake

U.S. Army Corps of Engineers
5625 Anderson Hwy (Hwy-29)
Hartwell, GA 30643
Phone: 706-856-0300
District: Savannah

Note: There are 4 campgrounds on the South Carolina side of the project, see South Carolina for more information.

The Hartwell Lake project is located just off US-29 on the GA/SC border. The Operations Manager's Office and Visitor Center is one mile past the dam on the Georgia side, or 5 miles north of Hartwell, Georgia. The project includes 24,209 land acres, 55,950 water acres and 962 shoreline miles. Many lake access areas can easily be reached from I-85.

RV Camping

RV camping is available at 2 Corps-managed campgrounds on the Georgia side of the lake. There are also 4 campgrounds listed in the South Carolina section of this guide. A state park and a private resort also provide camping and lodging.

Paynes Creek: May-Sep, 43 sites with electric (50amp) and water hookups, some pull thrus, $22-$24. Many sites are waterfront. *Amenities*: Dump station, restrooms, showers, swimming, playground, boat ramp. *Directions*: Located on the Togaloo River arm of Hartwell Lake. From I-85 Exit 177, south on SR-77 for 5 miles, follow directional signs last 10 miles. 518 Ramp Rd, Hartwell, GA 30643 / 888-893-0678. *GPS*: 34.47917, -82.97528

Watsadler: All year, 49 lakefront sites with electric (50amp) and water hookups, $22. *Amenities*: Dump station, restrooms, showers, playground, birding, fishing, boat ramp. *Directions*: Located next to the Project Office adjacent to the dam. From I-85 Exit 177, SR-77 toward Hartwell, then Hwy-29 north (toward Anderson, SC) for 4 miles, follow signs, entrance on left. 286 Watsadler Rd, Hartwell, GA 30643 / 888-893-0678. *GPS*: 34.34389, -82.84139

4) J. Strom Thurmond Lake

U.S. Army Corps of Engineers
510 Clarks Hill Hwy
Clarks Hill, SC 29821
Phone: 864-333-1100 or 800-533-3478
District: Savannah

Note: There are 4 campgrounds on the South Carolina side of the project, see South Carolina for more information.

Thurmond Lake is a long, relatively narrow body of water that extends from the dam (just north of Augusta, GA) to 29 miles up the Savannah River, 46 miles up the Little River and 6 miles up the Broad River. With a shoreline of 1,200 miles and 71,000 acres of water, it straddles the SC/GA border. Thurmond Lake's Visitor Center is located on the South Carolina side of the dam. From I-20 Exit 183, the dam is north on US-221.

RV Camping

RV camping is available in eight Corps-managed campgrounds on the Georgia side of the lake. There are also four campgrounds listed in the South Carolina section of this guide. On the Georgia side of the lake, camping is also available at Bobby Brown State Park and Elijah Clark State Park. Historic sites are near many of the campgrounds.

Big Hart: Apr-Oct, 31 shaded sites with electric (50amp) hookups, some pull thrus, 7 basic sites, $22-$24. *Amenities*: Drinking water, dump station, restrooms, showers, boat ramp, dock. Campground is adjacent to a recreation area with swim beach and playground. *Directions*: From I-20 Exit 172 (Thomson/Hwy-78), north 8 miles on Hwy-78 to Russell Landing Rd, then right 4 miles, follow signs. 5258 Washington Rd, Thomson, GA 30824 / 706-595-8613. *GPS*: 33.61458, -82.50875

Broad River: Mar-Sep, 31 sites with electric & water hookups, some pull thrus, $18-$22. Double & triple sites ideal for family and friends traveling together. Campground is on the Broad River's south bank. *Amenities*: Dump station, restrooms, showers, boat ramp, dock, fish cleaning station. *Directions*: From I-85 Exit 173 (Hwy-17), go south 30 miles, then Hwy-72 (toward Calhoun Falls) for 11 miles, then right on Hwy-79 for 10 miles, cross Broad River, campground on right. 8181 Elberton Hwy, Tignall, GA 30668 / 706-359-2053. *GPS*: 33.97711, -82.62785

Clay Hill: Apr-Sep, 17 sites with electric & water hookups, non-reservables, $16-$20. Lakefront sites. *Amenities*: Drinking water, dump station, restrooms, showers, boat ramp. *Directions*: From I-20 Exit 172, go 4 miles on US-78 to SR-43, continue to Amity Woodlawn Rd, follow signs. 5701 Clay Hill Rd, Lincolnton, GA 30817 / 706-359-7495. *GPS*: 33.66578, -82.44083

Hesters Ferry: Apr-Sep, 16 shaded sites with electric & water hookups, 9 basic sites, $16-$18. All sites are waterfront, located on Fishing Creek. *Amenities*: Drinking water, dump station, restrooms, showers. *Directions*: From Lincolnton, Georgia, go 12 miles north on Hwy-79, then east 2 miles on Rt-44, follow signs. 1864 Graball Rd, Tignall, GA 30668 / 800-533-3478 or 706-359-2746. *GPS*: 33.93543, -82.5404

Petersburg: All year, 93 sites with electric (50amp) and water hookups, some pull thrus, $18-$24. *Amenities*: Dump station, restrooms, showers, laundry, boat ramp, dock, fish cleaning station, swimming beaches, hiking trail. *Directions*: From I-20 Exit 183 (Appling), north 6 miles on Hwy-221. At 4-way stop continue another 2 miles, follow signs, entrance on left. 3998 Petersburg Rd, Appling, GA 30802 / 706-541-9464. *GPS*: 33.66194, -82.26088

Raysville: Mar-Oct, 52 sites with electric (50amp) and water hookups, some pull thrus, $22-$24. On the Little River.

Amenities: Dump station, restrooms, showers, boat ramp. **Directions**: From I-20 Exit 172 (Thomson/Hwy-78), north 3 miles, then right on Hwy-43 for 6 miles, entrance on left. 6489 Lincolnton Rd NE, Thomson, GA 30824 / 706-595-6759.) **GPS**: 33.63223, -82.47387

Ridge Road: Apr-Sep, 63 sites with electric (50amp) and water hookups, some pull thrus, 6 tent sites, $18–$24. Beautiful scenery. **Amenities**: Dump station, restrooms, showers, boat ramp, dock, fish cleaning station, hiking. **Directions**: From I-20 Exit 183 (Appling), north 6 miles on US-221. At 4-way stop, left on SR-47, then 5 miles, follow signs. 5886 Ridge Rd, Appling, GA 30802 / 706-541-0282. **GPS**: 33.68, -82.25761

Winfield: Mar-Sep, 80 sites with electric (50amp) and water hookups, $22. Many sites are waterfront. **Amenities**: Dump station, restrooms, showers, boat ramp, fishing, hunting, playground, water skiing, wildlife viewing. **Directions**: From I-20 Exit 175, north 7 miles, then north on Hwy-150, left on Mistletoe Rd, 2 miles, then left, follow signs. 7701 Winfield Rd, Appling, GA 30802 / 706-541-0147. **GPS**: 33.65194, -82.42194

5) Lake Sidney Lanier

U.S. Army Corps of Engineers
1050 Buford Dam Rd
Buford, GA 30518
Phone: 770-945-9531
District: Mobile

Lake Sidney Lanier is nestled in the foothills of the Georgia Blue Ridge Mountains just 35 minutes northeast of Atlanta. From I-985 Exit 4 take SR-20 west to Suwanee Dam Road north 3 miles, then left on Buford Dam Rd. The Visitor Center is one mile on the right. The project has 19,288 land acres, 38,000 water acres and 540 shoreline miles.

The lake is well known for its aqua-blue colored water and spectacular scenery. Shopping malls, outlet centers, restaurants and golf courses are nearby. Seasonal festivals and special events are featured in local towns. Gas, propane, marinas, restaurants and convenience stores are near the campgrounds.

RV Camping

Bald Ridge: Mar-Oct, 82 sites with electric (some 50amp) and water hookups, some pull thrus, a few non-reservables, $32. **Amenities**: Dump station, restrooms, showers, laundry, fishing, boat ramp, playground, swimming. **Directions**: From Atlanta SR-400 north to Exit 16, then right on Pilgrim Mill Rd, then right on Sinclair Shoals Rd, then left on Bald Ridge Rd. 4100 Bald Ridge Rd, Cumming, GA 30041 / 770-889-1591. **GPS**: 34.20389, -84.08611

Bolding Mill: Apr-Sep, 92 sites with electric (50amp) hookups, 9 tent sites, $25-$27, some pull thrus. **Amenities**: Dump station, restrooms, showers, laundry, swimming, playground, fishing, boating. **Directions**: From Atlanta, take SR-400 north to Exit 17, right onto SR-306, then right onto SR-53 and left onto Old Sardis Rd and left on Chestatee Rd. 4055 Chestatee Rd, Gainesville, GA 50506 / 770-534-6960. **GPS**: 34.33793, -83.95114

Duckett Mill: Apr-Sep, 97 sites with electric (some 50amp) and water hookups, some pull thrus, 14 tent sites, a few non-reservables, $18–$32. **Amenities**: Drinking water, dump station, restrooms, showers, laundry, fishing, boat ramp, swimming, playground. **Directions**: From SR-400 Exit 17, turn right on SR-306, then right on SR-53, right on Duckett Mill Rd. 3720 Duckett Mill Rd, Gainesville, GA 30506 / 770-532-9802. **GPS**: 34.30828, -83.93132

Old Federal: Mar-Oct, 30 sites with electric (some 50amp) hookups, 12 tent sites, $18–$32. **Amenities**: Drinking water, dump station, restrooms, showers, laundry, fishing, boat ramp, swimming. **Directions**: From I-985 Exit 8, turn left on Hwy-347/Friendship Rd, turn right on McEver Rd, then left on Jim Crow Rd, follow signs. 6219 Old Federal Rd, Flowery Branch, GA 30542 / 770-967-6757. **GPS**: 34.22222, -83.94944

Sawnee: Apr-Sep, 34 sites with electric hookups, 9 tent sites, $22–$30. **Amenities**: Drinking water, dump station, restrooms, showers, laundry, boat ramp, fishing, swimming, playground. **Directions**: From SR-400 Exit 14, turn left on SR-20 east, then left on Sanders Rd, at first stop sign go right on Buford Dam Rd. 3200 Buford Dam Rd, Cumming, GA 30041 / 770-887-0592. **GPS**: 34.17667, -84.07528

6) Walter F. George Lake

U.S. Army Corps of Engineers
427 Eufala Rd
Fort Gaines, GA 39851
Phone: 229-768-2516
District: Mobile

Note: There are 3 campgrounds on the Alabama side of the project, see Alabama for more information.

Walter F. George Lake, sometimes referred to as Lake Eufala, extends 85 miles along the Chatahoochee River and borders Alabama and Georgia. From Fort Gaines, Georgia, take Hwy-39 north for 2 miles; the W.F. George Resource Building is on the left. With

640 miles of shoreline, the lake offers plenty of room for water-related activities. Gracious antebellum mansions are located in nearby historic towns, including Cuthbert, GA and Eufala, AL.

RV Camping

RV camping is available at 1 Corps-managed campground on the Georgia side of the lake. There are also 3 campgrounds listed in the Alabama section of this guide.

Cotton Hill: All year, 91 sites with full hookups, some pull thrus, non-reservables, $20-$24. *Amenities*: Drinking water, dump station, restrooms, showers, laundry, fish cleaning station, playground, boat ramp, swimming, hiking, interpretive trail, water skiing. *Directions*: From Fort Gaines, follow SR-39 north 7 miles, follow signs. 229-768-3061. *GPS*: 31.67444, -85.06417

7) West Point Lake

U.S. Army Corps of Engineers
500 Resource Management Dr
West Point, GA 31833
Phone: 706–645–2937
District: Mobile

Note: There is one campground on the Alabama side of the project, see Alabama for more information.

West Point Lake straddles the AL/GA border, just north of Interstate 85. From I-85 Exit 2 follow US-29 north. The Visitor Center is on the left where information and maps are available. The project includes 32,282 land acres, 26,864 water acres and 539 miles of shoreline. Surrounded by deep forests and rolling hills, West Point Lake extends along the Chattahoochee River. A wildlife management area of 10,000 acres is located at the upper end of the lake, providing a habitat for many kinds of game and non-game wildlife.

Fishing is the most popular activity at the lake. A dozen creeks and more than 40 square miles of lake provide plenty of good fishing spots. The lake abounds with bass, catfish, crappie and bream. Bank fishing is excellent at most locations. Personal watercraft and water safety courses are offered from February to September in the Visitor Center.

RV Camping

There are three Corps-managed campgrounds on the Georgia side of the lake. Another campground is listed in the Alabama section.

Holiday: Feb-Sep, 77 sites with electric (some 50amp) hookups, 36 tent sites, $16–$24. *Amenities*: Drinking water, dump station, restrooms, showers, laundry, boating, fishing, hiking, hunting, playground, tennis courts, basketball & volleyball courts. *Directions*: From LaGrange, Georgia, west on Hwy-109, after crossing the First Lake Bridge across the lake, go one more mile, turn left on Thompson Rd, at the next intersection bear left, follow signs. 954 Abbotsford Rd, Lagrange, West Point, GA 30240 / 706-884-6818. *GPS*: 33.02611, -85.17889

R. Shaefer Heard: All year, 117 sites with electric (some 50amp) & water hookups, $24. *Amenities*: Dump station, restrooms, showers, laundry, boat ramp, amphitheater, boating, fishing, hiking, playground, swimming, tennis courts. *Directions*: From West Point, Georgia, go 4 miles north on US-29, follow signs. 101 Shaefer Heard Park Rd, West Point, GA 31833 / 706-645-2404. *GPS*: 32.92722, -85.16389

Whitetail Ridge: Mar-Nov, 58 sites with electric & water hookups, some pull thrus, $24. *Amenities*: Dump station, restrooms, showers, laundry, hiking trails, boat ramp. *Directions*: From LaGrange, Georgia, west on Hwy-109, after crossing the first bridge across the lake, go 1 mile, then left on Thompson Rd, follow signs. 565 Abbotsford Rd, Legrange, GA 30240 / 706-884-8972. *GPS*: 33.02222, -85.19167

Idaho

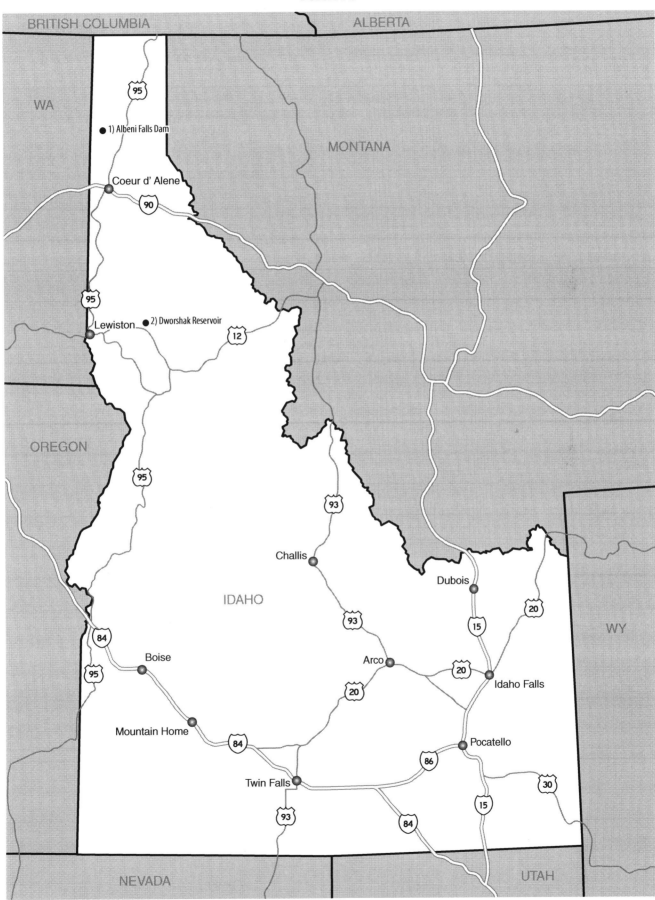

Activities	Auto Touring	Biking	Boating	Climbing	Cultural / Historic Sites	Educational Programs	Fishing	Groceries / Supplies	Hiking	Horseback Riding	Hunting	Lodging	Off Highway Vehicles	Visitor Center
1) Aleni Falls Dam & Lake Pend Oreille	◆	◆	◆	◆			◆	◆	◆		◆			◆
2) Dworshak Reservoir			◆					◆	◆		◆			◆

Idaho Projects

1) Albeni Falls Dam & Lake Pend Oreille

U.S. Army Corps of Engineers
2376 East Hwy 2
Oldtown, ID 83822
Phone: 208-437-3133
District: Seattle

Located in the panhandle of Idaho, the Albeni project includes 4,844 land acres, 94,600 water acres and 226 shoreline miles. The Albeni Visitor Center is located 2 miles east of the WA/ID border on US-2. History and natural history exhibits are featured. The Center offers tours of the Albeni Falls Dam four times daily from Memorial Day to Labor Day.

Albeni Falls Dam sits on the Pend Oreille River (pronounced pond-o-ray). Behind the dam, the waters of the Pend Oreille stretch 65 miles through a glacially-carved valley that separates three mountain ranges. Rimmed by mountains that rise 6,500 feet, Lake Pend Oreille is one of the largest and deepest natural lakes in western U.S. A popular day trip for visitors is the Pack River area to observe wildlife. Shopping, restaurants and a theme park are near Springy Point.

RV Camping

Albeni Cove: May-Sep, 10 sites, no hookups, some pull thrus, $18. **Amenities**: Restrooms, showers, boat ramp, fishing, swimming. **Directions**: From SR-41 in Oldtown, follow 4th St east for 2.2 miles. **GPS**: 48.1759, -116.9999

Priest River: May-Sep, 20 sites, no hookups, some pull thrus, $18. The park is also known as the "Mudhole." **Amenities**: Dump station, restrooms, showers, boat ramp, fishing, swimming, playground, wildlife viewing. **Directions**: One mile east of the town of Priest River on US-2. **GPS**: 48.17917, -116.88889

Riley Creek: May-Sep, 67 sites with electric (50amp) & water hookups, some pull thrus, $24-$26. Gates close at 10pm. **Amenities**: Drinking water, dump station, restrooms, showers, amphitheater, interpretive programs, boat ramp, fishing, hiking, biking, playground, swimming. **Directions**: From US-2 in Laclede, south on Riley Creek Rd 1 mile. **GPS**: 48.16111, -116.77028

Springy Point: May-Oct, 38 sites, no hookups, some pull thrus, $18. Gates close at 10pm. **Amenities**: Dump station, restrooms, showers, boat ramp, fishing, swimming. **Directions**: From Sandpoint, south on US-95, across the Long Bridge, turn west onto Longshore Dr for 3 miles, then right in Springy Point. **GPS**: 48.2375, -116.58333

2) Dworshak Reservoir

U.S. Army Corps of Engineers
P.O. Box 48
Ahsahka, ID 83520
Phone: 208-476-1255 or 208-476-1268
District: Walla Walla

Dworshak Reservoir is located in scenic forested and mountainous country in central Idaho. The Visitor Center is 5 miles west of Orofino on Hwy-7. After entering the project, follow signs to the Visitor Center, which is adjacent to the north dam abutment. The lake with 19,824 water acres and 54 shoreline miles is surrounded by abundant wildlife on 27,035 land acres. There is excellent wildlife viewing throughout. Lewis and Clark camped in this area, where they rested from their trip over the Bitterroot Range and built canoes for their trip on to the Pacific Ocean.

Fishing on the lake is excellent for salmon, trout and bass. The Dworshak National Fish Hatchery is the largest steelhead trout hatchery in the world.

RV Camping

Additional camping is available at Dworshak State Park.

Dent Acres: May-Sep, 50 sites with full hookups, some pull thrus, $18, 35-foot RV length limit. All sites are non-reservable, first-come first-serve. Call the Visitor Center (208-476-1255) for more information. *Amenities*: Dump station, restrooms, showers, boat ramp, tie-up dock in season, fish cleaning station, playground, hiking trail, group camping facility. *Directions*: From Hwy-12, cross the bridge at Orofino and turn left onto Hwy-7. Travel 200 yards, turn right and go 19 miles, follow signs. The road into the campground has some sharp curves and steep grades. 208-476-9029.

Illinois

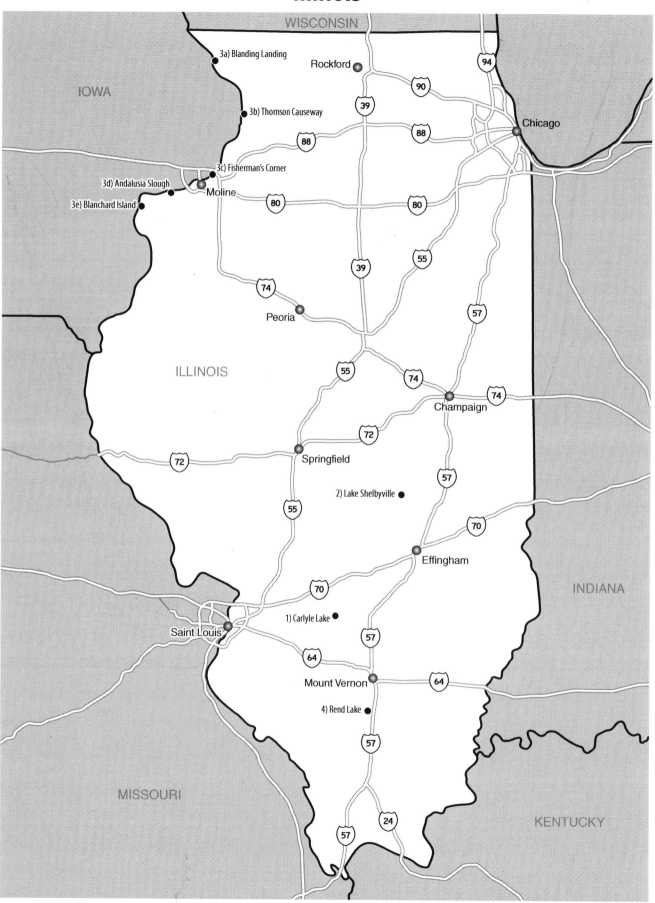

Activities

	Auto Touring	Biking	Boating	Climbing	Cultural / Historic Sites	Educational Programs	Groceries / Supplies	Fishing	Hiking	Horseback Riding	Hunting	Off Highway Vehicles	Lodging	Visitor Center
1) Carlyle Lake		♦	♦				♦	♦	♦		♦	♦	♦	♦
2) Lake Shelbyville			♦				♦	♦	♦				♦	♦
3) Mississippi River Camping	♦	♦	♦		♦	♦	♦	♦	♦					♦
4) Rend Lake	♦	♦	♦			♦	♦	♦	♦	♦	♦	♦	♦	♦

Illinois Projects

1) Carlyle Lake

U.S. Army Corps of Engineers
801 Lake Rd
Carlyle, IL 62231
Phone: 618-594-2484
District: St. Louis

Easy access to Carlyle Lake can be found from I-70, I-64 or I-57. The Visitor Center is located in the Dam West Recreation Area just northeast of Carlyle off SR-127. Exhibits at the Center include a 215-gallon aquarium with native fish and a snake exhibit featuring the massasauga rattlesnake. Lake information and maps of hiking and biking trails are available at the Center.

Carlyle, the largest lake in Illinois, has 24,988 water acres and 88 shoreline miles. It is one of the top inland sailing destinations in the nation. Boat rentals are offered at marinas.

RV Camping

In addition to Corps-managed campgrounds, there are also a number of private and state campgrounds around the lake.

Boulder: Apr-Sep, 83 sites with electric (most 50amp) hookups, some full hookup sites, $16–$24. **Amenities**: Drinking water, dump station, restrooms, showers, laundry, boat ramp, fishing, playground, marina. **Directions**: From I-57 take Old US-50 west 19 miles to Boulder Rd, then north 7 miles. 618-226-3586. **GPS**: 38.69472, -89.23361

Coles Creek: May-Sep, 119 sites with electric hookups, 20 full hookup sites (50amp throughout), $16–$24. **Amenities**: Drinking water, dump station, restrooms, showers, laundry, boat ramp, swimming. **Directions**: From I-57 take Old US-50 for 19 miles west, then north on Boulder Rd for 4 miles, then west on CR-1700N and continue until the road connects with CR-2400, continue to the campground. 618-226-3211. **GPS**: 38.65694, -89.26028

Dam West: Apr-Nov, 89 sites with electric (50amp) hookups, 28 full hookup sites, some pull thrus, $18–$28. **Amenities**: Drinking water, dump station, restrooms, showers, laundry, boat ramp, fishing, biking, interpretive trails, swimming, playground, marina. **Directions**: 618-594-4410. **GPS**: 38.62778,-89.35833

2) Lake Shelbyville

U.S. Army Corps of Engineers
RR 4, Box 128B
15 E. Main St
Shebyville, IL 62565
Phone: 217-774-3951
District: St. Louis

Lake Shelbyville is located in central Illinois, 35 miles south of Decatur. The Visitor Center is on the east side of the dam (south side of the lake) just outside the town of Shelbyville. Maps and information are available. The project consists of 11,100 acres of water and 29,408 acres of land. Popular game fish species include crappie, largemouth bass, muskie, walleye, white bass and bluegill. In the Okaw Bluff Wetlands there are nine photo blinds, a viewing stand and a one-mile nature trail.

Throughout the season, park rangers present free weekend interpretive programs at the Visitor Center, campground amphitheaters and on beaches.

RV Camping

RV camping may be found at five Corps-managed

locations. A resort on the lake has lodging and an 18-hole golf course. Eagle Creek State Park also has camping.

Bo Wood: Apr-Oct, 138 sites with electric (50amp) hookups, some full hookup, some pull thrus, $18-$22. **Amenities**: Drinking water, dump station, restrooms, showers, laundry, boat ramp, fish cleaning stations, playground. **Directions**: From Sullivan, go 2.6 miles south on SR-32, then west for .5 mile, follow signs. 217-774-3951. **GPS**: 39.55139, -88.62222

Coon Creek: Apr-Oct, 199 sites with electric (a few 50amp) hookups, 8 full hookup sites, all non-reservables - first come first serve, $18-$22. **Amenities**: Drinking water, dump station, restrooms, showers, laundry, boat ramp, courtesy dock, fish cleaning station, playground, swimming beach, basketball courts, interpretive trail. **Directions**: From Shelbyville, 4.5 miles north on SR-128 to CR-1750N, then .9 mile east to CR-1900E, then north .35 mile to CR-1785N, then east 1.75 miles to CR-2075E, then south 1.75 miles. 217-774-3951. **GPS**: 39.45139, -88.7625

Lithia Springs: Apr-Oct, 113 sites with electric (50amp) hookups, $18–$22, some sites are lakefront. **Amenities**: Drinking water, dump station, restrooms, showers, laundry, playground, swimming, boat ramp, fishing, hiking. **Directions**: Located on the east side of the lake. From Shelbyville, go 3 miles east on SR-16, then north 2 miles on CR-2200E, then west 1.4 miles on CR-1500N. 217-774-3951. **GPS**: 39.43444, -88.76

Lone Point: May-Sep, 55 sites with electric hookups, 2 full hookup sites, $16. **Amenities**: Drinking water, dump station, restrooms, showers, playground, boat ramp, fishing, hiking. **Directions**: Located on the west side of the lake. From Shelbyville go 4.5 miles north on SR-128 to CR-1750, then .9 mile east to CR-1900, then north .35 mile to CR-1785, then east 2.5 miles to CR-2150, then south .7 mile to CR-1725N, then east .25 mile to CR-2175E, then south .7 mile to the campground. 217-774-3951. **GPS**: 39.45222, -88.74028

Opossum Creek: May-Sep, 51 sites with electric hookups, 22 tent sites, $16. **Amenities**: Drinking water, dump station, restrooms, showers, playground, boat ramp, fishing, fishing dock, wildlife viewing. **Directions**: On the west side of the lake. From Shelbyville 3.5 miles north on SR-128 to CR-1650N, then .9 mile east to CR-1880E, then south .5 mile to CR-1600N, then east 1 mile. 217-774-3951. **GPS**: 39.44556, -88.7725

3) Mississippi River Camping
    a) Blanding Landing
    b) Thomson Causeway
    c) Fisherman's Corner
    d) Andulsuia Slough
    e) Blanchard Island

U.S. Army Corps of Engineers
P.O. Box 2004
Rock Island, IL 61204
Phone: 309-794-5338 or 309-794-4522
District: Rock Island

The Mississippi River Project of the Corps' Rock Island District maintains public recreation areas along a 314-mile stretch of the River. The Illinois portion of the project runs from the Wisconsin state line south to Lock & Dam 22 (near I-72). The Mississippi River Visitor Center is located on Rock Island, which can be accessed from I-74 in Illinois (River Dr or 7th Ave exit). The Center offers the best view of "locking through," where visitors can watch pilots as they skillfully maneuver tons of cargo through. Up to 2,500 bald eagles winter along the Mississippi near the locks and dams. They can be seen from mid-December through early March. Watching river traffic is a popular pastime. Historic sites can be found along the river as well as scenic drives.

Note: Another interesting Mississippi River location is the National Great Rivers Museum, located just north of St. Louis in East Alton, IL. The modern museum, visited by millions of travelers each year, tells the story of the great river, its history and impact on the nation. From I-270 Exit 34 (north of St. Louis and two miles east of the river in Illinois), take SR-3 north for about 11 miles to SR-143. The museum is just off SR-143 at Melvin Price Lock & Dam. The facility is operated by the Corps St. Louis District. For more information call 877-462-6979.

RV CAMPING

There are five Corps-managed campgrounds along the river in Hanover, Thomson and Hampton, IL and in the Quad Cities area.

3a) Blanding Landing

Blanding Landing: May-Oct, 30 sites with electric (50amp) hookups, some non-reservables, $14. **Amenities**: Drinking water, dump station, restrooms, showers, playground. **Directions**: From Hanover, Illinois, on US-84, turn west on Fulton Street next to Apple River Bridge, follow signs 8 miles. 5720 South River Rd, Hanover, IL 61041 / 563-582-0881 or 800-645-0348. **GPS**: 42.28583, -90.40333

3b) Thomson Causeway

Thomson Causeway: Apr-Oct, 126 sites with electric (50amp) hookups, 5 tent sites, $10–$16. Located on an island on the Mississippi River. **Amenities**: Drinking water, dump station, restrooms, showers, playground, interpretive trail, biking, boat ramp, fishing, hunting. **Directions**: From Thomson, IL on US-84 turn west onto Main St, then south on Lewis Ave, follow signs. Lewis Ave, Thomson, IL 61285 / 815-259-3628. **GPS**: 41.95167, -90.11083

3c) Fisherman's Corner

Fisherman's Corner: Apr-Oct, 28 sites with electric (50amp) hookups, some pull thrus, 6 tent sites, $10–$16. **Amenities**: Drinking water, dump station, restrooms, showers, playground, amphitheater, fishing, hiking, bike trail. **Directions**: On US-84 just north of Hampton, close to Rock Island. Route 84 North, Hampton, IL 61256 / 309-496-2720 or 815-259-3628. **GPS**: 41.56972, -90.39

3d) Andalusia Slough

Andalusia Slough: May-Oct, 16 sites, no hookups, some pull thrus, non-reservable, $4. **Amenities**: Drinking water, restrooms, dump station, boat ramp. **Directions**: Across the river from Davenport, Iowa, 2 miles west of Andalusia, IL on SR-92. 563-263-7913.

3e) Blanchard Island

Blanchard Island: May-Oct, 34 sites, no hookups, non-reservable first-come first-serve, $4. **Amenities**: Drinking water, dump station, restrooms, concrete boat ramp, fishing. **Directions**: Off the beaten path area located off the main channel of the Mississippi River on the Illinois side 4 miles south of Muscatine, IA. From Muscatine, IA bridge, 1.5 miles east on SR-92, south 4 miles, second right past Copperas Creek Bridge. 563-263-7913.

4) Rend Lake

U.S. Army Corps of Engineers
12220 Rend City Rd
Benton, IL 62812
Phone: 618-724-2493
Visitor Center: 618-439-7430
District: St. Louis

Located in the heart of southern Illinois, Rend Lake is a haven for wildlife and a recreational haven for visitors. It consists of 18,900 acres of water, 162 shoreline miles and 21,962 acres of land. The Visitor Center, located at the south side of the lake, has educational programs throughout the warm weather months and maps for hiking and biking trails.

A wildlife viewing adventure awaits visitors on any of the nature trails and quiet early risers will see deer as they feed at the forest edge. Abundant nature viewing is featured at the Wildlife Refuge. The Rend Lake Demonstration Garden has interesting exhibits on local plants and animals. Rend Lake is one of the best areas for birding. Horseback riding and trail riding are available at Wayne Fitzgerrel State Park. Other attractions include the 27-hole championship Rend Lake Golf Course and Southern Illinois Artisans Shop.

RV CAMPING

Ranger-led programs are held at campgrounds in season. Trap shooting and sporting clays are available near the campgrounds.

Gun Creek: Apr-Oct, 74 sites with electric and 26 with full hookups, some pull thrus, $16. **Amenities**: Drinking water, dump station, restrooms, showers, swimming, boat ramp, fishing, biking, trails, playground. **Directions**: From I-57 Exit 77, west on SR-154 for .25 mile, then left on Gun Creek Trail, south .25 mile, then right on Golf Course Rd, 1/2 mile. 12165 Golf Course Dr, Whittington, IL 62897 / 618-629-2338. **GPS**: 38.07861, -88.93028

North Sandusky: Apr-Oct, 103 sites with electric hookups, 15 full hookup sites, $16–$22. **Amenities**: Drinking water, dump station, restrooms, showers, playground, swimming, boat ramp, fishing, birding. **Directions**: From I-57 Exit 77, west 4.5 miles on SR-154 to Rend City Rd, then south 1 mile to stop sign. Park entrance is on the south side of the intersection. 8420 Loon Ln, Sesser, IL 62884 / 618-625-6115. **GPS**: 38.07111, -89.00556

South Marcum: Apr-Oct, 147 sites with electric (50amp) hookups, many have full hookup, 14 tent sites, non-reservables, $12–$24. **Amenities**: Drinking water, dump station, restrooms, showers, boat ramp, playground, hiking trail, dock, fishing, marina. **Directions**: From I-57 Exit 71, west for 3 miles on SR-14, then north on Rend City Rd. Turn right onto Main Dam and go 3 miles to the park entrance on left. 11623 Trailhead Ln, Benton, IL 62812 / 618-435-3549. GPS: 38.0375, -88.93611

South Sandusky: Apr-Oct, 121 sites with electric hookups, 18 full hookup sites, some pull thrus, 8 tent sites, $16–$24. **Amenities**: Drinking water, dump station, restrooms, showers, interpretive trail, birding, bicycle trails, fishing, playground, amphitheater with ranger programs in season. **Directions**: From I-57 Exit 71, go west on SR-14 for 3 miles to Rend City Rd for 6 miles, park entrance on right. 7820 Red Oak Ln, Sesser, IL 62884 / 618-625-3011. GPS: 38.06038, -89.00472

Iowa

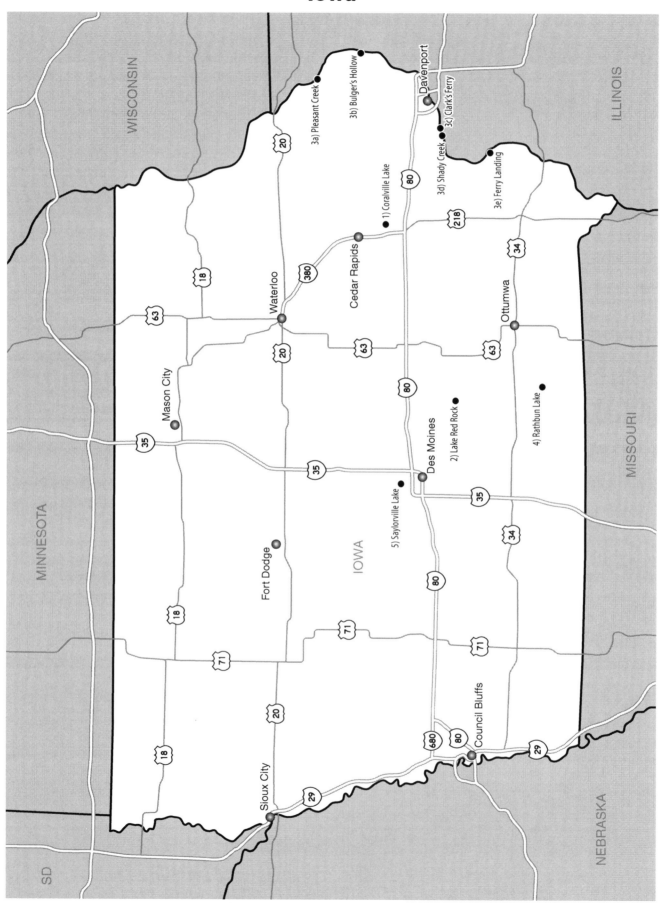

Activities

	Auto Touring	Biking	Boating	Climbing	Cultural / Historic Sites	Educational Programs	Fishing	Groceries / Supplies	Hiking	Horseback Riding	Hunting	Lodging	Off Highway Vehicles	Visitor Center
1) Coralville Lake	♦	♦	♦				♦		♦	♦	♦			
2) Lake Red Rock	♦	♦	♦		♦		♦		♦	♦	♦			♦
3) Mississippi River Camping			♦				♦		♦					♦
4) Rathbun Lake			♦	♦			♦	♦	♦			♦		
5) Saylorville Lake			♦	♦	♦		♦		♦	♦	♦			♦

Iowa Projects

1) Coralville Lake

U.S. Army Corps of Engineers
2850 Prairie De Chien Rd NE
Iowa City, IA 52240
Phone: 319-338-3543
District: Rock Island

The 5,430-acre Coralville Lake is six miles north of Iowa City on the Iowa River with easy access from Interstates 80 and 380. From I-80 Exit 244 (Dubuque Street) go north 3 miles to West Overlook Road, then one-quarter mile to the park areas.

Public golf courses are nearby as is the state's largest shopping mall in Iowa City. Other local attractions include the Herbert Hoover Presidential Library, the Amana Colonies and Devonian Fossil Gorge.

RV CAMPING

Corps-managed camping is available in three areas. Advance reservations are recommended for summer weekends. Camping is also available at nearby Lake McBride State Park.

Dam Complex: Apr 15-Oct 15, 136 wooded sites with electric hookups, 9 full hookup sites, 36 tent sites, some pull thrus, $12–$24. **Amenities**: Drinking water, dump station, restrooms, showers, boat ramp, fishing, hiking, marina, swimming, playground. **Directions**: From I-80 Exit 244, take Dubuque Street north 3 miles to West Overlook Rd, then 1/4 mile to the park. 2850 Prairie De Chien Rd NE, Iowa City, IA 52240 / 319-338-3543. **GPS**: 41.72444, -91.52944

Sandy Beach: May-Sep, 48 sites with electric hookups, 2 full hookup sites, 8 tent sites, $12–$22. **Amenities**: Drinking water, dump station, restrooms, showers, boat ramp, fishing, playground, swimming. **Directions**: From I-380 Exit 10, east onto 120th Street then south on Curtis Bridge Rd, then east on Sandy Beach Rd. 3369 Sandy Beach Rd NE, Solon, IA 52333 / 319-338-3543. **GPS**: 31.81361, -91.59528

Sugar Bottom: May-Sep, 214 sites with electric (some 50amp) hookups, 16 full hookup sites, some pull thrus, 17 tent sites, $12–$24. **Amenities**: Drinking water, dump station, restrooms, showers, boat ramp, fishing, hiking, horseback riding trails, playground, swimming, disk golf. **Directions**: From I-380 Exit 4, east on Penn Street to N Front Street (turns into Mehaffey Bridge Rd). After crossing the bridge go south into the campground. 2192 Mehaffey Bridge Rd, Solon, IA 52333 / 319-338-3543. **GPS**: 41.75639, -91.55917

2) Lake Red Rock

U.S. Army Corps of Engineers
1105 Highway T15
Knoxville, IA 50138
Phone: 641-828-7522
District: Rock Island

The 19,000-acre Lake Red Rock, Iowa's largest lake, has 100 shoreline miles surrounded by more than 60,000 land acres. The project is located about 30 miles southeast of Des Moines and 4 miles southwest of Pella on CR-T15. Red Rock's Visitor Center, open daily in season, features wildlife exhibits and a gift shop.

Large numbers of deer can be seen throughout the lake area. White pelicans migrate through the area every spring and fall. Large numbers of Bald Eagles can be observed during winter months. There is a

13-mile paved hiking and biking trail at the lake and equestrian trails are at the South Elk Rock Park area. Interpretive programs are featured Memorial Day through Labor Day at the amphitheater. Nearby towns include: Pella, Iowa, known for its Dutch heritage and Knoxville, Iowa, the Sprint Car Capital of the World. Visitors will find shopping malls, museums, a zoo and many other attractions in Des Moines, Iowa's capital.

RV Camping

Howell Station: Mar-Oct, 143 sites with electric (some 50amp) hookups, non-reservables, $20. *Amenities*: Drinking water, dump station, restrooms, showers, boat ramp, fishing, hiking, playground, wildlife viewing. *Directions*: From Pella, IA take Hwy-T15 southwest for 5 miles, then east on Idaho Dr to 198th Pl, south to the campground. 1081 198th Pl, Pella, IA 50138 / 641-828-7522. *GPS*: 41.365, -92.97361

North Overlook: Apr-Sep, 46 wooded sites with electric (50amp) hookups, 1 full hookup site, 8 tent sites, $8–$16. *Amenities*: Drinking water, dump station, restrooms, showers, playground, amphitheater, fishing, hiking, boating, biking, swimming. *Directions*: From Pella, Iowa, go 3 miles southwest on CR–T15. 1007 Highway T15, Pella, IA 50219 / 641-828-7522. *GPS*: 41.38028, -92.96972

Wallashuck: Apr-Oct, 80 sites with electric (some 50amp) hookups, $16. *Amenities*: Drinking water, dump station, restrooms, showers, playground, fishing, boat ramp, biking. *Directions*: From Pella, Iowa, go 4 miles west on CR-G28, then south on 190th Ave. 890 190th Ave, Pella, IA 50219 / 641-828-7522. *GPS*: 41.4, -92.99437

Whitebreast: Apr-Sep, 113 sites with electric (some 50amp) hookups, some pull thrus, $16. *Amenities*: Drinking water, dump station, restrooms, showers, 2 group camping areas, fish cleaning station, playground, swimming beach, amphitheater, boat ramp, fishing, biking. *Directions*: From Knoxville, IA go 8 miles northeast on CR-T15, then north 2 miles on CR-S71. 971 Highway S71, Knoxville, IA 50138 / 641-828-7522. *GPS*: 41.36417, -93.025

3) Mississippi River Camping
  a) Pleasant Creek
  b) Bulger's Hollow
  c) Clark's Ferry
  d) Shady Creek
  e) Ferry Landing

U.S. Army Corps of Engineers
PO Box 2004

Rock Island, IL 61204
Phone: 309-794-5338
District: Rock Island

Fifteen campgrounds dot the shoreline along the Upper Mississippi River Project. Five of these are in Iowa, from the Dubuque area to south of the Quad Cities area. There is an observation deck at the Visitor Center (Lock & Dam #15) in Rock Island. The riverfront area has an abundance of wildlife including songbirds, turkeys, herons, eagles, woodpeckers and deer. Fishing is a popular activity.

RV Camping

3a) Pleasant Creek

Pleasant Creek: May-Oct, 55 sites, no hookups, non-reservable, $4. *Amenities*: Drinking water, dump station, boat ramp. *Directions*: From Dubuque, 24 miles south on US-52, follow signs to Lock & Dam #12. Pleasant Creek is located 3 miles south of Bellevue, Iowa and offers good views of Mississippi River traffic. 563-582-0881.

3b) Bulger's Hollow

Bulger's Hollow: May-Sep, 26 sites (9 tent-only), non-reservable, no hookups, $4. Located at the bottom of a classic Mississippi River ravine, offers the best view of the widest point on the upper river basin, a 3.5-mile expanse from the Iowa to Illinois shorelines. *Amenities*: Drinking water, dump station, restrooms, boat launch, playground, horseshoe pits. *Directions*: From Clinton, 3 miles north on US-67, then 1 mile east on 170th Street. 563-582-0881.

3c) Clark's Ferry

Clark's Ferry: Apr-Oct, 27 sites with electric (50amp) hookups, $16. *Amenities*: Drinking water, dump station, restrooms, showers, boat launch, playground, horseshoes, amphitheater. *Directions*: From Davenport, Hwy-22 west about 15 miles, turn at Clarks Ferry sign in Montpelier, follow signs. 3860 Sunset Beach, Montpelier, IA 52759 / 563-381-4043 or 563-263-7913. *GPS*: 41.46639, -90.80944

3d) Shady Creek

Shady Creek: May-Oct, 53 sites with electric (50amp) hookups, $16. *Amenities*: Drinking water, dump station, restrooms showers, boat ramp, playground, horseshoe pit, hiking and a golf course nearby. *Directions*: From Davenport, west about 17 miles on Hwy-22, turn at Shady Creek sign. 3550 Hwy 22,

Muscatine, IA 52761 / 563-263-7913 or 563-262-8090. *GPS*: 41.4475, -90.87722

3e) Ferry Landing

Ferry Landing: Open all year, non-reservable, 22 free sites, no hookups. *Amenities*: Drinking water, dump station. *Directions*: Ferry Landing sits at the mouth of the Iowa River near the northern edge of Oakville, Iowa. From Muscatine, south on US-61, east on SR-99, follow signs to Lock & Dam #17. 563-263-7913.

4) Rathbun Lake

U.S. Army Corps of Engineers
20112 Hwy J–5T
Centerville, IA 52544
Phone: 641-647-2464
District: Kansas City

The 11,013-acre lake is located in the rolling hills of southern Iowa. Rathbun Lake, also known as "Iowa's ocean," has 155 shoreline miles and is surrounded by 24,925 land acres. From Des Moines, go 85 miles southeast on SR-5.

RV Camping

Five Corps-managed areas provide RV camping. Additional camping can be found at Honey Creek State Park and at private campgrounds at the lake.

Bridge View: May-Sep, 103 sites with electric (some 50amp) hookups, 8 basic sites, $12–$18, some pull thrus. *Amenities*: Drinking water, dump station, restrooms, showers, boat ramp, playground, horseshoe pit. ATV park nearby on the south bank of the South Fork Chariton River. *Directions*: From Moravia, 10 miles west on Hwy-J18, follow signs. 11456 Bridgeview Pl, Melrose, IA 52569 / 641-647-2464.) *GPS*: 40.87861, -93.02667

Buck Creek: May-Sep, 42 sites with electric (some 50amp) hookups, $16–$18. *Amenities*: Drinking water, dump station, restrooms, showers, boat ramp, marina, playground, swimming. *Directions*: From Centerville, 5 miles north on Hwy-5 to Hwy-J29, then 4 miles northwest to Hwy-J5T, north 2 miles, follow signs. 13796 Crappie Circle, Moravia, IA 52571 / 641-724-3206. *GPS*: 40.86278, -92.86778

Island View: May-Sep, 191 sites with electric (some 50amp) hookups, $16–$18. *Amenities*: Drinking water, dump station, restrooms, showers, boat ramp, marina, playground, swimming. *Directions*: From Centerville, 2.5 miles on Hwy-5, then 4 miles northwest on Hwy-J29, then .1 mile north on Hwy-J5T. 19357 Island View Pl, Centerville, IA 52544 / 641-647-2079. *GPS*: 40.8325, 92.91797

Prairie Ridge: May-Sep, 54 sites with electric (50amp) hookups, $18. *Amenities*: Drinking water, dump station, showers, boat ramp, playground, horseshoes. *Directions*: From Moravia, 4 miles west on Hwy-J18, then south 2.5 miles on 200th Ave (gravel), follow signs. 12755 200th Ave, Moravia, IA 52571 / 641-724-3103. *GPS*: 40.87694, -92.88722

Rolling Cove: May-Sep, 31 sites, no hookups, $12. *Amenities*: Drinking water, dump station, restrooms, showers, boat ramp, marina nearby. *Directions*: From Centerville, 2 miles west on Hwy-2, then north on Hwy-T14 for 5.5 miles, then west on Hwy-J5T for 2 miles, then north on 160th Ave for 1.5 miles, follow signs. 16017 Ranger Circle, Mystic, IA 52574 / 641-647-2464. *GPS*: 40.82528, -92.98306

5) Saylorville Lake

U.S. Army Corps of Engineers
5600 NW 78th Ave
Johnston, IA 50131
Phone: 515–276–4656
Visitor Center: 515-964-0672
District: Rock Island

The Saylorville Lake Project covers 26,000 acres and stretches for over 50 miles up the Des Moines River Valley, northwest of Des Moines. From I-35/80 Exit 127 in Des Moines take Hwy-141 north for about 6 miles to Hwy-415 (NW Saylorville Dr). The Visitor Center, located on the east side of the dam, features exhibits on the history and natural resources of the area. Maps and brochures are available and there is a gift shop.

The 24-mile paved, multi-purpose Neal Smith Trail runs from Des Moines to Big Creek State Park and connects the campgrounds to all recreation areas on the east side of the lake. It is used for biking, hiking, jogging, walking and in-line skating (no motor vehicles allowed). The Des Moines River is within easy walking distance. Interpretive programs are presented in season. There are golf courses nearby. Other nearby activities include Frisbee disc golf course, accessible fishing pier and swimming. Equestrian trails are in Jester County Park on the northwest shore.

RV Camping

Bob Shetler, Cherry Glen and Prairie Flower camping areas are on the east side of the lake near the trail. Bob Shetler is the campground of choice for many shore fishermen. Acorn Valley campground is on the heavily wooded west side of the lake.

Acorn Valley: May-Sep, 29 RV sites with electric hookups, 58 walk-in, tent only sites, $12–$22. Gate is closed 10pm to 6am. *Amenities*: Drinking water, dump station, restrooms, showers, fishing, hiking, playground. *Directions*: From Interstate 35/80 Exit 131 (Johnston/Saylorville Lake) north on Merle Hay Rd through Johnston for 2.8 miles. At 4-way stop, turn left on NW Beaver Dr for 3.7 miles. At National Weather Service Building, turn right on NW Coryden Dr, then right into campground. 9615 NW Beaver Dr, Johnston, IA 50131 / 515-276-0429. *GPS*: 41.73778, -93.72361

Bob Shetler: May-Sep, 67 sites with electric (some 50amp) hookups, some pull thrus, $16–$22. *Amenities*: Drinking water, dump station, restrooms, showers, fishing, fish cleaning stations, hiking, playground. *Directions*: From I–35/80 Exit 131 go 2.8 miles north on Merle Hay Rd through Johnson. At 4-way stop, turn left and go 1 mile northwest on Beaver Dr. At the large concrete water storage tank on right, go .8 mile northwest (right) on 78th Ave. Turn right at the T-intersection. 5200 NW 78th Ave, Johnston, IA 50131 / 515-276-0873. *GPS*: 41.70167, -93.68528

Cherry Glen: Apr-Oct, 125 sites with electric (some 50amp) hookups, 3 full hookup sites, $18–$24. Waterfront sites. *Amenities*: Drinking water, dump station, restrooms, showers, boat ramp, fishing, hiking, sailing, water skiing. *Directions*: From I-35 Exit 90 (Ankeny Industrial Pkwy), take Hwy-160 west for 2.4 miles (it becomes Hwy-415). Take Hwy-415 north for 4.1 miles. At the campground sign, get into the left lane and take NW 94th Ave for one-half mile. 4586 NW 94 Ave, Polk City, IA 50325 / 515-964-8792. *GPS*: 41.73139, -93.68

Prairie Flower: Apr-Oct, 159 sites with electric (some 50amp) hookups, $16-$20. Many of the family sites in the south end offer a pleasant view of the lake, while the north end is mostly for group camping in circle-the-wagon style. *Amenities*: Drinking water, dump station, marina, fishing, educational programs, playgrounds, swimming, volleyball, hiking, biking. Bike rentals, firewood. *Directions*: From I-35 Exit 90 (Ankeny Industrial Pkwy) take Hwy-160 west for 2.4 miles (it becomes Hwy-415), continue on Hwy-415 for 5.6 miles. At the campground sign, get into the left turn lane and take NW Lake Dr for .2 mile. 10370 NW Lake Dr, Polk City, IA 50325 / 515-984-6925. *GPS*: 41.74833, -93.6875

Kansas

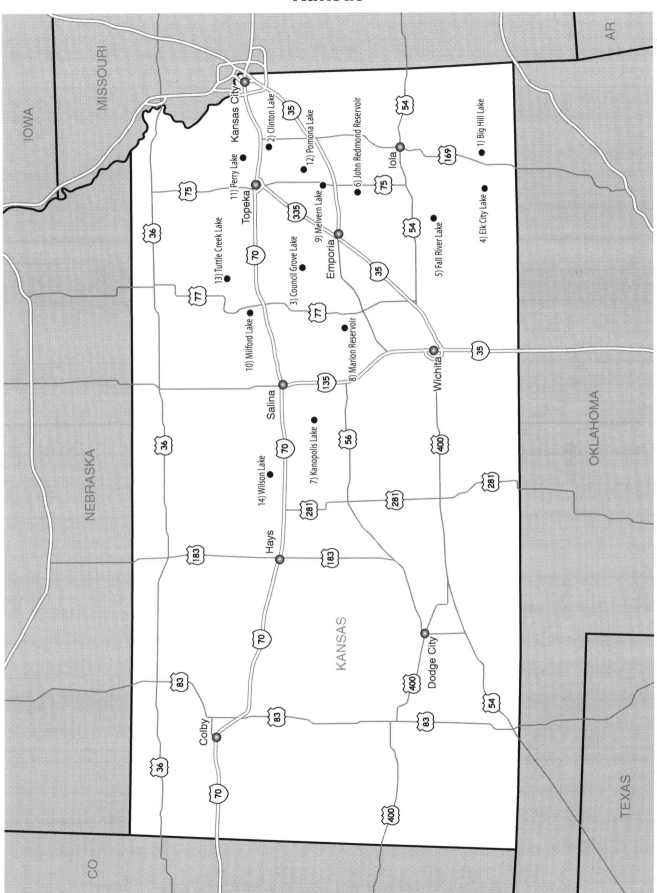

Activities

	Auto Touring	Biking	Boating	Climbing	Cultural / Historic Sites	Educational Programs	Fishing	Groceries / Supplies	Hiking	Horseback Riding	Hunting	Lodging	Off Highway Vehicles	Visitor Center
1) Big Hill Lake			♦				♦		♦	♦	♦		♦	
2) Clinton Lake	♦	♦	♦		♦		♦		♦	♦	♦			♦
3) Council Grove Lake	♦		♦		♦		♦		♦		♦		♦	
4) Elk City Lake			♦				♦		♦		♦			
5) Fall River Lake			♦			♦	♦	♦	♦		♦			
6) John Redmond Reservoir	♦	♦	♦				♦		♦	♦	♦		♦	♦
7) Kanapolis Lake	♦	♦	♦		♦		♦	♦	♦	♦	♦		♦	
8) Marion Reservoir			♦				♦				♦			
9) Melvern Lake			♦			♦	♦		♦	♦	♦			
10) Milford Lake		♦	♦			♦	♦		♦		♦	♦		♦
11) Perry Lake			♦				♦		♦	♦	♦		♦	♦
12) Pomona Lake		♦	♦		♦		♦		♦	♦	♦		♦	♦
13) Tuttle Creek Lake		♦	♦				♦		♦	♦	♦		♦	♦
14) Wilson Lake		♦	♦				♦		♦	♦	♦			♦

Kansas Projects

1) Big Hill Lake

U.S. Army Corps of Engineers
P.O. Box 426
Cherryvale, KS 67335
Phone: 620-336-2741
District: Tulsa

From Independence, travel 7 miles east on US-160, then 4 miles north on KS-169, then 5 miles east on the county road. The project office is on the west side of the dam. The project has 1,404 land acres, 1,204 water acres and 20 shoreline miles. Big Hill Lake is a productive, popular fishing spot. Big Hill Lake Horse Trail, 17 miles long with varied terrain, is also popular.

RV Camping

Cherryvale Park: All year, 10 sites with electric only and 14 full hookup sites (50amp throughout), some pull thrus, $20. **Amenities**: Drinking water, dump station, restrooms, showers, fishing, boating, hiking, hunting, horseback riding trails, playground, swimming, group camping area. **Directions**: From US-169 at Cherryvale, Kansas, go east on Main St through Cherryvale. At the end of Main St, turn south onto Olive St, go one-half block and turn east onto CR-5000. Follow paved road 4.5 miles, follows signs. Located on the west side of the dam, north of the project office. 620-336-2741 **GPS**: 37.26944, -95.45833

Mound Valley: Apr-Oct, 85 sites with electric (some 50amp) hookups, 8 basic sites, $10–$25. Many waterfront sites. **Amenities**: Drinking water, dump station, restrooms, showers, swimming, boat ramp, fishing, hiking, horseback riding trails, hunting, group camping. **Directions**: Located on the east side of the lake. Exit off US-169 at Cherryvale, then go east through Cherryvale on Main St, turn south at the end of Main St onto Olive St, go one-half block (follow sign), turn east onto CR-5000 and follow the paved road for 4.5 miles. 620-336-2741 **GPS**: 37.26944, -95.45833

Timber Hill: Apr-Oct, 20 sites, no hookups, some pull thrus, non-reservable, $10. **Amenities**: Drinking water, dump station, restrooms, fishing dock, boat ramp, equestrian trail with separate camping area. **Directions**: From the east side of the dam, go 3 miles north, then west on the gravel road. 620-336-2741.

2) Clinton Lake

U.S. Army Corps of Engineers
872 N 1402 Rd
Lawrence, KS 66049
Phone: 785-843-7665
District: Kansas City

From Lawrence, travel one mile west on Clinton Parkway. The Visitor Center, located on the northwest side of the dam, features displays on the history and wildlife of the area as well as the reasons for the dam. The project has 16,361 land acres, 7,000 water acres and 85 shoreline miles.

There is a marina on the north shore. A golf course, model plane airport and the Clinton Lake Historical Society Museum are nearby. The University of Kansas is in Lawrence.

RV Camping

RV camping is found at Corps-managed campgrounds and Clinton State Park where there is also a swimming beach.

Cedar Ridge: Apr-Oct, 84 sites with electric (some 50amp) hookups, some pull thrus, $18. **Amenities**: Drinking water, dump station, restrooms, showers, laundry, fishing, playground, horseshoe pit, swimming, volleyball. **Directions**: From Lawrence take Hwy-40 (6th St) west 4 miles, then left on CR-442, go west 5 miles to Stull. Go left onto CR-1023, go south about 6 miles to CR-6, turn left, 3.5 miles. 1205 E 700 Rd, Lawrence, KS 66047 / 785-843-7665. **GPS**: 38.91278, -95.37472

Hickory/Walnut: May-Sep, 220 sites (94 with electric hookups), some pull thrus, $10–$16. **Amenities**: Drinking water, dump station, restrooms, showers, laundry, boat ramp, fishing, biking, playground, swimming. **Directions**: From Lawrence, take Hwy-40 (6th St) west 4 miles, then left onto CR-442 and go 5 miles to Stull, then left on CR-1023, go 6 miles to CR-6, turn left and go 4 miles through Clinton. The park is next to town, follow signs. 1184 E 700 Rd, Lawrence, KS 66047 / 785-843-7665. **GPS**: 39.9125, -93.37444

Rockhaven: Apr-Nov, 50 sites (12 with electric hookups), non-reservable, $8–$12. Horse/mule camping in separate equestrian-only camping area. **Amenities**: Drinking water, restrooms, riding trails for campers and day use. **Directions**: From Stull, 6 miles south on SR-1023, then 3 miles east on SR-458, then .8 mile north on CR-700E (gravel). 1050 E 700 Rd, Lawrence, KS 66047 / 785-843-7665.

3) Council Grove Lake

U.S. Army Corps of Engineers
945 Lake Rd
Council Grove, KS 66846
Phone: 620-767-5195
District: Tulsa

Council Grove Lake is located about 30 miles southwest of Topeka. From the Kansas Turnpike (I-335) go west 26 miles on US-56 to Council Grove. In the famous Flint Hills region of Kansas, the project is on the Neosho River with over 3,310 acres of water, 40 shoreline miles and 5,887 land acres. The lake is named for the town of Council Grove where the Osage Indians signed a treaty to establish the Old Santa Fe Trail. A marker in town indicates the place where the treaty was signed.

An ATV area is below the dam in Outlet Channel East. Sightseeing is in the nearby historic town of Council Grove.

RV Camping

Canning Creek: All year, 40 sites with electric (some 50amp) and water hookups, 3 basic sites, $17–$20. **Amenities**: Dump station, restrooms, showers, playground, boat ramp, fishing, hiking, hunting, scenic drive, group camping area. **Directions**: Located 1.5 miles north of Council Grove on SR-177. Go west across Dam Road at the west end of the dam, turn right on to City Lake Rd and travel 2 miles west. 1130 City Lake Rd, Council Grove, KS 66846 / 620-767-6745. **GPS**: 38.69247, -96.53731

Kit Carson Cove: Mar-Nov, 14 sites with electric & water, 1 basic site, non-reservable, $8–$14. **Amenities**: Drinking water, restrooms, boat ramp, nature trail. **Directions**: From US-56 in Council Grove, 2 miles north on SR-177, then west. 620-767-5195.

Marina Cove: Apr-Oct, 3 sites with electric hookups, 1 basic site, non-reservable, $8–$12. **Amenities**: Drinking water, restrooms, boat ramp, marina. **Directions**: From Council Grove, 1.5 miles north on SR-177, then 1 mile west on Dam Road, 1.5 miles west on right. 620-767-5195.

Neosho: All year, 7 sites with electric hookups, 1 site with electric and water hookups, non-reservable, $12–$14. **Amenities**: Drinking water, restrooms, boat ramp. **Directions**: From Council Grove, 1.5 miles north on SR-177, 1 mile west on Dam Road, right on City Lake Road 1 mile, then .3 mile west on right. City Lake Rd, Council Grove, KS 66846 / 620-767-5195.

Richey Cove: Apr-Oct, 43 sites with electric (some 50amp) and water hookups, 16 electric-only, $11–$20. *Amenities*: Dump station, restrooms, showers, playground, swimming, hiking trail, boat ramp, fishing, hiking, scenic drive. *Directions*: From Council Grove go 3 miles north on SR-177, entrance on west side of highway. 1268 Hwy 177, Council Grove, KS 66846 / 620-767-5800. *GPS*: 38.70119, -96.49756

Santa Fe Trail: Apr-Oct, 35 sites with electric & water hookups, 1 full hookup, 5 electric-only, $11–$18. *Amenities*: Dump station, restrooms, showers, playground, boat ramp, hiking, fishing, hunting, scenic drive. *Directions*: From Council Grove go north 1.5 miles on SR-177, then west on Dam Road 1 mile to City Lake Rd, turn right and go 1 mile west to the campground. 1026 City Lake Rd, Council Grove, KS 66846 / 620-767-7125. *GPS*: 38.68189, -96.52486

4) Elk City Lake

U.S. Army Corps of Engineers
P.O. Box 426
Cherryvale, KS 67335
Phone: 620-336-2741
District: Tulsa

Located 127 miles east of Wichita in southern Kansas, 5 miles northwest of the town of Independence. From Independence, go 7 miles north on US-75, then 4 miles west and 2 miles south on county road. The project includes 15,336 land acres, 3,122 water acres and 50 miles of shoreline.

Elk City Lake features six scenic hiking trails through colorful forests and through some of the most interesting rock formations in the state. Elk City State Park is nearby. The State of Kansas uses 11,680 acres of project lands for wildlife management and public hunting.

RV CAMPING

Card Creek: All year, 15 sites with electric hookups, 4 basic, some pull thrus, all non-reservable on first come first serve basis, $12–$16. Close to public hunting areas. *Amenities*: Drinking water, dump station, restrooms, showers, boat ramp, fishing, nature trail, boat dock. *Directions*: From Elk City junction SR-39, go 7 miles southeast on US-160, then 1.3 miles north and 1.7 miles northwest. 620-336-2741.

Outlet Channel: Apr-Dec, 14 sites (7 with electric & water hookups and 7 basic sites), reservations not accepted, $10-$16. *Amenities*: Drinking water, dump station, restrooms, fishing, playground, near hiking and bike trails. *Directions*:

From Elk City, go 7 miles northwest of Independence on the county road below the dam. Sites are located on the west side of the spillway. 620-336-2741.

5) Fall River Lake

U.S. Army Corps of Engineers
RR 1 Box 243E
Fall River, KS 67047
Phone: 620-658-4445
District: Tulsa

Fall River Lake is located 70 miles east of Wichita and 4 miles west of the town of Fall River just off US-400. From junction US-77/US-400 (east of Wichita) go east on US-400 to mile marker 344 (250 Road), then northeast. The project office is on the west side of the dam. The lake is about a mile wide at the dam site and stretches up the picturesque Fall River for 15 miles.

Flowers, birds and game enhance the project situated in rolling prairie country. There is good wildlife viewing. The 10,900-acre Fall River Game Management Area is located within the project. Note: There are some low water crossings in some areas.

RV CAMPING

Damsite: Apr-Oct, 18 full hookup sites (some 50amp), 10 electric-only sites, 5 basic, $17–$21. Waterfront sites. *Amenities*: Drinking water, dump station, restrooms, showers, laundry, fishing, hunting, hiking, birding, canoeing, jet skiing, swimming, playground, wildlife viewing. *Directions*: From US-400 turn north at mile marker 344 (250 Road), then turn east for 2.4 miles, turn south at the park entrance, follow signs. 620-658-4445. *GPS*: 37.6443, -96.06927

Rock Ridge North: 23 sites with electric hookups, 2 sites with electric & water, 19 basic sites, non-reservable, $9–$16. *Amenities*: Drinking water, dump station, restrooms, boat ramp, nature trail. *Directions*: From junction US-400 & Hwy-99, go 7.8 miles east, 1.7 miles north and 1.5 miles west. Low water crossing. 620-658-4445.

Whitehall Bay: Apr-Oct, 9 full hookup sites (50amp), 15 electric-only sites, $17–$21. *Amenities*: Drinking water, dump station, restrooms, showers, laundry, boat ramp, fishing, canoeing, hiking, hunting, swimming, jet skiing, water skiing. *Directions*: From US-400 turn north at mile marker 344 and go about 1 mile, then turn east and go 2.8 miles across the dam, turn north .8 mile, then west .7 mile, then north 1.8 miles across the low water crossing, west .4 mile, then south 1 mile to campground. 620-658-4445. *GPS*: 37.66717, -96.07268

6) John Redmond Reservoir

U.S. Army Corps of Engineers
1565 Embankment Rd SW
Burlington, KS 66839
Phone: 620-364-8613
District: Tulsa

John Redmond Reservoir is located in the broad Neosho River Valley. From I-35 Exit 155, go south on US-75 to Embankment Road (3.5 miles north of Burlington), travel west and follow signs to the Dam area and Visitor Center. The project includes 30,693 land acres, 9,710 water acres and 69 shoreline miles.

The spillway area, a popular place for fishing, can be accessed from Riverside East campground. The multi-use Hickory Creek Trail is open to hikers, horseback riders and mountain bikers. There are 140 acres of trails for ATVs and dirt bikes. Numerous wildlife viewing areas are located around the reservoir. Sightseers will enjoy the Flint Hills Wildlife Refuge or wandering the old Indian grounds.

RV Camping

Riverside East: Apr-Oct, 43 sites with electric hookups, some pull thrus, $15. On the east bank of the Neosho River. Good wildlife viewing from the hiking trail. **Amenities**: Dump station, restrooms, showers, fishing, biking, hiking, hunting. **Directions**: From Burlington, travel 3.5 miles north on US-75, then 1.5 miles west on Embankment Rd, follow signs. 620-364-8613. **GPS**: 38.23333, -95.75

Riverside West: May-Sep, 36 sites with electric (some 50amp) hookups, 6 basic, $8–$15. On the west bank of the Neosho River. **Amenities**: Drinking water, dump station, restrooms, showers, playground, interpretive trail, boat ramp, fishing, hiking, biking, hunting. **Directions**: From Burlington, travel 3.5 miles north on US-75, then 2.5 miles west on Embankment Rd, follow signs. 620-364-8613. **GPS**: 38.22917, -95.76667

7) Kanopolis Lake

U.S. Army Corps of Engineers
105 Riverside Dr
Marquette, KS 67464
Phone: 785-546-2294
District: Kansas City

From Salina, go 20 miles southwest on KS-140, then 10 miles south on KS-141. Kanopolis Lake is located on the Smoky Hill River and is one of the oldest lakes in Kansas. The project has 18,580 land acres, 3,427 water acres and 41 shoreline miles.

Nearby, the Fort Hanker Museum at Kanapolis and the Rogers Art Gallery and Museum at Ellsworth portray the settlement of the American West.

RV Camping

Horse Thief and Langly State Parks also have camping as well as horseback riding and mountain biking.

Riverside: Apr-Oct, 16 sites with electric (some 50amp) hookups and 12 basic sites, $12–$18. River access for fishing. Caution: Steep river banks may be dangerous for unattended children. **Amenities**: Drinking water, dump station, restrooms, showers, playground, fishing, basketball court. **Directions**: On the southeast end of the dam. From Salina, west on Hwy-140 for 19 miles to Hwy-141, then 14 miles south to the end of the dam to Riverside Dr. Follow for .5 mile east. 785-546-2294. **GPS**: 38.599972, -97.93333

Venango: All year, 134 sites with electric (some 50amp) hookups, 24 basic sites, some pull thrus, $12–$18. **Amenities**: Drinking water, dump station, restrooms, showers, boat ramp, hiking, off-road (ATV) vehicle trail, volleyball court, playground, swimming. **Directions**: On the northwest end of the dam. From Salina, go west for 19 miles on Hwy-140, then 12 miles south on Hwy-141, then .5 mile west, follow signs. 785-546-2294. **GPS**: 38.63306, -97.9875

8) Marion Reservoir

U.S. Army Corps of Engineers
2105 North Pawnee
Marion, KS 66861
Phone: 620-382-2101
District: Tulsa

Marion Reservoir is 46 miles northeast of Wichita. From I-135 east in Newton, 24 miles north on KS-15, then 12 miles east on US-56. The reservoir encompasses 6,200 acres of water surrounded by another 6,000 acres of public lands. Wildlife observers will enjoy the Willow Walk Nature Trail located at Cottonwood Point campground.

RV CAMPING

Cottonwood Point: Mar-Nov, 109 sites with electric (some 50amp) and water hookups, 21 electric-only, some pull thrus, $17–$20. **Amenities**: Drinking water, dump station, boat ramp, restrooms, showers, dock, fishing, interpretive trail, playground, swimming. **Directions**: Located 4 miles northwest of Marion, KS off US-56, turn north on Old Mill Rd and go 2.8 miles north. Follow signs. 620-382-2101. **GPS**: 38.38889, -97.08889

French Creek Cove: Mar-Nov, 20 sites with electric hookups, $12. **Amenities**: Drinking water, restrooms, boat ramp, dock, all non-reservables. **Directions**: From Marion, go 7 miles west on US-56, then 1 mile north on KS-15 and 1 mile east on 210th St. 620-382-2101.

Hillsboro Cove: Mar-Nov, 30 sites with electric & water hookups, 21 electric-only, some pull thrus, $17-$19. **Amenities**: Drinking water, dump station, restrooms, showers, fishing, boating, hiking, hunting, playground, boat dock. **Directions**: From Marion, go 5 miles northwest on US-56, turn north on Night Hawk, then east, follow signs. 620-382-2101. **GPS**: 38.36278, -97.09972

Marion Cove: Mar-Nov, 6 basic sites, $8, all non-reservables. **Amenities**: Drinking water, restrooms, boat ramp, swimming. **Directions**: From Marion, go 3 miles west on US-56, then 1 mile north on Pawnee past the project office on left. 2125 North Pawnee Rd, Marion, KS 66861 / 620-382-2101.

9) Melvern Lake

U.S. Army Corps of Engineers
31051 Melvern Lake Pkwy
Melvern, KS 66510
Phone: 785-549-3318
District: Kansas City

From Topeka, go 40 miles south on US-75. The Project Information Center is located 1/4 mile west of the KS-31 exit off US-75 at the south end of the dam. Exhibits, brochures and pamphlets are available. Melvern Lake project is situated on the eastern edge of the Kansas Flint Hills Region and covers 6,900 acres of water and 18,000 acres of land open for public use. There is a stocked fishing pond at the Outlet campground.

RV CAMPING

Eisenhower State Park also offers camping and horseback riding.

Arrow Rock: May-Sep, 19 sites with electric hookups, 25 basic sites, $12–$18, some pull thrus. **Amenities**: Drinking water, dump station, restrooms, showers, laundry, boat ramp, fishing, fish cleaning stations, hunting, playground. **Directions**: From US-75, Olivet exit, go 1 mile west on KS-276 to South Fairlawn Rd, then 1 mile north to Arrow Rock Pkwy, then west 1 mile. 22862 Arrow Rock Pkwy, Lebo, KS 66856 / 785-549-3318. **GPS**: 38.49085, -95.75952

Coeur D'Alene: May-Sep, 33 sites with electric (50amp) hookups, 1 full hookup site, 25 basic sites, $12–$17. **Amenities**: Drinking water, dump station, restrooms, showers, swimming beach, fishing, fish cleaning stations, dock, marina, boat ramp, hiking, playground. **Directions**: From US-75, Melvern exit, go 2 miles south on Melvern Lake Pkwy, then 1 mile northwest on Coeur D'Alene Pkwy. 785-549-3318. **GPS**: 38.4976, -95.71791

Outlet: Apr-Oct, 61 sites with electric hookups, 89 full hookup sites, $18–$20. **Amenities**: Drinking water, dump station, restrooms, showers, laundry, boat ramp, fishing, fish cleaning station, hiking, swimming beach, playground. **Directions**: From US-75 Melvern exit, go 1/4 mile west on Melvern Lake Pkwy to cut off road, then 1/4 mile west to River Pond Pkwy, then 1/2 mile north. 30442 River Pond Pkwy, Melvern, KS 66510 / 785-549-3318. **GPS**: 38.51371, -95.70624

Turkey Point: May-Sep, 44 sites with electric (some 50amp) hookups, 16 basic sites, $12–$19. **Amenities**: Drinking water, dump station, restrooms, showers, laundry, boat ramp, fishing, fish cleaning station, hunting, playground. **Directions**: From Osage City, go south on KS-170 to 301st St, then 2 miles east, then 1 mile south on Indian Hills Rd to Turkey Point Pkwy, then 1/2 mile south. 30967 Turkey Point Pkwy, Osage City, KS 66523 / 785-549-3318. **GPS**: 38.49862, -95.78975

10) Milford Lake

U.S. Army Corps of Engineers
4020 West KS-57 Hwy
Junction City, KS 66441
Phone: 785-238-5714
District: Kansas City

Milford Lake, the largest man-made lake in Kansas, is located just north of I-70, about 65 miles west of Topeka. From I-70 Exit 295, go north on US-77 for 4 miles, then left on KS-57, then left and 1.5 miles to the Milford Lake Information Center where displays and exhibits are featured and maps and directions are available. The lake has 163 shoreline miles and the project encompasses 15,600 water acres and 32,263 land acres.

The Milford Nature Center is located at the project.

ATV areas at School Creek and Timber Creek are for vehicles less than 50 inches wide only. Restaurants are in the nearby town of Milford.

RV Camping

In addition to the Corps managed camping areas a county park, state park, city park and other private campgrounds offer RV camping.

Curtis Creek: Apr-Sep, 48 sites with electric hookups, 28 basic sites, $12–$18. **Amenities**: Dump station, restrooms, showers, playground, boat ramp, fishing dock. **Directions**: From I-70 Exit 290, go north 5 miles, then west on 837 for 6 miles. 6902 Curtis Creek Rd, Junction City, KS 66441 / 785-238-4636. **GPS**: 39.09278, -96.955

Farnum Creek: Apr-Sep, 30 sites with electric (some 50amp) hookups and 15 basic sites, some pull thrus, $12-$19. **Amenities**: Drinking water, restrooms, dump station, showers, boat ramp, fish cleaning stations, playground. **Directions**: Take I-70 to Exit 295, then north on Hwy 77 for 11 miles. 785-463-5791. **GPS**: 39.07778, -95.89167

School Creek: Apr-Oct, 44 sites, no hookups, primitive camping, non-reservable, $8. **Amenities**: Drinking water, restrooms, boat launch, pier, off-road/ATV area. **Directions**: From Wakefield, 1 mile west on SR-82. 785-238-5714.

Timber Creek: Apr-Oct, 45 sites, no hookups, non-reservable, $8. **Amenities**: Drinking water, restrooms, boat launch, playground, off-road/ATV area. **Directions**: From Wakefield, 1 mile east on SR-82. 785-238-5714.

West Rolling Hills: Apr-Sep, 44 sites with electric hookups, 12 basic sites, some pull thrus, tent area adjacent to beach, $12–$19. **Amenities**: Dump station, restrooms, showers, swimming, marina, boat ramp, playground. **Directions**: From I-70 Exit 290, go 5 miles to 244, then east .5 mile. 5028 West Rolling Hills Rd, Junction City, KS 66441 / 785-238-4636. **GPS**: 39.075, -96.92333

11) Perry Lake

U.S. Army Corps of Engineers
10419 Perry Park Dr
Perry, KS 66073
Phone: 785-597-5144
District: Kansas City

From Topeka take US-24 east for 17 miles to Perry. Turn left on Ferguson Road north of Perry for about 2 miles. Turn left at 39th Street (Spillway Rd) and travel about a mile, then turn right on Perry Park Dr. The brick building on the right is the Corps information center. The project has 31,641 land acres, 11,148 water acres and 160 miles of shoreline. A 30-mile National Recreation Trail follows the eastern shoreline of Perry Lake.

RV Camping

Four Corps-managed campgrounds, as well as Horse Trail State Park (with a 25-mile equestrian trail) and Perry State Park (with a mountain bike trail), are located at the lake.

Long View: May-Sep, 26 wooded sites with electric hookups, 13 basic sites and 6 tent sites, some pull thrus, $12–$16. **Amenities**: Drinking water, dump station, restrooms, showers, boat ramp, fishing, hiking. **Directions**: From Oskaloosa, go 6 miles west on KS-92, then 2 miles south on Ferguson Rd, then 2 miles west on 86th St. 7752 Longview Park Rd, Ozawkie, KS 66070 / 785-597-5144. **GPS**: 39.18472, -95.44444

Old Town: May-Sep, 29 shaded sites with electric hookups, 44 basic, some pull thrus, $12–$17. **Amenities**: Drinking water, dump station, restrooms, showers, boat ramp, fishing, hiking, biking, playground. **Directions**: From Ozawkie, travel 1.5 miles east on KS-92, follow signs. 9952 Old Town Trail, Ozawkie, KS 66070 / 785-597-5144. **GPS**: 39.225, -95.4375

Rock Creek: Apr-Oct, 64 sites with electric (some 50amp) hookups, 53 basic and 25 tent sites, $12–$18. **Amenities**: Drinking water, dump station, restrooms, showers, boat ramp, fishing, hiking, playground, horseback riding trails, scenic drive. **Directions**: From Hwy-24 west of the town of Perry, travel 3 miles north on KS-237, then east on Rock Creek Park Rd. 785-597-5144. **GPS**: 39.12083, -95.45417

Slough Creek: Apr-Oct, 85 sites with electric (some 50amp) and water hookups, 121 sites with no hookups, some pull thrus, 18 tent sites, $12–$18. **Amenities**: Drinking water, dump station, restrooms, showers, boat ramp, fishing, biking, hiking, horseback riding trails, interpretive trail, playground, group camping area. **Directions**: From Perry, junction Hwy-24, go 7 miles north on Ferguson Rd, then 1 mile southwest on Slough Creek Rd. 785-597-5144. **GPS**: 39.13472, -95.43056

12) Pomona Lake

U.S. Army Corps of Engineers
5260 Pomona Dam Rd
Vassar, KS 66524
Phone: 785-453-2201
District: Kansas City

From Topeka, go 24 miles south on US-75, then 7 miles east on KS-268. The Project Information & Visitor Center has displays about the lake and the environment and maps and brochures. Pomona has 4,000 water acres, 52 miles of shoreline and 8,025 land acres.

Located near the Santa Fe Trail, the lake has scenic beauty as well as an abundance of wildlife. Excellent fishing can be found at the lake's many bank fishing areas. Power boating and sailing are also popular at the lake. Two marinas provide fuel and boating services and supplies. Designated swimming beaches are at Michigan Valley campground and Pomona State Park.

RV CAMPING

Camping is also available at Pomona State Park.

Carbolyn Park: May-Sep, 29 sites with electric (some 50amp) hookups, 3 basic sites, some pull thrus, $16. Lots of shade in a secluded location. *Amenities*: Drinking water, dump station, restrooms, showers, playground, boat ramp. *Directions*: 25 miles south of Topeka on US-75. Park entrance is 4.5 miles south of Lyndon, on the east side of the highway, follow signs. 785-453-2201. *GPS*: 38.675, -95.67917

Cedar: All year, 8 primitive sites, free, non-reservable, *Amenities*: Restrooms, rock base boat ramp. *Directions*: Park is located on the north side of the lake. From Michigan Valley, 2 miles west on East 213th St, 1 mile on South Shawnee Heights Rd. 785-453-2201.

Michigan Valley: May-Sep, 51 sites with electric & water hookups, 36 basic sites, $12–$18. *Amenities*: Dump station, restrooms, showers, playground, swimming, marina. *Directions*: From US-75, east on KS-268 for 7 miles to Pomona Dam Rd, then north for 2.5 miles across the dam, turn west on Wolf Creek Pkwy for 500 feet, then south to the park entrance. 785-453-2201. *GPS*: 38.66472, -95.54889

Outlet Park: All year, 36 sites with electric & water hookups, $10-$18. *Amenities*: Dump station, restrooms, showers, laundry, playground, nature trail. *Directions*: Located along 110 Mile Creek. From US-75 go east on KS-268 for 7 miles, turn north on Pomona Dam Rd and go .5 mile to 229th St (just before the dam), turn east to the park entrance. 785-453-2201. *GPS*: 38.64583, -95.55972

Wolf Creek: Apr-Oct, 45 sites with electric & water hookups, $12–$16. *Amenities*: Dump station, restrooms, showers, playground, ball field, boat ramp, bank fishing area, group

camping area. *Directions*: From US-75, go east on KS-268 for 7 miles to Pomona Dam Rd, then north 2.5 miles across the dam. Turn west on Wolf Creek Pkwy for 1.2 miles. 785-453-2201. *GPS*: 38.67639, -95.56806

13) Tuttle Creek Lake

U.S. Army Corps of Engineers
5020 Tuttle Creek Blvd
Manhattan, KS 66502
Phone: 785-539-8511
District: Kansas City

Tuttle Creek Lake is situated some 55 miles northwest of Topeka. From I-70 Exit 313, go 9 miles north on KS-177, then 5 miles north on US-24 to the dam project office. The lake's long narrow shoreline stretches for 100 miles. The project has 12,500 surface acres of water and 16,000 acres of land. Tuttle, the second largest lake in Kansas, is located in the scenic Flint Hills. An off road vehicle area is just below the east end of the dam with access from Dyer Road.

RV CAMPING

The Corps manages two campgrounds, both on the west side of the lake. There are four state parks, the River Pond unit of Tuttle Creek State Park is the most popular for RV camping. The county operates a primitive campground. Random camping elsewhere is prohibited.

Stockdale: Apr-Sep, 11 sites with 50amp electric hookups, 2 pull thrus, $18. Tuttle Creek State Park is nearby. *Amenities*: Drinking water, dump station, restrooms, showers, boat ramp, fishing, biking, hiking, horseback riding trails, hunting, swimming, playground, off-road vehicle trails. *Directions*: From junction US-24/KS-13 at the west end of the dam, travel north and west 5 miles, then right on Riley County Rd (CR-895), then two miles, right on CR-396, then 2.5 miles to the campground. Entrance road is minimally maintained and can be flooded. 785-539-8511. *GPS*: 39.30611, -96.65222

Tuttle Creek Cove: Apr-Oct, lakefront sites, 44 with electric (some 50amp) hookups and 11 basic sites, some pull thrus, $12–$18. *Amenities*: Limited availability of drinking water, dump station, restrooms, showers, boat ramp, fishing, biking, hiking, playground, horseback riding trails, off road vehicle trails. *Directions*: From junction US-24/KS-13, east on KS-13 for 200 yards, then north on Tuttle Creek Rd, 3 miles. 6000 Tuttle Creek Cove Rd, Manhattan, KS 66503 / 785-539-8511. *GPS*: 39.27694, -96.63028

14) Wilson Lake

U.S. Army Corps of Engineers
4860 Outlet Rd
Sylvan Grove, KS 67481
Phone: 785-658-2551
District: Kansas City

From Salina, go west on I-70 to the Wilson exit (#206), then 7 miles north on SR-232 to the Visitor Center. Located in the Post Rock Country of north-central Kansas, the lake has 9,000 water acres and 100 shoreline miles. There are 25,574 land acres within the project.

Wildlife viewing is excellent from the Burr Creek Nature Trail at Sylvan Park, especially at dawn and dusk. Wilson State Park and a golf course are nearby.

RV CAMPING

Three Corps-managed camping areas include Minooka on the south side of the lake, Sylvan Park located below the dam near the administration building and Lucas Park on the north side of the lake.

Lucas Park: Apr-Oct, 71 sites with electric (some 50amp) hookups, 33 basic sites, $12–$24, some pull thrus. **Amenities**: Drinking water, dump station, restrooms, showers, boat ramp, dock, fishing, hiking, swimming, hunting. **Directions**: From I-70 Exit 206, go 9 miles north on SR-232, park is on left. 785-658-2551. **GPS**: 38.95556, -98.51944

Minooka: Apr-Oct, 106 sites with electric (some 50amp), 44 basic sites, some pull thrus, $12–$24. **Amenities**: Drinking water, dump station, restrooms, showers, boat ramp, fishing, fish cleaning station, hiking, swimming, playground. **Directions**: From I-70 Exit 199, go north on Dorrance Rd 7 miles. 785-658-2551. **GPS**: 39.93278, -98.575

Sylvan Park: All year, 27 sites with electric hookups, some pull thrus, $12–$18. **Amenities**: Drinking water, dump station, restrooms, showers, boat ramp, fishing, hiking, swimming, biking, volleyball, horseshoe pit, jet skiing, marina, wildlife viewing. **Directions**: From I-70 Exit 206, go 8 miles north on SR-232, before crossing the dam turn right at KS-181, go east 100 yards, then turn left, follow the road past the Visitor Center. 785-658-2551. **GPS**: 38.96833, -98.49167

Kentucky

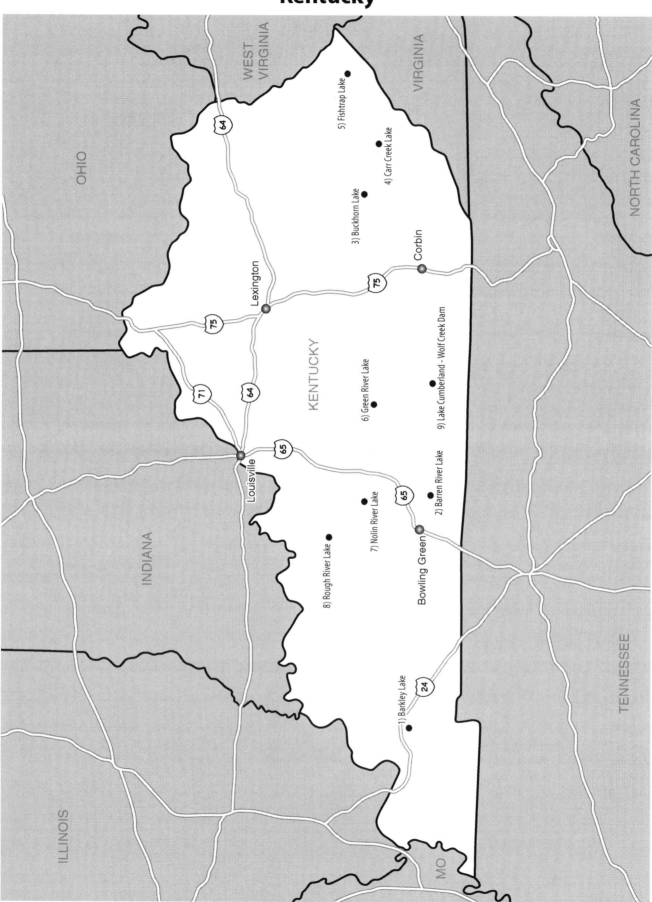

Activities

		Auto Touring	Biking	Boating	Climbing	Cultural / Historic Sites	Educational Programs	Fishing	Groceries / Supplies	Hiking	Horseback Riding	Hunting	Lodging	Off Highway Vehicles	Visitor Center
1)	Barkley Lake	♦	♦	♦		♦	♦	♦		♦	♦	♦	♦		♦
2)	Barren River Lake	♦		♦		♦		♦		♦		♦	♦		♦
3)	Buckhorn Lake	♦	♦	♦		♦		♦	♦	♦		♦	♦		
4)	Carr Creek Lake			♦				♦		♦		♦			
5)	Fishtrap Lake		♦	♦				♦				♦			
6)	Green River Lake			♦				♦		♦		♦			♦
7)	Lake Cumberland - Wolf Creek Dam		♦	♦		♦		♦	♦	♦		♦			♦
8)	Nolin River Lake	♦		♦		♦		♦		♦	♦	♦	♦	♦	
9)	Rough River Lake	♦		♦		♦		♦		♦		♦			♦

Kentucky Projects

1) Barkley Lake

U.S. Army Corps of Engineers
Box 218, 200 Barkley Lake Overlook
Grand Rivers, KY 42045
Phone: 270-362-4236
District: Nashville

Barkley Lake is the eastern part of the Land Between the Lakes, a National Recreation Area managed by the U.S. Forest Service. The Corps project includes 51,043 land acres, 57,920 water acres and 1,004 miles of shoreline. From Western Kentucky Parkway Exit 4, travel west on US-62 for 13 miles through Eddyville and follow US-62 to the Resource Office and Visitor Center located just below the dam. A "Steamboating on the Cumberland" exhibit is featured at the Visitor Center. Maps and brochures are available.

Local points of interest include a Civil War Monument and historic relics. Good wildlife viewing can be found throughout the project. Full service marinas, restaurants and golf are nearby. Fort Donelson National Battlefield is on Lake Barkley's western shore.

RV CAMPING

Corps-managed camping areas include one in Tennessee and three in Kentucky. Other camping is available at the state park and private marinas and resorts on the lake.

Bumpus Mills: Apr-Sep, 15 sites with electric & water hookups, non-reservable, $18-$20. **Amenities**: Dump station, restrooms, showers, laundry, swimming, boat ramp, fishing, hiking, swimming, playground, marina. **Directions**: Located in Tennessee. From I-24 Exit 65 (Cadiz), travel south on Hwy-139 (turns into SR-120). Go through Bumpus Mills, then west on Tobaccoport Rd, follow signs, go 1 mile on gravel road, continue straight at the "Y" and follow signs. Campground is 20 miles from Clarksville, Tennessee. 931-232-8831. **GPS**: 36.61972, -87.88306

Canal: Apr-Oct, 97 sites with electric (some 50amp) hookups, 17 full hookup sites, some pull thrus, $16–$29. **Amenities**: Dump station, restrooms, showers, laundry, playground, swimming, boat ramp, fishing, amphitheater. **Directions**: From I-24 Exit 31, go south on Hwy-453 for 2 miles. 270-362-4840. **GPS**: 36.99556, -88.20972

Eureka: Apr-Sep, 23 sites with electric & water hookups, $17–$23. **Amenities**: Dump station, restrooms, showers, boat ramp, fishing, biking, playground, swimming, water skiing. **Directions**: From I-24 Exit 40 (Kuttawa), go west on Hwy-62/641, then south on Hwy-810, then west on SR-1271, follow signs. 270-388-9459. **GPS**: 37.02514, -88.19401

Hurricane Creek: Apr-Sep, 51 sites with electric (some 50amp) & water hookups, 6 tent sites, some pull thrus, $12–$22. **Amenities**: Dump station, restrooms, showers, laundry, boat ramp, fishing, playground, swimming. *Directions*: From I-24 Exit 45, turn right on Hwy-293 west for .3 mile. Turn left on Hwy-93 south for 5.3 miles. Turn right on Hwy-274 south for 5.7 miles, then right on Hurricane Camp Road. Campground is 12 miles from Cadiz. 270-522-8821. *GPS*: 36.92, -87.97583

2) Barren River Lake

U.S. Army Corps of Engineers
1088 Finney Rd
Glasgow, KY 42141
Phone: 270-646-2055
District: Louisville

The project, some 20 miles southeast of Bowling Green and about 15 miles southwest of Glasgow, encompasses 14,667 land acres, 10,000 water acres and 140 shoreline miles. From I-65 Exit 53 (Cave City), travel 10 miles south on KY-90 to Glasgow, then 5 miles south on US-31 to KY-252 for 9 miles to the dam. The project office and Visitor Center are located on the north end of the dam. Maps, brochures and information on area attractions are available.

Cool water near the dam provides for good fishing for hybrid striped bass and rainbow trout when stocked. Barren River State Park on US-31 also has camping plus lodging, marina and golf. Area attractions include Mammoth Caves National Park and many federally protected Native American villages and burial sites.

RV Camping

Bailey's Point: Apr-Oct, 149 sites with electric (some 50amp) hookups, 52 basic sites, $16–$22. Largest Corps campground, scenic views of the lake. *Amenities*: Drinking water, dump station, restrooms, showers, hiking, swimming, interpretive trails. *Directions*: From Glasgow, Kentucky, take US-31E south for 15 miles to Hwy-252. Turn right and go 1.5 miles to Hwy-517, turn right, follow signs. 270-622-6959. *GPS*: 36.89083, -86.09528

Tailwater: Apr-Sep, 46 sites with electric (50amp) hookups, some pull thrus, $18. *Amenities*: Restrooms, drinking water, boat ramp, hiking, fishing, marina, playground. *Directions*: From Glasgow, Kentucky, take US-31E south for 4 miles, turn right on SR-252 which will cross the dam in 8 miles. Tailwater entrance road is at the south end of the dam, follow signs. Campground is approximately 19 miles from Bowling Green. 270-622-7732. *GPS*: 36.89444, -86.13306

The Narrows: Apr-Sep, 86 gravel sites with electric (50amp) & water hookups, $22. *Amenities*: Restrooms, showers, boat ramp, amphitheater, interpretive trails, marina, playground, swimming area. *Directions*: From Glasgow, Kentucky, take US-31E south for 10 miles, turn right on Hwy-1318, follow signs. 270-646-3094. *GPS*: 36.90417, -86.07083

3) Buckhorn Lake

U.S. Army Corps of Engineers
804 Buckhorn Dam Rd
Buckhorn, KY 41721
Phone: 606-398-7251
District: Louisville

The Buckhorn project encompasses 4,646 land acres, 1,230 water acres and 65 shoreline miles. From Hazard, Kentucky, travel 9 miles north on KY-15, then 20 miles east on KY-28. Maps and brochures are available at the Corps office located near the town of Buckhorn (north side of the lake).

Buckhorn offers the scenic beauty of the Appalachian Mountain Range. Attractions in the area include Daniel Boone National Forest, Red River Gorge Geological Area and Buckhorn State Resort where there is lodging, dining and an 18-hole golf course. Restaurants and miniature golf are nearby.

RV Camping

Buckhorn: Apr-Oct, 28 sites with electric (50amp) hookups, 4 tent sites, $12–$22. *Amenities*: Cable TV, dump station, restrooms, showers, laundry, boat ramp, horseshoe pit, interpretive trails, playground, soccer field, swimming. *Directions*: From I-64 Exit 98 take Mountain Pkwy to Exit 33 at Slade, then KY-11S through Beattyville. Continue on KY-11 to Boonville, go straight past the courthouse to KY-28W. Follow KY-28 about 23 miles to Buckhorn. 104 Tailwater Camp Rd, Buckhorn, KY 41721 / 606-398-7220. *GPS*: 37.35083, -83.47278

Trace Branch: May-Sep, 18 sites with electric (some 50amp) hookups, $22. *Amenities*: Dump station, restrooms, showers, boat ramp, dock, fishing, horseshoe pit, playground, swimming, jet skiing, basketball courts. *Directions*: From I-75 Exit 41 (London) or Exit 38, take Daniel Boone Pkwy east for 44 miles to Hyden Spur, exit to Tim Couch Pass and immediate left toward Thousandsticks onto Bull Creek Rd, 2.5 miles to KY-257, then north for 5 miles to Dryhill, go right across Dryhill Bridge, then left on Toulouse Rd for 5 miles to Mosley Bend Rd intersection, continue straight 1/2 mile to Trace Branch area on left. 606-398-7251. *GPS*: 37.24167, -83.37278

4) Carr Creek Lake

U.S. Army Corps of Engineers
843 Sassafras Creek Rd
Sassafras, KY 41759
Phone: 606-642-3308
District: Louisville

Carr Creek is located in the mountainous region of southeastern Kentucky, 16 miles east of Hazard and 18 miles north of Whitesburg. From Hazard, travel 16 miles south on KY-15, then 1 mile north on KY-1089. The project office is located below the dam, behind the Little Dove Church at Sassafras. Information and maps are available. The project includes 3,196 land acres, 710 water acres and 24 shoreline miles.

Fishing and boating are primary activities at the lake. Nearby attractions include the Daniel Boone National Forest and Buckhorn Lake.

RV Camping

Carr Creek State Park on Hwy-15 also has camping.

Littcarr: Apr-Oct, 45 sites with electric (50amp) & water hookups and 6 basic sites, $20. **Amenities**: Dump station, restrooms, showers, laundry, boat ramp, fishing, marina, grocery store, playground, horseshoes, shuffleboard, nature trail. **Directions**: From I-75 Exit 38 (SR-192) east to Daniel Boone Pkwy. Follow the Parkway to SR-15, then south on SR-15 to SR-160. Turn north and follow for 4 miles. 606-642-3052. **GPS**: 37.2375, -82.94972

5) Fishtrap Lake

U.S. Army Corps of Engineers
2204 Fishtrap Rd
Shelbiana, KY 41562
Phone: 606-437-7496
District: Huntington

There are 14,858 land acres, 1,131 water acres and 43 shoreline miles at Fishtrap. From Pikeville, travel 12 miles east on US-460, then 2 miles east on SR-1789 to the project office located just downstream of the dam.

Located in rich coalfield country, near the Virginia state line, steep mountains surround the project area.

Boat ramps and a marina are at the lake. A mountain biking trail is popular.

RV Camping

Grapevine: May-Sep, 10 sites with electric and water, 18 basic sites, reservations not accepted, $8–$12. **Amenities**: Dump station, restrooms, showers, playground. **Directions**: From the town of Phyllis (north of the lake), go .5 mile west on SR-194. 606-835-4564.

6) Green River Lake

U.S. Army Corps of Engineers
544 Lake Rd
Campbellsville, KY 42718
Phone: 270-465-4463
District: Louisville

The Green River project has 25,583 land acres, 8,210 water acres and 147 miles of shoreline. From I-65 Exit 43, go east on the Cumberland Pkwy toward Glasgow/Somerset. Stay on Cumberland/Louie Nunn Pkwy (portions toll) to Exit 49. Take KY-55 toward Columbia. Turn left onto KY-55/Jamestown Street and follow KY-55. Turn right onto KY-1061/Lake Road to the Visitor Center. The Center features interpretive exhibits.

RV Camping

Holmes Bend: Apr-Oct, 101 sites with electric (most 50amp) hookups, 23 basic sites, $17–$23. **Amenities**: Drinking water, dump station, restrooms, showers, interpretive trail, playgrounds. **Directions**: From Columbia, Kentucky, take Exit 49 off the Cumberland Pkwy, then go north on KY-55 for 1.5 miles, turn right on KY-551 and continue 1 mile, turn left on Holmes Bend Rd, follow signs. Holmes Bend Rd/KY-682, Columbia, KY 42728 / 270-384-4623. GPS: 37.21389, -85.26667

Pikes Ridge: Apr-Sep, 20 sites with electric (50amp) & water hookups, 1 full hookup site and 39 basic sites, $15–$21. Some waterfront sites. **Amenities**: Drinking water, dump station, restrooms, boat ramp, fishing, hiking, hunting, interpretive trails, playground, swimming. **Directions**: From Campellsville KY, take KY-70 east for 4 miles, turn right on KY-76 and continue for 4.8 miles, turn right on Pikes Ridge Rd, follow signs. 270-465-6488. **GPS**: 37.28056, -85.29167

Smith Ridge: Apr-Sep, 62 sites with electric (50amp) hookups and 18 basic sites, some pull thrus, $17–$21. **Amenities**:

Drinking water, dump station, restrooms, showers, hiking, hunting, playground, swimming. *Directions*: From Campbellsville, Kentucky, take KY-70 east for 1 mile, turn right on KY-372 and continue 3 miles, turn right on County Park Rd, follow signs. 1500 County Park Rd, Campbellsville, KY 42719 / 270-789-2743. *GPS*: 37.29583, -85.3

7) Lake Cumberland – Wolf Creek Dam

U.S. Army Corps of Engineers
855 Boat Dock Rd
Somerset, KY 42501
Phone: 606-679-6337
District: Nashville

The Cumberland project is located south of Lexington near the Tennessee state line and south of the Cumberland Pkwy. It encompasses 48,580 land acres, 50,250 water acres and 1,085 shoreline miles. The Lake Cumberland Visitor Center is located at the Resource Manager's office on Boat Dock Rd, about 4 miles south of Somerset on US-27 at red light #29. A self-guided study in nature overlooks the lake at the Visitor Center. Tours of the dam are available in summer and the educational fish hatchery is next door.

During the recreation season, the Corps conducts an interpretive demonstration of an 1877 grist mill, which is on the National Register of Historic Places. Other places of interest nearby include the Mill Springs National Historical Landmark, Natural Arch, Yahoo Falls and Big Fork National River and Recreation Area.

RV CAMPING

Five Corps-managed areas provide camping at Cumberland. Other campgrounds can be found at Burnside State Park and at marinas and private resorts around the lake.

Cumberland Point: Apr-Sep, 30 sites with electric (some 50amp) hookups, $20. *Amenities*: Dump station, restrooms, showers, laundry, playground, boat ramp, fishing. *Directions*: From Nancy, Kentucky, take Hwy-235 south for 1 mile, then right onto Hwy-761 and go 9 miles. 1000 Hwy 761, Nancy, KY 42544 / 606-871-7886. *GPS*: 39.96556, -84.84222

Fall Creek: Apr-Oct, 10 sites, non-reservable, $18. *Amenities*: Drinking water, dump station, restrooms, showers. *Directions*: Located off Hwy-2393 about 4 miles from Conley Bottom Resort. 606-348-6042.

Fishing Creek: Apr-Sep, 46 sites with electric (50amp) hookups, $12–$20. *Amenities*: Drinking water, dump station, restrooms, showers, laundry, boat ramp, fishing, playground, swimming. *Directions*: From Somerset, Kentucky, take Hwy 80 west for 5 miles, turn right on Hwy 1248 and follow for 2 miles. Entrance is on the left at the bottom of the hill. 1611 Hwy 1248, Somerset, KY 42501 / 606-679-5174 or 606-679-6337. *GPS*: 37.07139, -84.68917

Kendall: All year, 116 sites with electric (50amp) hookups, $20–$22. *Amenities*: Dump station, restrooms, showers, laundry, boat ramp, fishing, fish cleaning stations, playground, horseshoe pit, basketball courts, hiking and bike trails. *Directions*: From Jamestown, KY take US-127 south for 10 miles, turn right on Kendell Rd, just before crossing the dam, follow signs. 80 Kendall Rd, Jamestown, KY 42629 / 270-343-4660. *GPS*: 36.8725, -85.14667

Waitsboro: Apr-Oct, 21 sites with 50amp electric hookups, 4 tent sites, $20. *Amenities*: Drinking water, dump station, restrooms, showers, laundry, boat ramp, fishing, playground. *Directions*: From Somerset, KY, take US-27 south for 5 miles, turn right on Waitsboro Rd, follow signs. 500 Waitsboro Dr, Somerset, KY 42501 / 606-561-5513. *GPS*: 37.00361, -84.62306

8) Nolin River Lake

U.S. Army Corps of Engineers
2150 Nolin Dam Rd
Bee Spring, KY 42207
Phone: 270-286-4511
District: Louisville

Located north of Bowling Green, the lake is accessible from I-65 or from the Western Kentucky Pkwy. Known for its blue-green water, the lake has 5,795 water acres and 172 miles of shoreline. There are 12,155 land acres within the project. From I-65 Exit 53, go west into Brownsville, then north for 5 miles on KY-259, then right on KY-728, follow signs.

Portions of Nolin River path are within Mammoth Cave National Park, making it scenic for canoe trips. Canoe rentals are available locally. Golf and riding stables are nearby.

RV Camping

Nolin Lake State Park also has camping.

Dog Creek: May-Sep, 50 sites with electric (50amp) hookups, 20 basic sites, $15–$22. **Amenities**: Drinking water, dump station, restrooms, boat ramp, hiking, marina, playground, swimming area. **Directions**: From Louisville take I-65 Exit 76 at Upton, then Hwy-224 west for 9 miles to Millerstown, turn left on Hwy-479, go 8 miles to Hwy-88, turn left and go 2.1 miles, then right on Hwy-1015, then 1.1 miles. 890 Dog Creek Rd, Cub Run, KY 42729 / 270-524-5454. **GPS**: 37.32083, -86.12917

Moutadier: Apr-Oct, 81 sites with electric (some 50amp) hookups, 86 basic sites, $15–$22. **Amenities**: Drinking water, dump station, restrooms, showers, boating, hiking, marina, playground. **Directions**: From Louisville, take I-65 south to the Western Kentucky Pkwy. Take the Parkway west for about 30 miles to Hwy-259 at Leitchfield, KY. Take Hwy-259 south for about 12 miles to Hwy-2067, turn left on Hwy-2067, follow signs. 1343 Moutadier Rd/KY-2067, Leitchfield, KY 42754 / 270-286-4230. **GPS**: 37.31639, -86.23306

Wax: Apr-Sep, 56 sites with electric (50amp) hookups, 54 basic sites, some pull thrus, $15–$22. **Amenities**: Drinking water, dump station, restrooms, showers, boat ramp, fishing, hiking, marina, playground. **Directions**: From Louisville, take I-65 south to Exit 76 at Upton, then Hwy-224W to Millerstown 9 miles. Turn left on Hwy-479 and go 8 miles to Hwy-88, turn left for .5 mile. 14069 Peonia Rd, Clarkson, KY 42726 / 270-242-7578. **GPS**: 37.34167, -86.12917

9) Rough River Lake

U.S. Army Corps of Engineers
14500 Falls of Rough Rd
Falls of Rough, KY 40119
Phone: 270-257-2061
District: Louisville

Located 51 miles north of Bowling Green, the Rough River project encompasses 8,974 land acres, 4,860 water acres and has 220 miles of shoreline. From Louisville, travel west on US-60 to Harned, then south for 10 miles on KY-79 to the project office/Visitor Center, which is on KY-79. Information, maps and brochures are available.

Local attractions include the historic Green Farm and Pine Knob Theater featuring outdoor dramas based on folklore of the area, June through September. There are many caves in the area including the Mammoth Caves, the longest cave system in the world.

RV Camping

There are four Corps-managed campgrounds with a large number of lakefront sites. Camping is also available at Rough River Dam State Park, where visitors will also find 18-hole and 9-hole golf courses and miniature golf.

Axtel: Apr-Sep, 82 sites with 50amp electric hookups, 57 basic sites, $15–$22. **Amenities**: Drinking water, dump station, restrooms, showers, boat ramp, fishing, boating, marina, playground, swimming area. **Directions**: From Louisville, take US-60 to Harned, then south on Hwy-259. Travel 9 miles and turn west on Hwy-79 for .5 mile. 270-257-2584. **GPS**: 37.6225, -86.45306

Cave Creek: Apr-Sep, 16 sites with 50amp electric hookups, 65 basic sites, $17–$22. 35-foot RV length limit. **Amenities**: Drinking water, dump station, restrooms, showers, playground, boat ramp, fishing pier. **Directions**: From Elizabethtown, Kentucky, take Western Kentucky Pkwy to the Leitchfield exit (#107), then north to Hwy-259 to Hwy-54, travel west on Hwy-54 for 11 miles, then 6 miles on Hwy-79, then east on Hwy-736 for 2 miles. 502-879-4304. **GPS**: 37.57333, -86.49528

Laurel Branch: Apr-Sep, 26 sites with 50amp electric hookups and 45 basic sites, $17. **Amenities**: Drinking water, dump station, restrooms, boat ramp, fishing, playground. **Directions**: From Louisville, take US-60 to Harned, then 10 miles west on Hwy-79, then east on Hwy-259 for .5 mile to Hwy-110, then west on Hwy-110 for 1 mile, follow signs. 435 Laurel Branch Rd, McDaniels, KY 40152 / 270-257-8839. **GPS**: 37.6075, - 86.45361

North Fork: Apr-Sep, 44 sites with electric (50amp) hookups, and 44 basic sites, some pull thrus, $17–$22. **Amenities**: Drinking water, dump station, restrooms, showers, playground, swimming, boat ramp, dock, fishing. **Directions**: From Louisville, take US-60 to Harned, then take Hwy-79 west for 9 miles. 9077 South Hwy 259, McDaniels, KY 40152 / 502-257-8139. **GPS**: 37.62972, -86.43667

Minnesota

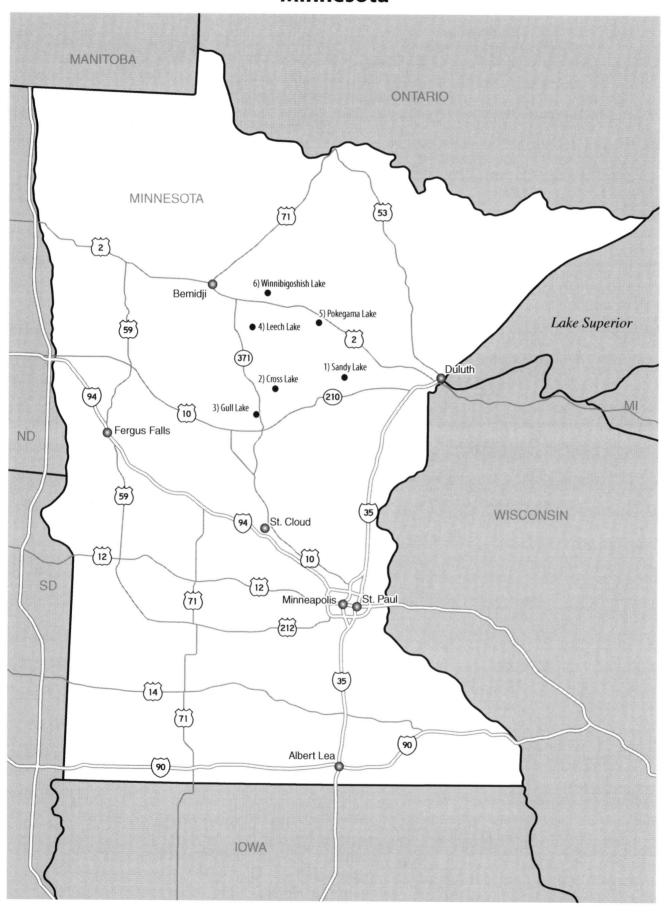

Activities

	Auto Touring	Biking	Boating	Climbing	Cultural / Historic Sites	Educational Programs	Fishing	Groceries / Supplies	Hiking	Horseback Riding	Hunting	Lodging	Off Highway Vehicles	Visitor Center
1) Cross Lake		♦	♦				♦		♦		♦			
2) Gull Lake			♦		♦		♦		♦		♦			♦
3) Leech Lake			♦			♦	♦		♦		♦			
4) Pokegama Lake			♦				♦				♦			
5) Sandy Lake			♦		♦		♦		♦		♦			♦
6) Winnibigoshish Lake			♦				♦				♦			

Minnesota Projects

1) Cross Lake

U.S. Army Corps of Engineers
35507 County Rd 66
Crosslake, MN 56442
Phone: 218-692-2025
District: St. Paul

Located 22 miles north of Brainerd, Minnesota, Cross Lake is in the Whitefish chain of lakes. It has 13,660 water acres and 119 miles of scenic shoreline. From Hwy-25 north, turn right on CR-3, then north to Crosslake, Minnesota. Fishing and hunting are popular sporting activities within the project.

RV Camping

Cross Lake: May-Sep, 72 sites with electric (some 50amp) hookups and 46 basic sites, $20-$26. The campground is in a wooded setting with some lakefront sites. **Amenities**: Drinking water, dump station, restrooms, showers, laundry, boat ramp, fishing, swimming, playground. **Directions**: From Brainerd, MN, on Hwy-25, turn right on CR-3 and travel north to Crosslake. Entrance is on the left directly across from junction of CR-3 & CR-66. 35507 County Road 66, Crosslake, MN 56442 / 218-692-2025. **GPS**: 46.66972, -94.10833

2) Gull Lake

U.S. Army Corps of Engineers
10867 East Gull Lake Dr NW
Brainerd, MN 56401
Phone: 218-829-3334
District: St. Paul

The Gull Lake project is located 130 miles north of St. Paul and 10 miles northwest of Brainerd. Take SR-210 west to SR-371, then north on SR-371 for about 6 miles, turn left at the Federal Recreation Area sign. The project office is on the southeast side of the lake; information is available. The original 7-room dam tender's house is listed on the National Register of Historic Places; prehistoric archaeology of the dam site is also significant with Aboriginal burial mounds on the National Register. An interpretive exhibit is featured at the Visitor Center.

The Corps-managed campground is in a wooded setting and has interpretive hiking trails through the forested areas. Boat and canoe rentals are available in the area. Nearby attractions include golf, shopping, restaurants and an amusement park.

RV Camping

Gull Lake: Apr-Oct, 39 sites with 50amp electric hookups, $26. **Amenities**: Drinking water, dump station, restrooms, showers, boat ramp, fishing, hiking, swimming, playground, interpretive trails. **Directions**: From junction MN-210 & MN-371 in Baxter, travel north on MN-371 for 5.8 miles. Turn left onto CR-125 (Gull Dam Rd), follow signs, about 3 miles. 10867 E Gull Lake Dr, Brainerd, MN 56401 / 218-829-3334. **GPS**: 46.41083, -94.35139

3) Leech Lake

U.S. Army Corps of Engineers
1217 Federal Dam Dr NE
Federal Dam, MN 56641
Phone: 218-654-3145
District: St. Paul

The 126,000-acre lake is located in the middle of the Chippewa National Forest, 200 miles northwest of Minneapolis. From Grand Rapids, Minnesota, take US-2 west for 33 miles to Bena, Minnesota, then CR-8 for 8 miles to Federal Dam, Minnesota.

The lake is well known for its excellent perch, walleye and muskie fishery. The Leech Lake Indian Reservation is nearby.

The Corps-managed campground is located in a wooded setting and offers a variety of recreation within the campground as well as nature trails and a marina. Ranger programs are presented in season. Firewood is available for a fee.

RV Camping

Leech Lake: 64 sites with electric (some 50amp) hookups, 5 full hookup sites and 4 tent sites, $10–$22. *Amenities*: Drinking water, dump station, restrooms, showers, laundry, boat ramp, fishing, fish cleaning stations, boat dock, hiking, playground, shuffleboard, volleyball, basketball, badminton. *Directions*: From Grand Rapids, MN, take US-2 west for 33 miles to Bena, MN, then CR-8 south for 8 miles. 01217 Federal Dam Dr NE, Federal Dam, MN 56641 / 218-654-3145. *GPS*: 47.24472, -94.23083

4) Pokegama Lake

U.S. Army Corps of Engineers
34385 US Hwy-2
Grand Rapids, MN 55744
Phone: 218-326-6128
District: St.Paul

This 16,000-acre lake is near Grand Rapids just south of US-2. From Grand Rapids, travel west on US-2 for 2 miles, then south at sign.

Located near the Mississippi River headwaters, the Corps-managed campground is situated next to the river with good shoreline fishing. The campground is nestled in a scenic area and wildlife viewing is excellent. Birders enjoy seeing bald eagles, loons, duck, geese and many other species. The Forest History Center is nearby.

RV Camping

Pokegama Dam: Apr-Oct, 20 sites with 50amp electric hookups and 2 tent-only sites, $12–$26. *Amenities*: Drinking water, dump station, restrooms, showers, boat ramp, fish cleaning station, playground. *Directions*: From Grand Rapids, west on US-2 for 2 miles, turn left at sign. 218-326-6128. *GPS*: 47.25, -93.58333

5) Sandy Lake

U.S. Army Corps of Engineers
22205 531st Ln
McGregor, MN 55760
Phone: 218-426-3482
District: St. Paul

Located 120 miles north of St. Paul, on the canoe route that once linked Lake Superior and the Mississippi River, Sandy Lake is a part of the Corps' Mississippi River Headwaters Project. The dams that created the lakes were constructed in the 1800's. When the dam at Sandy Lake was built, it included a lock to pass boat traffic through. It was the northernmost lock on the Mississippi River and was the site of an early trading post. Today the lockhouse has been renovated to display interpretive exhibits and artifacts at the Visitor Center. From MN-65 travel to the north entrance of Sandy Lake and follow signs to the Visitor Center located at the dam.

RV Camping

At the Corps-managed campground, about half of the campsites are located near the shoreline of Sandy Lake and the Sandy River.

Sandy Lake: May-Sep, 43 sites with electric hookups, some pull thrus, 8 walk-in tent sites, $16–$24. *Amenities*: Drinking water, dump station, restrooms, showers, laundry, boat ramp, fishing pier, hiking, horseshoes, swimming, playground, volleyball & basketball courts, badminton. *Directions*: Take MN-65 north of McGregor and follow south entrance signs to the campground. 218-426-3482. *GPS*: 46.78833, -93.32833

6) Winnibigoshish Lake

U.S. Army Corps of Engineers
22205 531st Ln
McGregor, MN 55760

Phone: 218-426-3482
District: St. Paul

Winnibigoshish is 102 miles northwest of Duluth. Situated in the Chippewa National Forest, the lake is located northwest of Deer River and north of US-2. The lake is 67,000 acres in size and has 141 miles of shoreline. It was formed by a huge ice block left behind by a receding glacier. From Deer River, Minnesota, go 2 miles west on US-2, then turn right on MN-46 and go 12 miles north. Turn left on Itasca CR-9 and go two miles, follow signs.

The area has nesting bald eagles and is home to many other birds and mammals including black bear. Winnibigoshish is considered a world-class fishery. The camping area is east of the Mississippi River and the dam.

RV Camping

Winnie Dam: May-Oct, 22 sites with 50amp electric hookups, $20. **Amenities**: Drinking water, dump station, restrooms, no showers, boat ramp, fishing, fish cleaning stations, playground. **Directions**: From Deer River, MN, west on US-2, for 1 mile, then turn right on MN-46 for 12 miles, turn left on CR-9, follow signs, 2 miles. 218-326-6128. **GPS**: 47.43, -94.04917

Mississippi

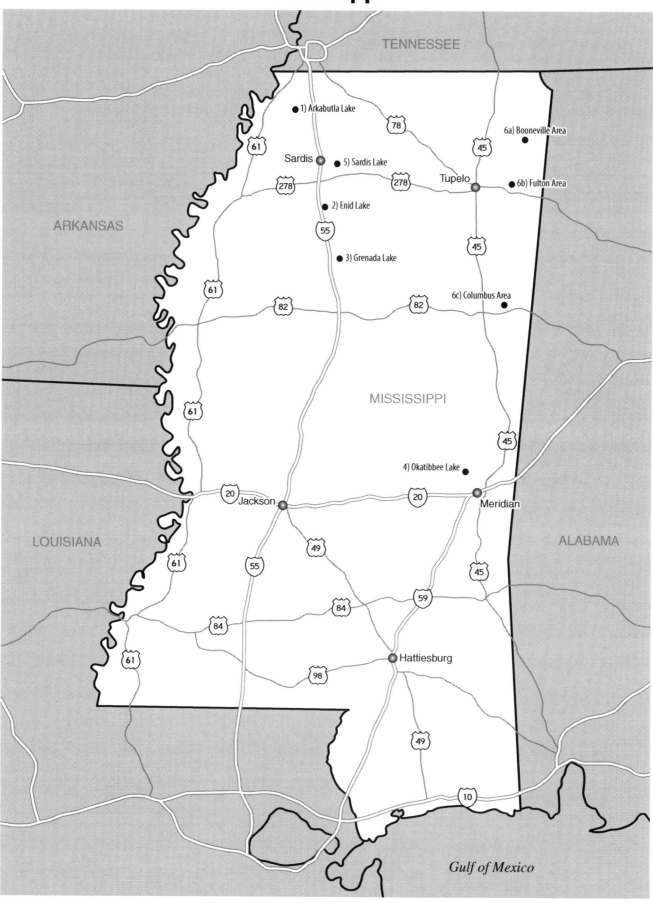

Activities

	Auto Touring	Biking	Boating	Climbing	Cultural/Historic Sites	Educational Programs	Fishing	Groceries/Supplies	Hiking	Horseback Riding	Hunting	Lodging	Off Highway Vehicles	Visitor Center
1) Arkabutla Lake		♦	♦				♦		♦		♦			
2) Enid Lake		♦	♦				♦		♦	♦	♦	♦		♦
3) Grenada Lake			♦			♦	♦		♦		♦	♦	♦	♦
4) Okatibbee Lake	♦	♦	♦				♦		♦		♦			♦
5) Sardis Lake			♦				♦		♦			♦		
6) Tennessee-Tombigbee Waterway			♦		♦	♦	♦		♦		♦			♦

Mississippi Projects

1) Arkabutla Lake

U.S. Army Corps of Engineers
3905 Arkabutla Dam Rd
Coldwater, MS 38618
Phone: 662-562-6261
District: Vicksburg

Located in northern Mississippi, 30 miles south of Memphis, Tennessee, the project includes 44,520 land acres, 12,730 water acres and 134 shoreline miles. From I-55 Exit 280 (Hernando), travel 13 miles west on Scenic Loop 304 to the project.

On the Coldwater River, the lake is known for its large crappie and excellent sailing conditions.

RV Camping

Corps campgrounds at the lake include Dub Patton on the north end of the dam near the town of Eudora and Hernando Point on the east side of the lake.

Dub Patton: Mar-Oct, 81 sites with 50amp electric sites in a predominately pine forested area, $16–$20. **Amenities**: Drinking water, dump station, restrooms, showers, hiking, boat ramp, fishing, hunting, playground. **Directions**: From I-55 Exit 280 (Hernando) travel west on Scenic Route 304, follow signs. 662-562-6261.

Hernando Point: All year, 84 sites with 50amp electric hookups, $16–$20. **Amenities**: Drinking water, dump station, restrooms, showers, boat ramp, fishing, hiking, hunting, playground, swimming, interpretive trails. **Directions**: From

I-55 Exit 280 (Hernando) travel west to US-51, then south on US-51 to area sign, then west on Wheeler Rd and follow signs. 788 Wheeler Rd, Hernando, MS 38632 / 662-562-6261. **GPS**: 37.73361, -90.06889

2) Enid Lake

U.S. Army Corps of Engineers
264 CR-39
Enid, MS 38927
Phone: 662-563-4571
District: Vicksburg

Enid Lake is 65 miles south of Memphis, Tennessee, and 26 miles north of Grenada. The project spans 28,476 land acres, 15,560 water acres and has 125 shoreline miles. From I-55 Exit 233, travel east on CR-36/Enid Dam Rd to the Project Office where information is available.

Located in the Hills region of the state, about 140 miles north of Jackson, the lake is noted for its fishing with several world records posted at the lake. It is also recognized for its family camping facilities.

RV Camping

The four campgrounds listed below all have trails for off-road vehicles and horseback riding trails. George P. Cossar State Park also has camping.

Chickasaw Hill: All year, 53 sites with 50amp electric hookups, some pull thrus, $14. **Amenities**: Drinking water, dump station, restrooms, showers, boat ramp, fishing, hiking, swimming, horseback riding, off road vehicle trails. **Directions**: From I-55 Exit 233, take CR-36 (Enid Dam Rd) east for 1 mile to the

Enid Lake Field Office, then north for 3 miles on Chapel Hill Rd, then east on Pope Water Valley Rd for 7 miles, then south on Chickasaw Rd for 1.5 miles. 662-563-4571. *GPS*: 34.16389, -89.82222

Persimmon Hill: All year, 72 sites with 50amp electric hookups, many sites also have water hookups, $16-$18. *Amenities*: Drinking water, dump station, restrooms, showers, boat ramp, fishing, hiking, playground, swimming, designated trails for horseback riding and off-road vehicles. *Directions*: From I-55 Exit 233, go 1 mile on Enid Dam Rd (CR-36) east, then south across the top of the dam 2 miles, follow signs. 662-563-4571. *GPS*: 34.13556, -89.88611

Wallace Creek: All year, 99 sites with 50amp electric hookups, $16–$18. *Amenities*: Drinking water, dump station, restrooms, showers, boat ramp, fishing, playground, swimming, off road vehicle and horseback riding trails. *Directions*: From I-55 Exit 233, travel east on Enid Dam Rd (CR-36) about 2.5 miles, follow signs. 662-563-4571. *GPS*: 34.16111, -89.89167

Water Valley Landing: Mar-Oct, 29 sites with 50amp electric hookups, $14. *Amenities*: Drinking water, dump station, restrooms, showers, boat ramp, fishing, hiking, designated trails for horseback riding and off-road vehicles, playground, swimming. *Directions*: On the south side of the reservoir. From I-55 Exit 227, go 17 miles east on SR-32, then 2 miles on CR-53, follow signs. 662-563-4571. *GPS*: 34.14306, -89.76389

3) Grenada Lake

U.S. Army Corps of Engineers
P.O. Box 903
Grenada, MS 38902
Phone: 662-226-5911
District: Vicksburg

Grenada Lake, about 100 miles south of Memphis, Tennessee, has 35,820 water acres, 148 shoreline miles and 54,559 land acres. From I-55 Exit 206 (Grenada), travel 4 miles east on MS-8, then follow Scenic Loop Drive 333 to the dam area. The Visitor Center, at the south end of the dam, features a film presentation and a multi media touch screen to access information about the lake. The Center also has a variety of exhibits and an observation deck overlooking the lake.

Grenada Lake is home to the "Thunder On Water" festival held annually in June. Civil War redoubts are located on project lands and Civil War Reenactments are held. Golf is nearby.

RV Camping

RV camping, with many lakefront sites, is available at the Corps facilities and at Hugh White State Park.

North Abutment: All year, 56 sites with 50amp electric & water hookups, some pull thrus, $18. *Amenities*: Drinking water, dump station, restrooms, showers, fishing, boating, waterfront sites. Amphitheater overlooks the lake. *Directions*: From I-55 Exit 206, take Hwy-8 east through the city of Grenada for 3 miles, then left on Scenic Loop 333 across the dam and take the second road to the right. 662-226-1679. *GPS*: 33.84694, -89.77444

North Graysport: All year, 50 sites with 50amp electric hookups, some pull thrus, $14. *Amenities*: Drinking water, dump station, restrooms, showers, boat ramp, amphitheater. *Directions*: From I-55 Exit 206, take Hwy-8 east for 4 miles across the lake, follow signs. 662-226-1679. *GPS*: 33.84417, -89.60361

4) Okatibbee Lake

U.S. Army Corps of Engineers
8604 Okatibbee Dam Rd
Collinsville, MS 39325
Phone: 601-626-8431
District: Mobile

Okatibbee Lake is located 8 miles north of Meridian, Mississippi, along SR-19. The project encompasses 7,494 land acres, 3,800 water acres and 28 shoreline miles. The Visitor Center is near the north end of the dam. Boating and fishing are popular. Anglers will find large populations of bass, crappie and catfish. The fishing platform at the tailrace below the dam is a popular place to drop in a line.

Sightseeing, golf and restaurants are available in nearby Meridian. A water park is on the east side of the lake. There are five beaches and swimming areas around the lake.

RV Camping

Camping is available at the Corps-managed facility listed below and at a park operated by the Harrison Waterway District.

Twiltley Branch: All year, 52 sites with 50amp electric hookups and 12 basic sites with water only, $18–$20.

Amenities: Dump station, restrooms, showers, laundry, boat ramp, fishing, hunting, hiking, playground, swimming, group camping area. **Directions**: From Meridian, take SR-19 north for 8 miles, follow signs. 9200 Hamrick Rd No, Collinsville, MS 39325 / 601-626-8068.

5) Sardis Lake

U.S. Army Corps of Engineers
29049 Hwy 315
Sardis, MS 38666
Phone: 662-563-4531
District: Vicksburg

The Sardis Lake project has 32,100 water acres and spans 163 shoreline miles. Surrounding project land encompasses 66,257 acres. The lake is 8 miles north of Oxford, Mississippi. From I-55 Exit 252 (Sardis), travel 10 miles east on MS-315 or from I-55 Exit 246 (Batesville) travel 10 miles east on MS-35.

Located on the Tallahatchie River, Sardis Lake is known for its sand beaches and fishing for its abundant bass and crappie.

RV CAMPING

Camping is found at the Corps-operated campgrounds and at John Kyle State Park. Golf is nearby. Rental cabins are also available at the state park.

Clear Creek: All year, 52 sites with electric hookups, some have water hookups, $18. **Amenities**: Drinking water, dump station, restrooms, showers, playground. **Directions**: From I-55 Exit 243A in Batesville, travel 21 miles east on MS-6 toward Oxford. Turn left at the West Oxford exit onto West Jackson Ave. Go about 3 miles, then left onto MS-315 and travel about 13 miles. 662-563-4531.

Oak Grove: All year, 82 sites with electric & water hookups, non-reservable, $16. **Amenities**: Drinking water, dump station, restrooms. **Directions**: From I-55 Exit 246, travel east on SR-35 to below the dam. 662-563-4531.

6) Tennessee-Tombigbee Waterway
  a) Booneville Area
  b) Fulton Area
  c) Columbus Area

6a) Booneville Area

Bay Springs Visitor Center
82 Bay Springs Resource Rd
Dennis, MS 38838
Phone: 662-423-1287
District: Mobile

The Visitor Center features 8,000 square feet of exhibits and artifacts of the Tenn-Tom project, the natural resources of the area and the history of the waterway. There are a number of films for visitors to view and rangers present programs on water safety. From Dennis, Mississippi, take Hwy-4 west for 5 miles to the Center, on the east side of the lake in Tishomingo County. The area around the building includes a nature trail, dogtrot cabin and an overlook.

RV CAMPING

Piney Grove: Mar-Nov, 144 sites with electric (50amp) & water hookups, $18–$20. **Amenities**: Drinking water, dump station, restrooms, showers, laundry, boat ramp, fishing pier, playground, swimming. **Directions**: From Booneville, MS, take SR-30 east for 11 miles to Burton, turn right on CR-3501 for 3 miles, follow signs. CR 3550, New Site, MS 38859 / 662-728-1134.

6b) Fulton Area

Jamie L. Whitten Historic Center
100 Campground Rd
Fulton, MS 38843
Phone: 662-862-5414
District: Mobile

The Visitor Center at Fulton features exhibits from the federal agencies that were involved in the economic development of northeast Mississippi. Outside the center, picnic areas and a long pier provide excellent views and vistas of the Tenn-Tom Waterway. The Center is 4.2 miles north of the junction of MS-25 & US-78 on the South Access Road.

RV CAMPING

Whitten Park: All year, 61 sites with electric & water hookups, some pull thrus, $18–$20. **Amenities**: Drinking water, dump station, restrooms, showers, laundry, boat ramp, fishing pier, nature trails, swimming. **Directions**: From US-78 Exit 104

(Fulton exit), go north 200 yards, turn left on Access Road at the first traffic light, go north 4 miles. Campground is on the left side of the road within the Whitten Historical area. 100 Campground Rd, Fulton, MS 38843 / 662-862-5414.

6c) Columbus Area

Waterway Management Center
3606 West Plymouth Rd
Columbus, MS 39701
Phone: 662-327-2142
District: Mobile

Information about the Tenn-Tom Waterway is available at the Corps Office in Columbus. From US-82 exit at US-45/Plymouth Bluff Access Rd and travel north, turn left on Old West Point Rd for 1 mile, right on Right Bank Access Rd & right on West Plymouth Rd.

RV Camping

Blue Bluff: All year, 92 shady sites with electric & water hookups, $16–$18. **Amenities**: Drinking water, dump station, restrooms, showers, hiking trails, swimming, 24-hour gate attendants. **Directions**: From junction of Hwy-145 and Meridian Street in downtown Aberdeen, travel north 2 miles on Meridian St and turn right on Lock & Dam Rd. Entrance road is on the left. 20051 Blue Bluff Rd, Aberdeen, MS 39730 / 662-369-2832.

DeWayne Hayes: All year, 100 sites with electric & water hookups, 10 basic sites, $16–$20. **Amenities**: Drinking water, dump station, restrooms, showers, laundry, boat ramp, fishing pier, fish cleaning station, hiking tails, game courts. **Directions**: From Columbus, MS, take US-45 north to junction US-373/50N. Turn left and follow US-373 for 1.5 miles to Stenson Creek Rd, left on Stenson Creek Rd, follow brown signs. Travel 2 miles to Barton's Ferry Rd and turn left 1/2 mile. 662-434-6939.

Town Creek: All year, 100 sites with electric & water hookups, 10 basic sites, $16–$20. **Amenities**: Drinking water, dump station, restrooms, showers, laundry, fish cleaning stations, hiking trails, playgrounds. **Directions**: From Columbus, MS, take US-45 north to Hwy-50. Turn left and follow Hwy-50 west past the Hwy-50 Waterway bridge. About 2 miles west of the bridge, turn north, follow signs. 10690 Witherspoon Rd, West Point, MS 39773 / 662-494-4885.

Missouri

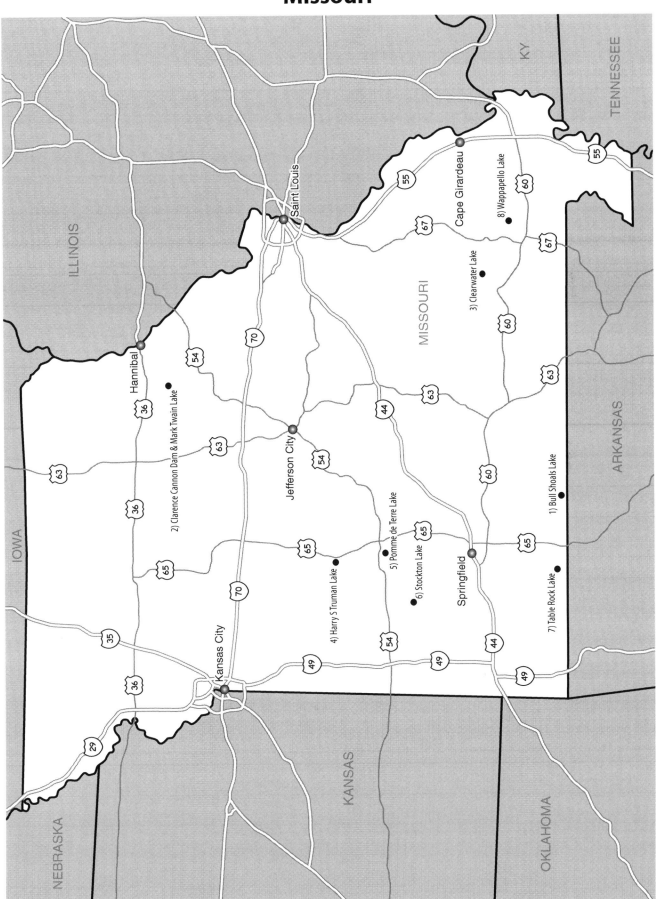

TENNESSEE

KY

ILLINOIS

Saint Louis

55

Cape Girardeau

60

8) Wappapello Lake

67

67

MISSOURI

3) Clearwater Lake

60

Hannibal

36

63

54

70

2) Clarence Cannon Dam & Mark Twain Lake

63

44

63

Jefferson City

54

60

ARKANSAS

63

1) Bull Shoals Lake

65

65

5) Pomme de Terre Lake

65

65

4) Harry S Truman Lake

6) Stockton Lake

Springfield

65

7) Table Rock Lake

70

54

44

IOWA

35

49

49

49

36

Kansas City

29

NEBRASKA

KANSAS

OKLAHOMA

Activities

		Auto Touring	Biking	Boating	Climbing	Cultural/Historic Sites	Educational Programs	Fishing	Groceries/Supplies	Hiking	Horseback Riding	Hunting	Lodging	Off Highway Vehicles	Visitor Center
1)	Bull Shoals Lake			♦				♦		♦		♦			
2)	Clarence Cannon Dam & Mark Twain Lake	♦	♦	♦		♦		♦		♦	♦	♦			
3)	Clearwater Lake			♦				♦		♦		♦			
4)	Harry S. Truman Lake	♦		♦		♦	♦	♦		♦	♦	♦		♦	♦
5)	Pomme De Terre Lake	♦		♦				♦		♦		♦			
6)	Stockton Lake			♦				♦	♦	♦	♦	♦	♦		
7)	Table Rock Lake		♦	♦				♦	♦	♦	♦		♦	♦	♦
8)	Wappapello Lake	♦	♦	♦				♦	♦	♦	♦	♦	♦	♦	♦

Missouri Projects

1) Bull Shoals Lake

U.S. Army Corps of Engineers
324 West 7th St
Mountain Home, AR 72653
Phone: 870-425-2700
District: Little Rock

Bull Shoals Lake is located 135 miles north of Little Rock, Arkansas, south of Branson near the MO/AR state line. From Little Rock, Arkansas, take US-65 north to junction US-62, then 50 miles east to Flippin and 4 miles north to the lake. Maps and information can be obtained at the Project Office in Arkansas. Bull Shoals has 62,326 land acres, 45,440 water acres and 740 shoreline miles. Its extensive area straddles the states of Arkansas and Missouri.

In the beautiful Ozark Mountains, the lake is known for its exceptional water quality and outstanding fisheries. Bull Shoals has hundreds of lake arms and coves, perfect for boating, fishing, swimming and water sports of all kinds. The area also has great appeal to bird-watchers, naturalists and hikers. Fall is a popular season at Bull Shoals when visitors are attracted to the spectacular autumn foliage in the Ozarks.

RV Camping

Of the 10 Corps-managed campgrounds, 5 are in Missouri and 5 in Arkansas. They are listed in their respective state sections in this guide. Most campgrounds at Bull Shoals have boat launches and public marinas.

Beaver Creek: Mar-Oct, 34 sites with electric (some 50amp) hookups, $18–$19. **Amenities**: Drinking water, dump station, restrooms, showers, boat ramp, playground, marina. **Directions**: From Mountain Home, AR, go north on SR-5 for 24 miles, then west for 42 miles on US-160 to Kissee Mills, MO, then left on Hwy-O, follow signs. 3480 Foxglove Rd, Kissee Mills, MO 65680 / 417-546-3708. **GPS**: 36.63972, -93.04583

Buck Creek: Apr-Sep, 37 sites with electric hookups, $12-$18. **Amenities**: Drinking water, dump station, restrooms, showers, boat ramp, fishing, marina, playground, swimming. **Directions**: From Mountain Home, AR, take SR-5 north for 24.4 miles, then west on US-160 for 21 miles, then south on SR-U for 5 miles to US-125 for 5.7 miles to Buck Creek Park access road. Follow signs. 10600 S. Stae Hwy 125, Protem, MO 65733 / 417-785-4313. **GPS**: 36.49444, -92.79611

Pontiac Park: Apr-Sep, 30 sites with electric hookups, 5 basic sites, $14–$18. **Amenities**: Drinking water, dump station, restrooms, showers, boat ramp, playground. **Directions**: From Mountain Home, AR, go north on SR-5 for 20 miles to junction of Hwy-W, then 7 miles west to Pontiac, MO, and southwest .3 mile to the access road, follow signs. Highway W, Pontiac, MO 65729 / 417-679-2222. **GPS**: 36.51, -92.60806

River Run: Mar-Oct, 32 sites with electric & water hookups, 5 basic sites, $18-$20. **Amenities**: Drinking water, dump station, restrooms, showers, marina, boat ramp, playground.

Directions: From junction US-160 & US-76 in Forsyth, MO, take US-76 south for .5 mile to River Run access road, follow signs. 138 River Run Rd, Forsyth, MO 65653 / 417-546-3646. **GPS**: 36.67444, -93.1125

Theodosia: Apr-Sep, 29 sites with electric (some 50amp) hookups, $18. **Amenities**: Drinking water, dump station, restrooms, showers, laundry, boat ramp, marina, playground, swimming, convenience store. **Directions**: From Mountain Home, AR, go north on SR-5 for 24 miles to US-160. Follow US-160 for 12 miles to the park access road, follow signs. 417-273-4626 or 870-425-2700. **GPS**: 36.57333, -92.65361

2) Clarence Cannon Dam & Mark Twain Lake

U.S. Army Corps of Engineers
20642 Hwy J
Monroe City, MO 63456
Phone: 573-735-4097
District: St. Louis

Located in northeast Missouri, the project spans the Salt River Valley and includes 18,000 water acres, 285 shoreline miles and 45,881 land acres. It is 28 miles southwest of Hannibal and 120 miles northwest of St. Louis. From Hannibal, take US-36 west for 17 miles, then Hwy-J south.

Equestrian camping is available at Frank Russell with easy access to the Joanna Multi-Use Trail. A shooting range is located below the dam near the spillway. Local attractions include the Mark Twain birthplace, shopping, sightseeing and restaurants in nearby towns.

RV Camping

Mark Twain State Park also has RV camping.

Frank Russell: Apr-Oct, 65 sites with electric hookups, $18. **Amenities**: Drinking water, dump station, restrooms, showers, shaded horse stalls. **Directions**: From Hannibal, MO, take US-36 west for 17 miles to Hwy-J, then south for 9 miles. 573-735-4097. **GPS**: 39.53556, -91.6475

Indian Creek: May-Nov, 215 sites with electric (some 50amp) hookups (some are full hookup sites), 12 basic RV sites, $16–$24. **Amenities**: Drinking water, dump station, restrooms, showers, boat ramp, biking, interpretive trails, playground, swimming, marina. **Directions**: From Hannibal, MO, take US-36 west for 20 miles, then southwest on US-24 for 6 miles, then south on Hwy-HH for 2 miles, east on Monroe CR-581 for 3 miles. 573-735-4097. **GPS**: 39.53917, -91.73306

Ray Behrens: Mar-Nov, 40 full hookup sites (50amp) and 122 electric-only (50amp), $18–$24. **Amenities**: Drinking water, dump station, restrooms, showers, boat ramp, amphitheater, playground, hiking trails, biking, marina. **Directions**: From Hannibal, MO, take US-36 west for 17 miles, turn south on Hwy-J and go 12 miles to the campground. 573-735-4097. **GPS**: 39.51583, -91.66306

3) Clearwater Lake

U.S. Army Corps of Engineers
RR 3 Box 3559-D
Piedmont, MO 63957
Phone: 573-223-7777
District: Little Rock

The project, 120 miles south of St. Louis, has 17,089 land acres, 1,630 water acres and 27 shoreline miles. Clearwater is located 7 miles west of Piedmont. From St. Louis go south on I-55 to Exit 174, then continue south on US-67 to MO-34 west through the town of Piedmont to the lake. Clearwater Lake is noted for the grandeur of its hills and natural springs.

Wildlife viewing is excellent from numerous walking and hiking trails. Historic sites, restaurants and sightseeing may be found in nearby towns.

RV Camping

RV camping is also available at the nearby state parks.

Bluff View: May-Sep, 49 sites with electric (some 50amp) hookups, $16–$20. **Amenities**: Drinking water, dump station, restrooms, showers, boat ramp, boating, canoeing, fishing, interpretive trails, playground, swimming. **Directions**: Located 8 miles west of Piedmont, MO. From Hwy-34 turn right on Hwy-49 and go 1 mile, then left on Hwy-AA for 7 miles. 93 Highway AA, Piedmont, MO 63957 / 573-223-7777. **GPS**: 37.18194, -90.78944

Highway K: Apr-Oct, 67 sites with electric (some 50amp) hookups and 61 basic sites, $16–$20. **Amenities**: Drinking water, dump station, restrooms, showers, fishing, canoeing, playground, swimming. **Directions**: From Annapolis, follow SR-K west for 5 miles to park entrance. 5347 County Road 452, Annapolis, MO 63620 / 573-223-7777. **GPS**: 37.32417, -90.76667

Piedmont Park: Apr-Sep, 78 sites with electric (some 50amp) hookups, $16–$20. *Amenities*: Drinking water, dump station, restrooms, showers, boat ramp, boating, canoeing, marina, playground. *Directions*: From Piedmont, MO, follow Hwy-34 for 7 miles, southwest to Hwy-HH, then 5 miles on HH to the dam, follow signs. 821 County Road 418, Piedmont, MO 63957 / 573-223-7777. *GPS*: 37.1425, -90.77028

River Road: May-Sep, 97 sites with electric, $12-$20. *Amenities*: Drinking water, dump station, showers, boat ramp, canoeing, boating, fishing, hiking, playground, swimming, water skiing. *Directions*: From Piedmont, MO, follow Hwy-34 southwest for 6 miles to Hwy-HH. Turn right and go 5.5 miles. The park is located below the dam. RR3 Box 3559D, Piedmont, MO 63957 / 573-223-7777. *GPS*: 37.13361, - 90.76694

4) Harry S. Truman Lake

U.S. Army Corps of Engineers
15968 Truman Rd
Warsaw, MO 65355
Phone: 660-438-7317
District: Kansas City

The project encompasses 55,600 water acres, 212,913 land acres and 958 shoreline miles. From Kansas City go 19 miles south on US-71, then 75 miles east on MO-7 to Warsaw, then 1 mile north. The Harry S. Truman Visitor Center sits atop Kaysinger Bluff and provides a spectacular view of the dam and reservoir. Exhibits feature information about the rich history of the Osage River Valley from pre-civilization to modern day. There is good wildlife viewing from the observation deck.

Area attractions include Benton County Museum in Warsaw, Henry County Museum in Clinton and the Lost Valley Hatchery & Aquarium just outside of Warsaw.

RV CAMPING

Berry Bend: Apr-Oct, 113 sites with electric hookups and 78 basic sites, $14–$18. *Amenities*: Drinking water, dump station, restrooms, showers, laundry, swimming, boat ramp, fishing, hiking, playground. *Directions*: Located on the Osage arm of the reservoir, 9 miles southwest of Warsaw. From Warsaw travel 4.4 miles west on MO-7, then 3 miles west on Hwy-Z, then 1.8 miles on paved access road. 660-438-3872. *GPS*: 38.19972, -93.51

Berry Bend Equestrian: All year, 24 sites with electric hookups and 65 basic sites, $14–$18, equestrian use only. *Amenities*: Drinking water, restrooms, showers, laundry, boat ramp, fishing, horseback riding trails, playground. *Directions*: Located in Benton County about 10 miles west of Warsaw. From Hwy-Z, travel 2 miles south on Berry Bend access road. 660-438-7317. *GPS*: 38.19972, -93.51

Bucksaw Park: Apr-Oct, 12 sites with electric (some 50amp) & water hookups, 1 full hookup, 114 electric-only and 181 basic sites, $14–$24, a few pull thrus. *Amenities*: Drinking water, dump station, restrooms, showers, laundry, boat ramp, fishing, playground, swimming, marina. *Directions*: From Clinton, MO, go 8 miles east on MO-7, then 3 miles south on Hwy-U, turn left at SE 803 Road, stay on the paved road, follow signs. 673 SE 803 Rd, Clinton, MO 64735 / 660-477-3402. *GPS*:38.26, -93.60556

Long Shoal Park: Apr-Oct, 2 full hookup sites, 97 electric-only and 27 basic, $14–$18. *Amenities*: Drinking water, dump station, restrooms, showers, laundry, boat ramp, fishing, hiking, playground, marina. *Directions*: From Warsaw, MO, go 4.4 miles west on MO-7, follow signs. 12733 Long Shoal Park Rd, Warsaw, MO 65355 / 660-438-2342. *GPS*: 38.27611, -93.46972

Osage Bluff: Apr-Oct, 41 electric-only sites and 27 basic, $14-$18. *Amenities*: Drinking water, dump station, restrooms, showers, laundry, boat ramp, fishing, playground, marina. *Directions*: Located 8 miles south of Warsaw. From Hwy-83 travel about 1 mile on Hwy-295, follow signs. 176 Osage Bluff Rd, Warsaw, MO 65355 / 660-438-3873. *GPS*: 38.19056, -93.39333

Sparrowfoot: Apr-Oct, 80 electric-only sites and 36 basic, $14-$18. *Amenities*: Drinking water, dump station, restrooms, showers, laundry, boat ramp, fishing, playground, swimming. *Directions*: Located in Henry County about 4 miles southeast of Clinton. From Hwy-13 travel about 1 mile east on SE 450 Rd, follow signs. 150 SE 450 Road, Clinton, MO 64735 / 660-885-7546. *GPS*: 38.29639, -93.72639

Talley Bend: Apr-Sep, 108 electric-only sites and 6 basic, $14-$18. *Amenities*: Drinking water, dump station, restrooms, showers, laundry, boat ramp, fishing, playground, swimming. *Directions*: Located in Saint Clair County about 13 miles northeast of Osceola. From Hwy-13 travel east on Hwy-C for 6 miles, follow signs. 8950 NE Highway C, Lowery City, MO 64763 / 417-644-2446. *GPS*: 38.13778, -93.61722

Thibaut Point: Apr-Sep, 18 electric-only sites and 20 basic, $14–$18. *Amenities*: Drinking water, dump station, restrooms, showers, laundry, swimming, boat ramp, fishing, playground. *Directions*: Located in Benton County 8 miles north of Warsaw. From Hwy-65 travel west on Hwy-T for 3 miles, turn south on Road 218 (gravel), follow 1 mile. 26773

Georgetown Ave, Warsaw, MO 65355 / 660-438-2767. *GPS*: 38.29639, -93.39639

Windsor Crossing: Apr-Sep, 47 basic sites, $8. *Amenities*: Drinking water, restrooms, swimming, boat ramp, fishing. *Directions*: Located in Henry County 20 miles west of Warsaw and 18 miles east of Clinton. From MO-7 travel north on Hwy-PP for 4 miles, follow signs. 12 NE PP Highway, Clinton, MO 64735 / 660-477-9275. *GPS*: 38.36444, -93.545

5) Pomme De Terre Lake

U.S. Army Corps of Engineers
Route 2, Box 2160
Hermitage, MO 65668
Phone: 417-745-6411
District: Kansas City

Located 60 miles north of Springfield, the lake is in the rugged, tree-covered hills of the west-central Missouri Ozarks. The project includes 7,790 water acres, 113 shoreline miles and 12,699 land acres. From Springfield, Missouri, go 53 miles north on US-65, then 5 miles west on US-54 and 4 miles south on MO-254. The project office is on the north side of the lake.

Fishing is a popular activity. The cool, clear spring waters make this lake an attractive destination for water recreation.

RV Camping

RV camping is also available at the two state parks on the lake.

Damsite Park: All year, 56 sites with electric (some 50amp) hookups, 15 basic sites, some pull thrus, $12–$20. *Amenities*: Drinking water, dump station, restrooms, showers, laundry, fishing dock, playground. *Directions*: From Springfield, MO, take US-65 north for 60 miles to Preston, MO, then US-54 west to Hermitage, then Hwy-254/64 south to Carsons Corner, then Hwy-254 west toward the dam. 417-745-2244. *GPS*: 37.90472, -93.30778

Lightfoot Landing: Apr-Oct, 29 sites with electric & water hookups, 6 basic and 5 tent sites, $14–$20. *Amenities*: Drinking water, dump station, restrooms, showers, laundry, boat ramp, playground. *Directions*: From Springfield, MO, take Hwy-13 north to Bolivar, then Hwy-83 north to RB Hwy east to the campground. 417-282-6890. *GPS*: 376.82611, -93.36139

Nemo Landing: All year, 58 sites with electric (some 50amp) hookups and 59 basic sites, $12-$20. *Amenities*: Drinking water, dump station, restrooms, showers, laundry, boat ramp, playground, swimming. *Directions*: From Springfield, MO, take US-65 north past Louisburg to Hwy-NN west to Nemo. Turn west at the 4-way stop, follow signs. 417-993-5529. *GPS*: 37.86611, -93.27389

Outlet Park: Apr-Oct, 14 sites with electric (some 50amp) & water hookups, 7 basic sites, $12–$20. *Amenities*: Drinking water, restrooms, boat ramp, playground, group camping, baseball field, multi-purpose courts. Harbor Marina nearby. *Directions*: From Springfield, MO, take US-65 north to Preston, take Hwy-54 west to Hermitage, then south on Hwy-254/64 about 4 miles to Carson Corner. Turn west toward Pomme de Terre dam. Cross the dam and turn north on the paved road at the far end of the dam and follow the road to the park below the dam. 417-745-2290. *GPS*: 37.90278, -93.32917

Wheatland Park: Apr-Oct, 64 sites with electric (some 50amp) hookups, 10 basic sites, $12–$20. *Amenities*: Drinking water, dump station, restrooms, showers, laundry, boat ramp, playground, swimming. *Directions*: From Springfield, MO, take Hwy-13 north to Bolivar, then travel north on Hwy-83 past Elkton to Hwy-254. Follow Hwy-254 to The Triangle and take CR-205 south, follow signs. County Road 205, Hermitage, MO 65668 / 417-282-5267. *GPS*: 37.87556, -93.37444

6) Stockton Lake

U.S. Army Corps of Engineers
16435 East Stockton Lake Dr
Stockton, MO 65785
Phone: 417-276-3113
District: Kansas City

Located 50 miles north of Springfield in the scenic Missouri Ozarks, the project covers 36,415 land acres and has 24,632 water acres and 298 shoreline miles. From Springfield travel 29 miles north on MO-13 and 22 miles west on MO-32.

Boating services and supplies and a restaurant can be found at three marinas on the lake. Equestrian trails are at Hawker Point and Orleans Trail. Stockton is popular for sailing, boating and scuba diving.

RV Camping

RV Camping and camping cabinsis are available at Stockton State Park.

Cedar Ridge: Apr-Sep, 23 sites with electric hookups, 20 basic sites, $12–$20. *Amenities*: Drinking water, dump station, restrooms, showers, boat ramp, fishing, sailing, scuba diving, swimming. *Directions*: From Bona, MO, take Hwy-245 north for 1/2 mile to Hwy-RA, turn left (north) on Hwy-RA for .7 mile. 21680 E. CR-1, Aldrich, MO 65601 / 417-995-2045. *GPS*: 37.57556, -93.68139

Crabtree Cove: Apr-Sep, 24 sites with electric hookups, 22 basic sites, $12–$18. *Amenities*: Drinking water, dump station, restrooms, showers, boat ramp, fishing, hiking, wildlife viewing. *Directions*: On the northeast corner of the lake. From Stockton take Hwy-32 for 3.5 miles, then south on the access road. 17630 E. C-1, Stockton, MO 65785 / 417-276-6799. *GPS*: 37.66972, -93.75306

Hawker Point: Apr-Sep, 25 sites with electric hookups and 22 basic sites, $12–$18. *Amenities*: Drinking water, dump station, restrooms, showers, boat ramp, fishing, horseback riding trails, wildlife viewing. *Directions*: On the northern end of Big Sac Arm of the lake. From Stockton, take Hwy-39 south for 6.2 miles, turn left on Hwy-H and continue for 5.2 miles. 16030 E. HP-1, Stockton, MO 65785 / 417-276-7266. *GPS*: 37.60639, -93.78111

Masters: May-Sep, 64 sites, no hookups, $10–$14. *Amenities*: Drinking water, dump station, restrooms, showers, boat ramp, fishing, primitive group camp area, swimming, wildlife viewing. *Directions*: Located on the Little Sac Arm of the lake. From Fair Play, MO, take Hwy-32 west for 5 miles, then south on Hwy-RA, follow for 4 miles, then west onto the park access road. 20291 S Hwy RA, Fair Play, MO 65649 / 417-276-6847 or 417-276-3113. *GPS*: 37.59917, -93.68

Orleans Trail: May-Sep, 108 sites, no hookups, $12. *Amenities*: Drinking water, dump station, restrooms, showers, boat ramp, group camp area with electric, fishing, marina, horseback riding trails, swimming, wildlife viewing. *Directions*: On the northeast part of the lake, just outside the town of Stockton. From Stockton, MO, take Hwy-39 south for 1/2 mile, then RB Road east 1/2 mile, then right on Blake St. 15365 E. OT-1, Stockton, MO 65785 / 417-276-6948. *GPS*: 37.65944, -93.78306

Ruark Bluff: Apr-Sep, 52 sites with electric hookups, 12 basic sites, $10–$18. *Amenities*: Drinking water, dump station, restrooms, showers, boat ramp, fishing, swimming, wildlife viewing. *Directions*: On the Big Sac Arm of the Sac River. From Greenfield, MO, take Hwy-H north for 6.4 miles, then east on the park access road, follow signs. 819 Hwy H, Stockton, MO 65661 / 417-637-5303. *GPS*: 37.52583, -93.80944

7) Table Rock Lake

U.S. Army Corps of Engineers
4600 State Hwy 165

Branson, MO 65616
Phone: 417-334-4101
District: Little Rock

The project, just 4 miles southwest of Branson, includes 24,846 land acres, 43,100 water acres and 745 shoreline miles. From Springfield, Missouri, go 40 miles south on US-65 to Branson, then take SR-165 west for 7 miles to Table Rock Dam. The Dewey Short Visitor Center features exhibits and audio-visual presentations. Located in the Ozark Mountains, the area provides extensive wildlife viewing.

Mark Twain National Forest has hiking and mountain biking opportunities. Other nearby attractions include cave tours, shopping, restaurants and a theme park. Five commercial boat cruises operate seasonally at the lake.

RV Camping

Table Rock State Park, as well as marinas and resorts on the lake also have camping.

Aunt's Creek: May-Oct, 55 sites with electric (some 50amp) hookups, $20, some pull thrus. *Amenities*: Drinking water, dump station, restrooms, showers, boat ramp, fishing, hiking, swimming, scuba diving. *Directions*: From Branson West, junction of Hwy-76, travel 3.9 miles south on Hwy-13, then 2.7 miles west on Hwy-OO. 2837 State Hwy OO, Reed Springs, MO 65737 / 417-739-2792. *GPS*: 36.67361, -93.45972

Baxter: Apr-Sep, 50 sites with 50amp electric hookups, a few basic and tent sites, $21. *Amenities*: Drinking water, dump station, restrooms, showers, boat ramp, fishing, marina, playground, swimming. *Directions*: From Lampe, MO, at junction of Hwy-13, travel 4.8 miles west on Hwy-H. 4631 State Hwy H, Lampe, MO 65616 / 417-779-5370. *GPS*: 36.56694, -93.50139

Big M: Apr-Sep, 14 full hookup sites, 4 electric-only and 35 basic sites, $16–$23. *Amenities*: Drinking water, dump station, restrooms, showers, boat ramp, fishing, hiking, marina, scuba diving, swimming, volleyball. *Directions*: From Cassville, travel east on SR-76 for 9 miles, then Hwy-M to the access road, follow signs. 417-271-3190. *GPS*: 36.55778, -93.67667

Campbell Point: Apr-Sep, 38 sites with electric (some 50amp) hookups and 38 basic sites, $16–$21, a few pull thrus. *Amenities*: Drinking water, dump station, restrooms, showers, boat ramp, fishing, hiking, playground, scuba diving, swimming, volleyball, water skiing. *Directions*: Located east of Cassville, travel east on SR-76 to SR-39 southeast to Hwy-

YY to the access road. 792 campbell Point Rd, Shell Knob, MO 65747 / 417-858-3903. *GPS*: 36.59583, -93.55028

Cape Fair: Apr-Oct, 36 sites with electric (some 50amp) & water hookups, 33 electric-only and 13 basic sites, $16–$21. *Amenities*: Drinking water, dump station, restrooms, showers, boat ramp, fishing, hiking, marina, playground, scuba diving, group camping. *Directions*: From Reeds Spring/junction SR-248, go south on Hwy-13 for 1.4 miles, then 8 miles west on Hwy-76 to Cape Fair, then southwest on Lake Road 76-82, follow signs, 1092 Shadrack Rd, Cape Fair, MO 65624 / 417-538-2220. *GPS*: 36.7225, -93.53167

Cricket Creek: Mar-Sep, 34 sites with electric (some 50amp) and 2 tent sites, some pull thrus, $20-$21. *Amenities*: Drinking water, restrooms, dump station, showers, boat ramp, fishing, hiking, marina, playground, swimming, volleyball, scuba diving. *Directions*: From Branson, take US-65 south for nearly 12 miles. Turn right on Boat Dock Rd West. Follow signs. 870-426-3331. *GPS*: 36.48306, -93.30028

Eagle Rock: Apr-Oct, 1 full hookup site, 25 sites with electric (some 50amp) hookups and 31 basic sites, $16–$21, some pull thrus. *Amenities*: Drinking water, dump station, restrooms, showers, boat ramp, fishing, hiking, marina, scuba diving, swimming, volleyball, water skiing. *Directions*: From Cassville, MO, take US-86 southeast for 4 miles to Eagle Rock Community, follow signs. 417-271-3215. *GPS*: 36.52722, -93.73

Indian Point: Apr-Oct, 74 sites with electric (many 50amp) hookups, $20–$21. *Amenities*: Drinking water, dump station, restrooms, showers, boat ramp, fishing, hiking, marina, scuba diving, swimming, wildlife viewing. *Directions*: Close to Silver Dollar City Theme Park. From Branson, MO, take Hwy-76 west for 3 miles to Indian Point Rd, then south for 2 miles. 3125 Indian Point Rd, Branson, MO 65616 / 417-338-2121. *GPS*: 36.63111, -93.34722

Long Creek: Apr-Oct, 37 sites with electric (some 50amp) hookups and 10 basic sites, $16–$21. *Amenities*: Drinking water, dump station, restrooms, showers, boat ramp, fishing, hiking, scuba diving, swimming. *Directions*: From Branson, MO, take US-65 south for 5 miles to Hwy-86 west for 3 miles to Long Creek Rd, follow signs. 1036 Long Creek Rd, Ridgedale, MO 65739 / 417-334-8427. *GPS*: 36.52056, -93.30417

Old Highway 86: Apr-Oct, 23 sites with electric (some 50amp) hookups, 40 electric-only sites and 8 basic sites, $12–$19. *Amenities*: Drinking water, dump station, restrooms, showers, boat ramp, fishing, hiking, playground, swimming, volleyball, wildlife viewing. *Directions*: From Branson, south on US-65 to Hwy-86 (near the Arkansas state line). Take Hwy-86 for 6 miles west, then north on Hwy-UU and follow to the campground. 1791 State Hwy UU, Blue Eye, MO 65611 / 417-779-5376. *GPS*: 36.55944, -93.31944.

Viney Creek: May-Sep, 24 sites with electric (some 50amp) & water hookups and 22 basic, $16–$21. *Amenities*: Drinking water, dump station, restrooms, showers, boat ramp, fishing, hiking, playground, swimming, volleyball, water skiing. *Directions*: From Cassville, MO, travel southeast on Hwy-39 for 7 miles to Hwy-39/48, then west to the campground. 417-271-3860. *GPS*: 36.56611, -93.67583

Viola: Apr-Sep, 22 sites with electric (some 50amp) & water hookups and 15 electric-only sites, $14–$19. *Amenities*: Drinking water, dump station, restrooms, showers, boat ramp, fishing, hiking, marina, swimming, playground, scuba diving, wildlife viewing. *Directions*: From Shell Knob, MO, travel south on Hwy-39 for 7 miles to Hwy-39/48, then west to the campground. RR5 Box 5210, Shell Knob, MO 65747 / 417-858-3904. *GPS*: 36.56167, -93.59472

8) Wappapello Lake

U.S. Army Corps of Engineers
10992 Hwy T
Wappapello, MO 63966
Phone: 573-222-8562
Visitor Center: 573-222-8773
District: St. Louis

This project, located in southeast Missouri, encompasses 36,120 land acres, 8,400 water acres and 180 shoreline miles. From St. Louis, travel south for 32 miles on I-55 to Exit 174, take US-67 south for 88 miles to Greenville, turn left at Hwy-D and travel south 20 miles. The Bill Emerson Memorial Visitor Center has exhibits and various programs that focus on the natural beauty found in southeastern Missouri. The lake is near Mark Twain National Forest and the Mingo National Wildlife Refuge.

RV Camping

RV camping and camping cabins are available at Lake Wappapello State Park.

Greenville: All year, 100 sites with electric hookups, 5 basic sites, $16. *Amenities*: Drinking water, dump station, restrooms, showers, river access, boat ramp, fishing, horseshoe pit, playground, volleyball. One mile historical trail to explore. *Directions*: From US-67 in Greenville, continue 1 mile south, follow signs. 573-224-3884. *GPS*: 37.10278, -90.45833

Peoples Creek: All year, 19 full hookup sites with electric (50amp), 38 electric-only sites $18–$20. The campground consists of two separate sections: 37 lakefront sites in the lower section and 20 sites in the upper. Reservations must be made at least 4 days in advance. **Amenities**: Drinking water, dump station, restrooms, showers, boat ramp, fishing dock, swimming. **Directions**: From St. Louis, take I-55 south to US-67, then south on US-67 to Hwy-D near Greenville, south about 15 miles, follow signs. From Poplar Bluff, east on US-60, north on SR-51, west on Hwy-T to campground. 573-222-8234. **GPS**: 36.92639, -90.28306

Redman Creek: All year, 108 full hookup sites (50amp) and 6 boat-in sites, $9–$20. **Amenities**: Drinking water, dump station, restrooms, showers, boat ramp, boat rentals, fishing, fish cleaning stations, horseshoe pit, interpretive trails, swimming, tennis, volleyball. **Directions**: From Poplar Bluff, take US-60 east to Hwy-T, travel north on Hwy-T, follow signs, 10270 Hwy T, Wappapello, MO 63966 / 573-222-8233. **GPS**: 36.92278, -90.2875

Montana

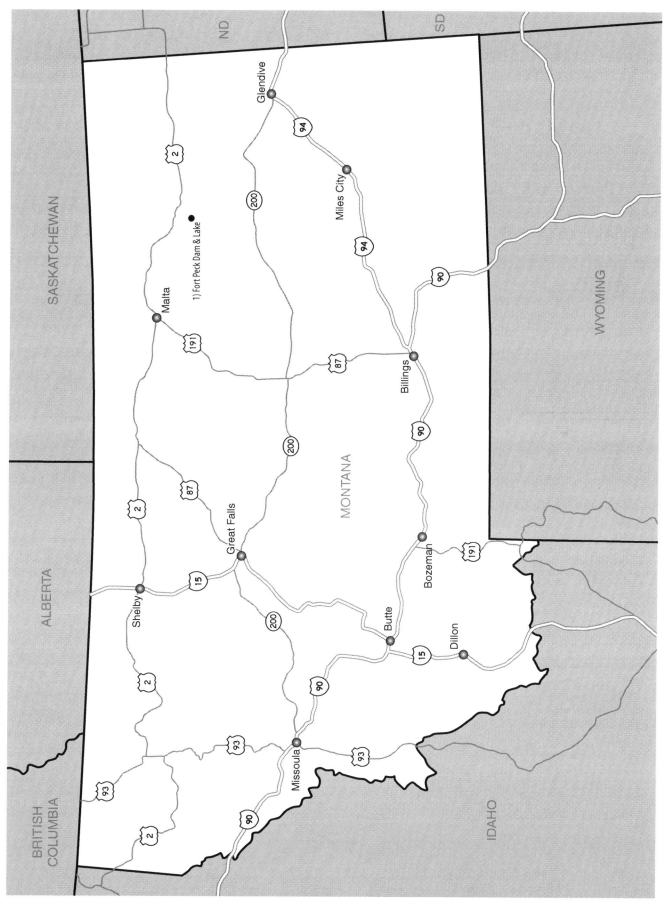

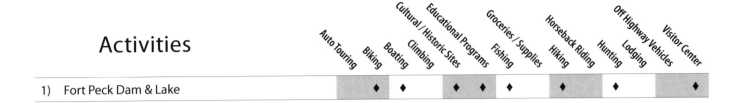

Activities	Auto Touring	Biking	Boating	Climbing	Cultural / Historic Sites	Educational Programs	Fishing	Groceries / Supplies	Hiking	Horseback Riding	Hunting	Lodging	Off Highway Vehicles	Visitor Center
1) Fort Peck Dam & Lake		♦	♦		♦	♦	♦		♦		♦			♦

Montana Projects

1) Fort Peck Dam & Lake

U.S. Army Corps of Engineers
P.O. Box 208
Fort Peck, MT 59223
Phone: 406-526-3411
District: Omaha

The Fort Peck project, located in northeast Montana south of US-2, features 240,000 water acres, 1,520 shoreline miles and 168,591 land acres. The Interpretive Center & Museum on site includes wildlife dioramas, aquariums, dinosaur fossils and the dam's construction history. The museum is open daily, Memorial Day to Labor Day. Powerhouse tours are also given.

Fort Peck Dam is the largest embankment dam in the United States, with the 5th largest man-made reservoir. The vast size of the project, plus its remote location, makes it an ideal destination for a high-quality outdoor experience.

RV Camping

Downstream: Apr-Oct, 75 sites with electric (some 50amp) hookups and 15 tent sites, $16–$20, some pull thrus. **Amenities**: Drinking water, dump station, restrooms, showers, fishing, fish cleaning stations, biking, hiking, marina, basketball. **Directions**: From Glasgow, MT, go south on SR-24 for 18 miles to the dam. Follow Highway 117 northeast and turn right at the intersection into the campground. 406-526-3224. **GPS**: 48.00889, -106.42889

Nelson Creek: All year, 16 basic sites, non-reservable, free. 40-foot RV length limit. **Amenities**: Boat ramp. **Directions**: From Fort Peck go 44 miles southeast on SR-24, then 7 miles west on the gravel road. 406-526-3411. **GPS**: 47.3423, -106.13449

West End: May-Sep, 13 sites with electric hookups, non-reservable, $10–$16. 35-foot RV length limit. **Amenities**: Drinking water, restrooms, showers. **Directions**: On the west side of the dam. 406-526-3411. **GPS**: 47.997, -106.494

Nebraska

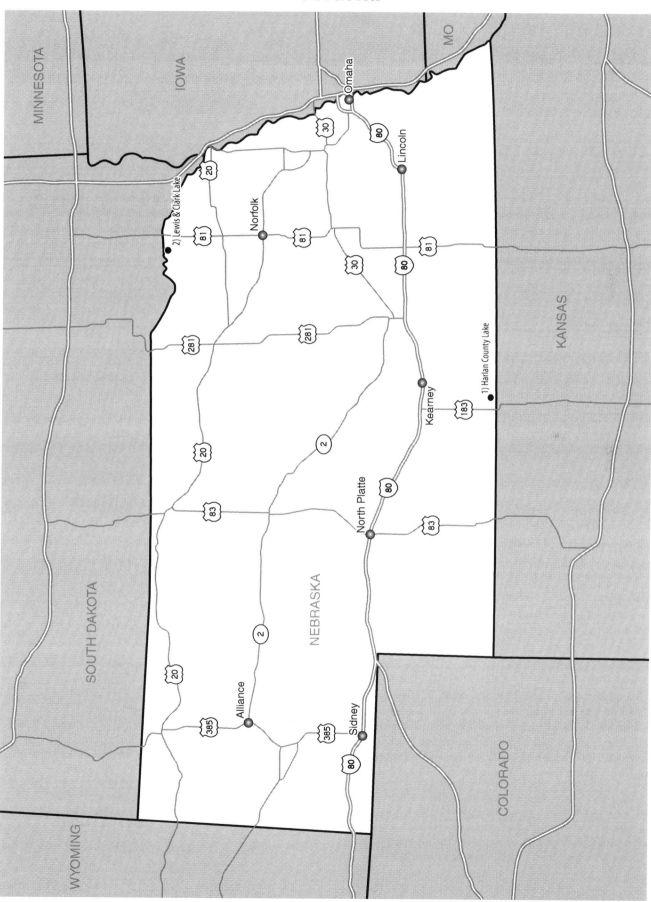

Activities

	Auto Touring	Biking	Boating	Climbing	Cultural / Historic Sites	Educational Programs	Fishing	Groceries / Supplies	Hiking	Horseback Riding	Hunting	Off Highway Vehicles	Lodging	Visitor Center
1) Harlen County Lake	♦		♦		♦		♦		♦					♦
2) Lewis & Clark Lake	♦	♦	♦		♦	♦	♦		♦		♦		♦	♦

Nebraska Projects

1) Harlan County Lake

U.S. Army Corps of Engineers
70788 Corps Rd A
Republican City, NE 68971
Phone: 308-799-2105
District: Kansas City

Harlan County Lake, the state's second largest lake, is located in south-central Nebraska just north of the Kansas state line. It has 18,217 land acres, 13,240 water acres and 75 shoreline miles. From I-80 Exit 257, travel 41 miles south on US-183 to the lake. Shopping and restaurants can be found in nearby towns.

RV Camping

Gremlin Cove: All year, 70 basic sites, non-reservable, $8-$10. **Amenities**: Drinking water, restrooms, showers, boat ramp, swimming beach. **Directions**: Located near the north end of the dam. From US-136 in Republican City, go 1.2 miles south on Hwy-A (Berrigan Rd) to the dam, north side. 308-799-2105. **GPS**: 40.086313, -99.21452

Hunter Cove: Apr-Nov, 84 sites with electric (some 50amp) hookups, 76 basic sites, some pull thrus, $14-$20. **Amenities**: Drinking water, dump station, restrooms, showers, laundry, boat ramp, fishing, fish cleaning stations, hiking, playground, volleyball. **Directions**: Located on the east end of the lake. From Republican City (on US-136), turn south on Berrigan Rd and travel 1.25 miles to Road B, then west 1 mile to the park. 308-799-2105. **GPS**: 40.08306, -99.2277

Methodist Cove: Apr-Nov, 32 full hookup sites and 16 electric only (some 50amp), 128 basic sites, some pull thrus, $14-$20. **Amenities**: Drinking water, dump station, restrooms, showers, boat ramp, fishing, boating, playground, hunting. **Directions**:

From Alma, go east on South Street and travel 2.5 miles to the park entrance. 308-799-2105. **GPS**: 40.08694, -99.31556

North & South Outlet: All year, 60 sites, no hookups, non-reservables, $8. Campsites are on the north and south sides of the Republican River below the dam. Access to the river and Stilling Basin from both areas. **Amenities**: Drinking water, restrooms. A nature trail is located at the east end of North Outlet Park. **Directions**: From Republican City on US-136 travel on Hwy-A to the North Outlet –or– on CR-1 to the South Outlet. 308-799-2105. **GPS** North Outlet: 40.072998, -99.210205; **GPS** South Outlet: 40.070313, -99.208984

2) Lewis & Clark Lake

U.S. Army Corps of Engineers
NE Hwy 121
Yankton, SD 57078
Phone: 402-667-7873
District: Omaha

Lewis and Clark Lake is formed behind the Gavins Point Dam. The lake is 25 miles long and has 90 miles of shoreline. The entire project, with 17,126 land acres around the lock and dam, straddles the Nebraska/South Dakota border just west of Yankton, South Dakota. The Visitor Center is located atop Calumet Bluff just downstream from the Gavins Point Powerplant. The Center provides a spectacular view of the lake, the dam and the Missouri River. Exhibits highlight the geology, exploration, early navigation, settlement and early history of the Missouri River. From Crofton, Nebraska, travel 13 miles north on Hwy-121. Powerplant tours are given on weekends and holidays.

RV Camping

Cottonwood: Apr-Oct, 75 sites with electric hookups, $16–$18. The campground is on the west side of Lake Yankton, a small lake below Gavins Point Dam. **Amenities**: Drinking water, dump station, restrooms, showers, boat ramp, fish cleaning stations, playground. *Directions*: From Yankton, South Dakota, travel 4 miles west on SD-52, then south on Dam Toe Rd and follow signs. 402-667-7873. *GPS*: 42.85861, -97.4825

Nebraska Tailwaters: May-Oct, 32 sites with electric hookups and 10 basic sites, $12–$16. The campground is on the bank of the Missouri River and provides good shore fishing. *Amenities*: Drinking water, dump station, restrooms, showers, boat ramp, fishing dock, playground. *Directions*: From Yankton, South Dakota, travel south on US-81 for 2 miles, then west on Hwy-121 for 4 miles. 402-667-7873. *GPS*: 42.84898, -97.47028

New Mexico

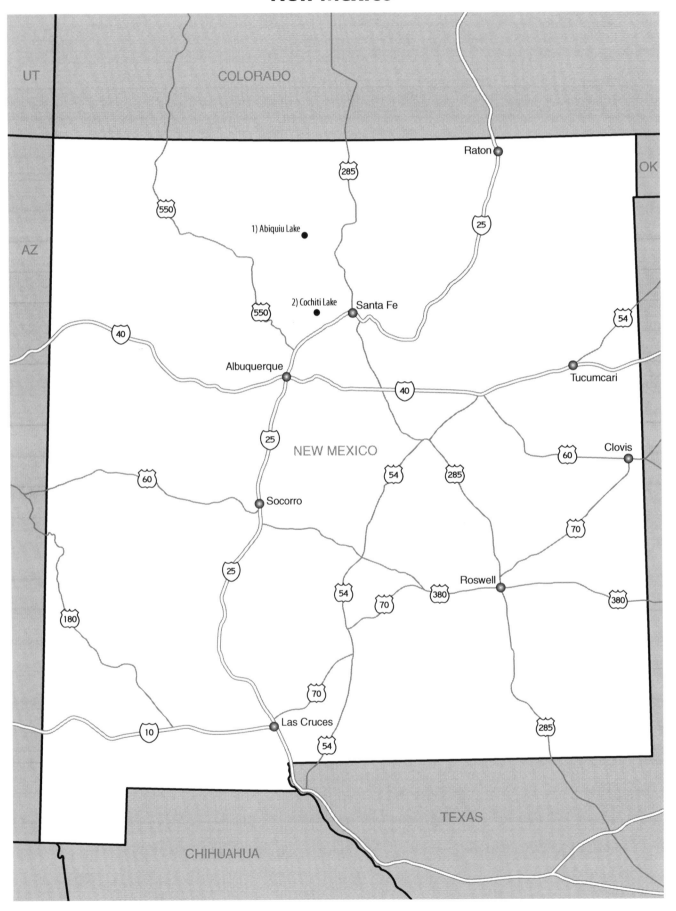

Activities

	Auto Touring	Biking	Boating	Climbing	Cultural / Historic Sites	Educational Programs	Fishing	Groceries / Supplies	Hiking	Horseback Riding	Hunting	Lodging	Off Highway Vehicles	Visitor Center
1) Abiquiu Lake	◆	◆	◆		◆		◆		◆					◆
2) Cochiti Lake	◆		◆		◆		◆		◆					◆

New Mexico Projects

1) Abiquiu Lake

U.S. Army Corps of Engineers
4631 State Hwy 96
Albiquiu, NM 87510
Phone: 505-685-4371
District: Albuquerque

Abiquiu has 2,104 land acres, 7,489 water acres and 51 shoreline miles. The lake is located on the Rio Chama, a tributary of the Rio Grande. The reservoir offers some of the finest fishing in northern New Mexico. From Santa Fe, travel 61 miles north on US-84 to SR-96 west. The project is located on SR-96 at the intersection of US-84.

The dam area provides a panoramic view of Cerro Pedernal (Flint Mountain). It is surrounded by red sandstone formations. Reptile fossils 200 million years old have been found in the area. Nearby attractions include Ghost Ranch, Georgia O'Keefe Museum, San Pedro Wilderness and sightseeing in Santa Fe.

RV Camping

Riana: Apr-Oct, 13 sites with electric (some 50amp) hookups, 24 basic and 15 tent sites, $10–$14. The campground is located on a 150-foot rock bluff overlooking the lake. **Amenities**: Drinking water, dump station, restrooms, showers, playground, biking, boating, fishing, hiking. **Directions**: From Espanol, New Mexico, travel 30 miles north on US-84. Turn west on SR-96 and continue 1 mile. 505-685-4561. **GPS**: 36.23333, -106.43333

2) Cochiti Lake

U.S. Army Corps of Engineers
82 Dam Crest Rd
Pena Blanca, NM 87041
Phone: 505-465-0307
District: Albuquerque

Cochiti Lake consists of 12,490 land acres, 1,200 water acres and 28 shoreline miles. Cochiti Dam is one of the largest earthfill dams in the U.S. From I-25 Exit 259, go northwest on NM-22 through Pena Blanca to the project office and Visitor Center. Cochiti Lake is five miles from Tent Rocks National Monument, which has fascinating geological formations.

The lake is located within the boundaries of the Pueblo de Cochiti Indian Reservation on the Rio Grande about halfway between Albuquerque and Santa Fe. Visitors are asked to observe and obey all Pueblo regulations. Good wildlife viewing can be found throughout the project including four osprey nesting platforms around the lake. Wind surfing is a popular activity. Cochiti is a no-wake lake. Sightseeing, shopping and restaurants are nearby.

RV Camping

Cochiti: All year, 40 sites with electric (some 50amp) hookups, 31 basic sites, $12–$20, some pull thrus. **Amenities**: Drinking water, dump station, restrooms, showers, boat ramp, fishing, playground, swimming, interpretive trail. **Directions**: On the west side of the lake. From I-25 Exit 259, go west on NM-22 through Pena Blanca to the project office and follow signs. 505-465-0307. **GPS**: 35.64167, -106.325

Tetilla Peak: Apr-Oct, 36 sites with electric (some 50amp) hookups and 9 basic sites, some pull-thrus, $12-$20. **Amenities**: Drinking water, dump station, restrooms, showers, boat ramp, fishing, hiking trail, swimming, playground. **Directions**: On the east side of the lake. From I-25 Exit 264, travel west on SR-16 to the Tetilla area and follow signs. 505-465-0307. **GPS**: 35.64722, -106.30444

North Carolina

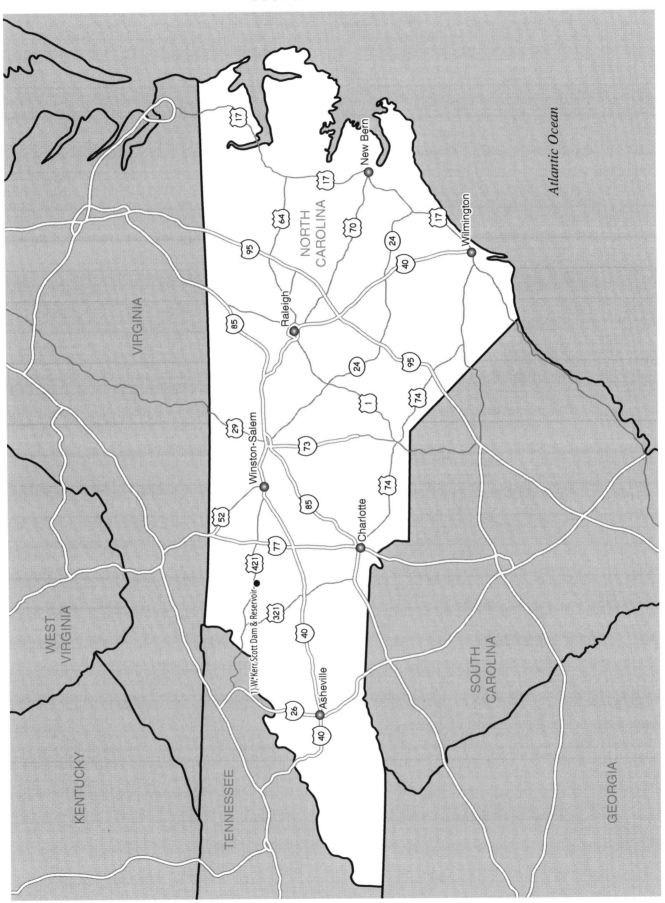

Activities

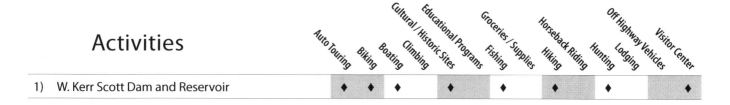

	Auto Touring	Biking	Boating	Climbing	Cultural / Historic Sites	Educational Programs	Fishing	Groceries / Supplies	Hiking	Horseback Riding	Hunting	Lodging	Off Highway Vehicles	Visitor Center
1) W. Kerr Scott Dam and Reservoir	♦	♦	♦		♦		♦		♦		♦			♦

North Carolina Projects

1) W. Kerr Scott Dam and Reservoir

U.S. Army Corps of Engineers
499 Reservoir Rd
Wilkesboro, NC 28697
Phone: 336-921-3750 or 336-921-3390
District: Wilmington

The W. Kerr Scott Reservoir is located in the Yadkin River Valley northwest of Charlotte. The project includes 4,305 land acres, 1,470 water acres and 66 shoreline miles. From Winston-Salem go northwest on US-421 to Wilkesboro, then 5 miles west on NC-268. Information is available from the Visitor Center.

RV Camping

Bandits Roost: Apr-Oct, 85 sites with electric (50amp) & water hookups, 17 tent sites, $18–$24, some pull thrus. **Amenities**: Drinking water, dump station, restrooms, showers, boat ramp, fishing, hiking, playground, swimming, basketball, amphitheater. **Directions**: Located on the south side of the lake. From Winston-Salem, take US-421 west to Wilkesboro, then SR-268 west 6 miles to the Goshen Volunteer Fire Department on SR-1141. Turn right on Jess Walsh Rd 1/2 mile and follow signs. 667 Jess Walsh Rd, Wilkesboro, NC 28697 / 336-921-3190. **GPS**: 36.11972, -81.24528

Fort Hamby Park: Apr-Oct, 26 sites with electric (50amp) hookups, 8 tent sites, $20-$22, some pull thrus. **Amenities**: Drinking water, dump station, restrooms, showers, boat ramp, fishing, hiking, horseshoe pit, basketball, playground, swimming, group camping. **Directions**: Located on the north side of the lake. From Winston-Salem, take US-421 west to Wilkesboro. About 5 miles past Wilkesboro, turn left on South Recreation Rd and travel 1.5 miles. 1534 Recreation Rd, Wilkesboro, NC 28697 / 336-973-0104. **GPS**: 36.13833, -81.27111

Warrior Creek: Apr-Oct, 53 sites with electric (some 50amp) hookups, 10 tent sites, $22, some pull thrus. **Amenities**: Drinking water, dump station, restrooms, showers, biking, birding, fishing, hiking, playground, swimming, group camping, basketball courts. **Directions**: Located on the south side of the lake. From Winston-Salem, take US-421 west to Wilkesboro, then SR-268 west 8 miles. After crossing the SR-268 bridge, turn right at the first road and follow signs. 336-921-2177. **GPS**: 36.11056, -81.30944

North Dakota

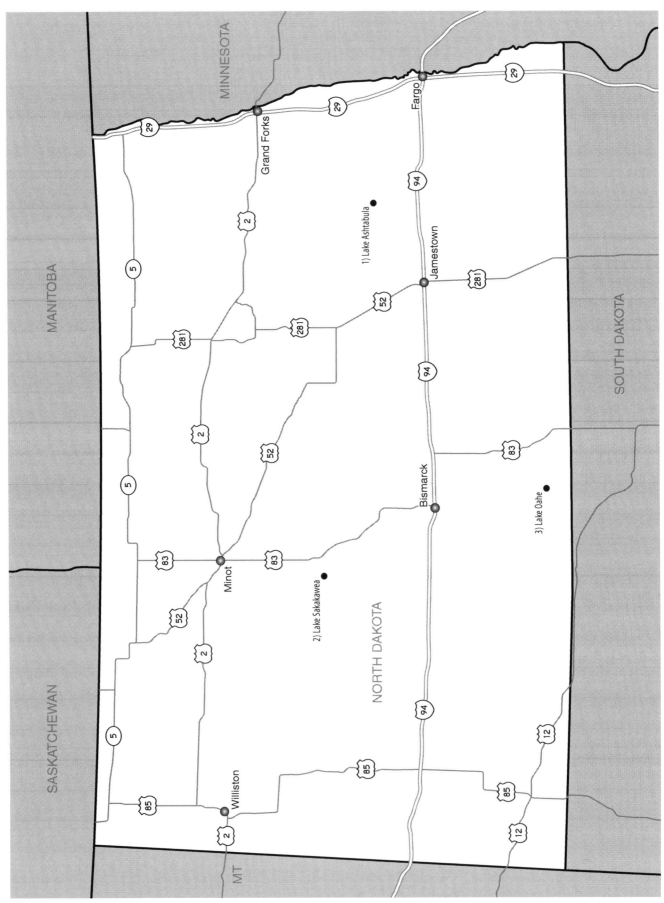

Activities

	Auto Touring	Biking	Boating	Climbing	Cultural/Historic Sites	Educational Programs	Fishing	Groceries/Supplies	Hiking	Horseback Riding	Hunting	Lodging	Off Highway Vehicles	Visitor Center
1) Lake Ashtabula		♦	♦				♦		♦					
2) Lake Oahe		♦	♦				♦		♦		♦			♦
3) Lake Sakakawea		♦	♦				♦		♦		♦			♦

North Dakota Projects

1) Lake Ashtabula

U.S. Army Corps of Engineers
2630-114th Ave SE
Valley City, ND 58072
Phone: 701-845-2970
District: St. Paul

Lake Ashtabula, in eastern North Dakota, includes 3,053 land acres, 6,430 water acres and 78 shoreline miles. It is located northwest of Fargo. From I-94 Exit 292, follow signs to CR-19 and travel northeast for about 12 miles. Year-round recreational opportunities are offered; wildlife viewing is excellent throughout the project.

RV Camping

Ashtabula Crossing East: May-Sep, 32 sites with electric hookups and 1 tent site, $22. **Amenities**: Drinking water, dump station, restrooms, showers, boat ramp, fishing pier, playground, swimming, hiking. Restaurant in walking distance. **Directions**: From I-94 Exit 292, go north through Valley City and 14 miles north on CR-21, follow signs. 790-845-2970. **GPS**: 47.1574, -98.0045

Ashtabula Crossing West: May-Sep, 26 sites with electric hookups and 12 basic sites, non-reservables, $22. **Amenities**: Drinking water, dump station, restrooms, showers, boat ramp, campfire programs, fishing pier, general store, hiking, playground. **Directions**: From I-94 Exit 292, go north through Valley City and 14 miles north on CR-21, follow signs. 790-845-2970. **GPS**: 47.1604, -98.0102

Eggerts Landing: May-Sep, 36 sites with electric hookups and 4 tent sites, $22. **Amenities**: Drinking water, dump station, restrooms, showers, boat ramp, fishing pier, playground, swimming, hiking. Restaurant in walking distance. **Directions**: From I-94 Exit 292, go north through Valley City and continue 14 miles north on CR-21, follow signs. 790-845-2970. **GPS**: 47.0956, -98.0085

Mel Reiman: May-Sep, 15 sites with electric hookups and 12 basic sites, $12–$16. **Amenities**: Drinking water, dump station, restrooms, showers, boat ramp, fishing, playground, swimming, hiking, visitor center. **Directions**: From I-94 Exit 292, go north through Valley City and then northwest on River Road for 9 miles. 790-845-2970. **GPS**: 47.0334, -98.0712

2) Lake Oahe

U.S. Army Corps of Engineers
28563 Powerhouse Rd
Pierre, SD 57501
Phone: 605-224-5862
District: Omaha

The vast Lake Oahe's 2,250 shoreline miles are located between Pierre, South Dakota, and Bismarck, North Dakota. It has some 53 recreation areas; most are managed by private concessionaires.

The project's Visitor Center is located in South Dakota and is situated on the east crest, providing an excellent view of the lake. The Center provides information about the history of the area, early navigation, settlement and natural history of the lake and Missouri River. Programs highlight the Lewis and Clark expedition and the fish of the area. The Center is open Memorial Day to Labor Day. Powerplant tours are given. To get to the Visitor Center from Pierre, South Dakota, follow SD-1804 north for 8 miles.

RV Camping

Beaver Creek: May-Sep, 37 sites with electric hookups, 15 non-reservable basic sites, $10–$14. **Amenities**: Drinking water, dump station, restrooms, showers, boat ramp, docks, fish cleaning stations, playground, swimming, hiking trails, horseshoe pit, wildlife viewing. **Directions**: From Linton, North Dakota, go west on Hwy-13 for 13 miles. After the highway changes to Hwy-1804, continue west for 1 mile, then follow the road south for 2 more miles. The campground is on the right. 701-255-0015. **GPS**: 46.2495, -100.5283

3) Lake Sakakawea

U.S. Army Corps of Engineers
P.O. Box 527
Riverdale, ND 58565
Phone: 701-654-7411
District: Omaha

Lake Sakakawea is located 75 miles northwest of Bismarck on the Missouri River. The lake is 178 miles long with 1,340 miles of shoreline. From I-94 Exit 159, go north 55 miles on US-83 then west 10 miles on SR-200. Exhibits in the power plant lobby display the construction and operation of Garrison Dam. Plant tours are given daily during summer months. The lake is an important resting spot for migrating whooping cranes.

There are 35 recreation areas around the large lake, including two Corps-managed campgrounds. Downstream is adjacent to a wooded wildlife management area and a National Fish Hatchery.

RV Camping

Downstream: May-Sep, 101 sites with electric (some 50amp) hookups and 16 tent sites, $16. **Amenities**: Drinking water, dump station, restrooms, showers, amphitheater, hiking, playground, swimming, volleyball, horseshoes, visitor center. **Directions**: From Riverdale, take Hwy-200 west to the dam. After crossing the Spillway Bridge, take the Tow Rd down the face of the dam. At the intersection at the bottom, turn left and go .25 mile east and turn right onto the campground access road. The campground is 1 mile south of the paved road. 701-654-7440. **GPS**: 47.48222, -101.42611

East Totten Trail: May-Sep, 30 sites with electric hookups and 10 basic sites, non-reservable, $14. **Amenities**: Drinking water, dump station, restrooms, boat ramp, playground. **Directions**: From Garrison, go 6 miles east on SR-37 and then 2.5 miles south on US-83. Campground is on east side of highway. 701-654-7411.

Ohio

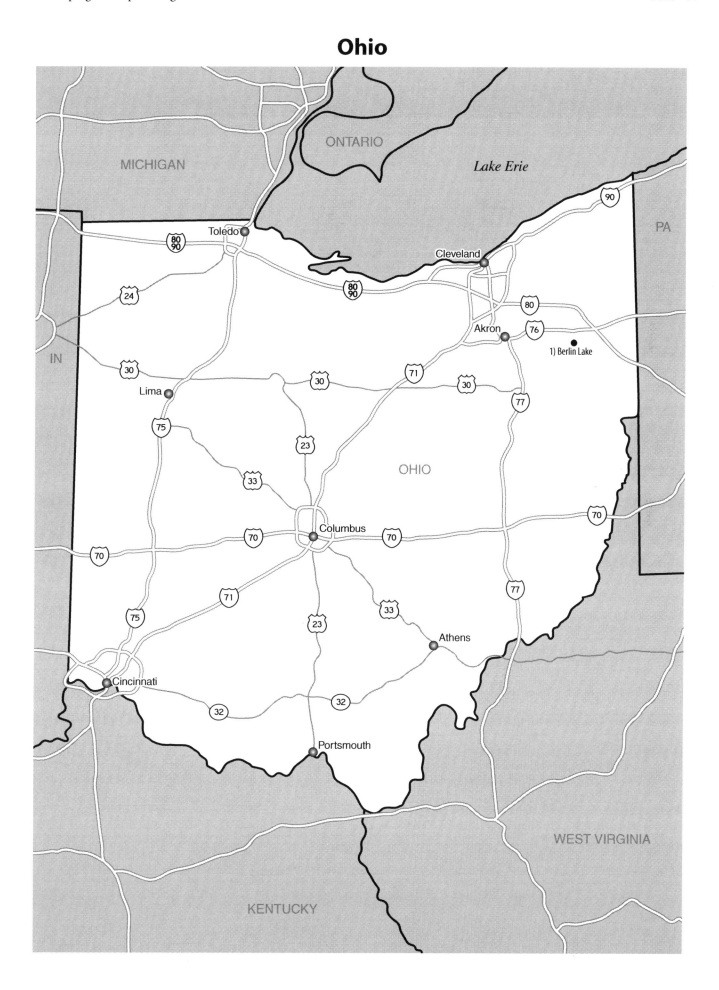

Activities

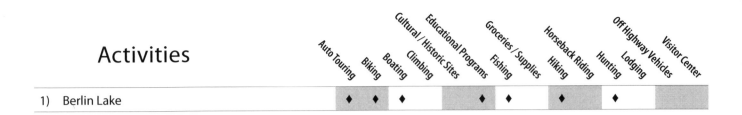

	Auto Touring	Biking	Boating	Climbing	Cultural / Historic Sites	Educational Programs	Fishing	Groceries / Supplies	Hiking	Horseback Riding	Hunting	Lodging	Off Highway Vehicles	Visitor Center
1) Berlin Lake	♦	♦	♦				♦	♦		♦		♦		

Ohio Projects

1) Berlin Lake

U.S. Army Corps of Engineers
7400 Bedell Rd
Berlin Center, OH 44401
Phone: 330-547-3781
District: Pittsburgh

Located in northeastern Ohio, the project includes 4,400 land acres, 3,580 water acres and 70 shoreline miles. Berlin Lake is on the Mahoning River about 35 miles upstream from Warren, Ohio; it is known for its walleye fishing. From Deerfield, Ohio, travel 2 miles east on OH-224.

The campground features ranger programs in the amphitheater in season, Memorial Day through Labor Day. The lake is a short distance from Akron and Youngstown, where restaurants and shopping can be found.

RV Camping

Mill Creek: May-Sep, 100 sites with electric (some 50amp) hookups, 248 basic sites, $14–$24. *Amenities*: Drinking water, dump station, restrooms, showers, boat ramp, biking, birding, canoeing, kayaking, sailing, water skiing, volleyball courts, playground, swimming, self-guided interpretive trail. *Directions*: From I-76 Exit 54, go south on SR-534 about 5.5 miles to US-224 in Berlin Center. Go west on US-224 for 2 miles to Bedell Rd, then south about .75 mile. 330-547-8180. *GPS*: 41.00694, -80.99806

Oklahoma

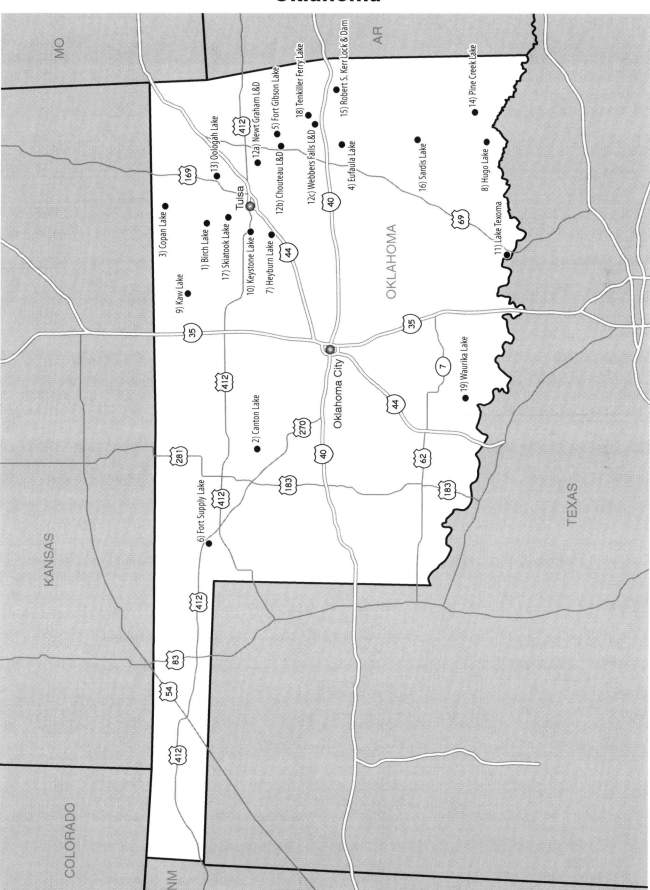

Activities

	Auto Touring	Biking	Boating	Climbing	Cultural / Historic Sites	Educational Programs	Fishing	Groceries / Supplies	Hiking	Horseback Riding	Hunting	Lodging	Off Highway Vehicles	Visitor Center
1) Birch Lake			♦				♦		♦	♦	♦			
2) Canton Lake		♦	♦				♦		♦		♦			♦
3) Copan Lake			♦				♦		♦	♦	♦			
4) Eufaula Lake	♦		♦				♦		♦		♦	♦		
5) Fort Gibson Lake	♦		♦				♦	♦	♦		♦			♦
6) Fort Supply Lake	♦		♦			♦	♦		♦		♦			♦
7) Heyburn Lake			♦				♦		♦		♦			
8) Hugo Lake		♦	♦				♦		♦	♦	♦			
9) Kaw Lake			♦				♦		♦	♦	♦		♦	
10) Keystone Lake			♦				♦		♦		♦	♦	♦	
11) Lake Texoma		♦	♦				♦		♦	♦	♦			
12) Locks & Dams on the Arkansas River	♦		♦				♦		♦					♦
13) Oologah Lake	♦		♦		♦		♦		♦	♦	♦			
14) Pine Creek Lake			♦				♦		♦		♦			
15) Robert S. Kerr Lock & Dam	♦		♦				♦		♦		♦			
16) Sardis Lake			♦				♦		♦		♦			
17) Skiatook Lake			♦				♦		♦		♦			
18) Tenkiller Ferry Lake	♦		♦		♦		♦		♦		♦	♦		
19) Waurika Lake		♦	♦				♦		♦	♦	♦			

Oklahoma Projects

1) Birch Lake

U.S. Army Corps of Engineers
5353 Lake Rd
Skiatook, OK 74070
Phone: 918-396-3107
District: Tulsa

Located just north of Skiatook Lake, Birch Lake has 2,584 land acres, 1,137 water acres and 27 shoreline miles. The lake is on Birch Creek in Osage County and its dam site is about 1.5 miles south of the town of Barnsdall. From Tulsa, go north on US-75, then west on SR-20 to the first light (Hwy-11), then go north to Barnsdall and turn left across from Big Heart grocery to the "T" then left to Birch Lake.

Boating, fishing and hunting are popular activities. Anglers will find walleye, crappie, catfish and several species of bass in the lake.

RV Camping

Birch Cove, A & B Sections: Apr-Oct, 85 sites with electric hookups, $18, some pull thrus. All campsites are on or near the waterfront. **Amenities**: Drinking water, dump station, restrooms, showers, boat ramp, fishing pier, playground, swimming, interpretive trail, horseback riding trail, hunting. **Directions**: From Barnsdall, OK, travel 3.1 miles to Hwy-11 across the spillway, then .7 mile west, follow signs. 918-847-2220 or 918-396-3170. **GPS**: 36.53444, -96.16222

Twin Cove: Apr-Sep, 11 sites, no hookups, non-reservable, $8. **Amenities**: Drinking water, restrooms, boat ramp, swimming beach, playground, hiking/nature trail. **Directions**: From Barnsdall, go 1.5 miles south to the camping area near the spillway. 918-396-3170.

2) Canton Lake

U.S. Army Corps of Engineers
HCR 65 Box 120
Canton, OK 73724
Phone: 580-886-2989
District: Tulsa

Located in western Oklahoma on the North Canadian River, the project is 2 miles north of the town of Canton. The lake has 7,910 water acres and 40 shoreline miles surrounded by 12,684 land acres. The project is accessible from I-40 Exit 108. Go north on US-270 to Watonga, continue on US-270/281, then north on SR-58 to Canton. From Canton, Oklahoma, go .5 mile west on OK-51, then north on OK-58A, follow signs. The project office is southwest of the dam. The Visitor Center has an overlook with excellent views of the lake. There are displays of animals native to the area, arrowheads and historic artifacts at the Center.

Canton is noted for its fishing, especially walleye. The annual "Walleye Rodeo" event is held in May. The lake has a sandy beach. Calm waters paralleling the dam are popular for water skiing. There is an active prairie dog town at the project.

RV Camping

Corps camping areas are located on both sides of the lake. Boat ramps and playgrounds are located at all campgrounds. Restaurants are nearby.

Big Bend: Apr-Oct, 86 sites with electric hookups, 19 basic sites, $15–$22. *Amenities*: Drinking water, dump station, restrooms, showers, playground, three boat ramps. *Directions*: On the west side of the lake, north of the dam. From Canton, OK, go 1.8 miles west on SR-51, then travel 4 miles north on the paved road, follow signs. 580-886-3576. *GPS*: 36.11833, -98.61444

Canadian: Apr-Sep, 123 sites with electric (some 50amp) hookups, $18–$22. *Amenities*: Drinking water, dump station, restrooms, showers, boat ramp, playground, amphitheater, fishing, water skiing. *Directions*: Near the west side of the dam. From Canton, OK, go .5 mile west on SR-51, then north on SR-58A. Travel for 2 miles, taking the left fork and go west where the highway joins a paved county road. Keep traveling west for .25 mile, then north to the campground. 580-886-3454. *GPS*: 36.09056,-98.60583

Longdale: Apr-Oct, 35 sites, no hookups, 3 tent sites, $11. *Amenities*: Drinking water, restrooms, boat ramp. *Directions*: On the east side of the lake. From Canton, OK, go west on SR-51 for .2 mile, then north on Hwy-58 for 6 miles to the south city limits of Longdale. Turn left on a paved county road for 2 miles to the campground. 580-274-3454. *GPS*: 36.12917, -98.58139

Sandy Cove: Apr-Oct, 35 sites with electric hookups, $18. *Amenities*: Drinking water, restrooms, showers, playground, swimming beach. *Directions*: On the east side of the dam. Located on the North Canadian River, 2.5 miles from the town of Canton. From Canton, go west on SR-51 for .5 mile, then north on Hwy-58A for 2 miles. Take the right fork at the "Y" and continue on Hwy-58A to the north end of the dam. 580-274-3576. *GPS*: 36.10417, -98.56944

3) Copan Lake

U.S. Army Corps of Engineers
Route 1 Box 260
Copan, OK 74022
Phone: 918-532-4334
District: Tulsa

The Copan project, located north of Tulsa near the Kansas state line, includes 12,997 land acres, 4,850 water acres and 30 shoreline miles. Maps and information are available at the project office. Wah Sha She State Park is nearby.

Swimming, boating and fishing are popular activities. Horse trails are at Washington Cove and Copan Point (day use).

RV Camping

Post Oak: Apr-Oct, 17 sites with electric hookups, $16–$18. *Amenities*: Drinking water, dump station, restrooms, showers, hiking trail. *Directions*: From US-75 travel 3 miles west on SR-10. 918-532-4334. *GPS*: 36.89753, -95.96973

Washington Cove: Apr-Oct, 100 sites with electric hookups, $16. *Amenities*: Drinking water, dump station, restrooms, showers, boat ramp, horseback riding trails, playground, hiking trails. *Directions*: From US-75 travel west 1 mile on SR-10 then 2 miles north. 918-532-4129. *GPS*: 36.90763, -95.93749

4) Eufaula Lake

U.S. Army Corps of Engineers
102 E. BK 200 Rd

Stigler, OK 74462
Phone: 918-484-5135
District: Tulsa

Eufaula Lake is located in east-central Oklahoma and is the largest lake located entirely in the state of Oklahoma. The 102,000-acre lake has over 600 miles of shoreline. The project is 31 miles south of Muskogee and spans across the junction of I-40 and US-69. From I-40 Exit 278 (Warner), go south on SR-2 for 10 miles then southwest 7 miles on SR-71. The project office is on the east side of the road.

The lake is situated on the Canadian River, 27 miles upstream from its confluence with the Arkansas River. Golf, restaurants, shopping and sightseeing are nearby.

RV CAMPING

Camping is available at these Corps-managed areas and at Robber's Cave State Park.

Belle Starr: Apr-Sep, 111 sites with electric (some 50amp) hookups, some pull thrus, $18–$20. *Amenities*: Drinking water, restrooms, dump station, boat ramp, fishing, hiking, playground, marina, swimming. *Directions*: From I-40 Exit 264, go south on US-69 to Texanna Rd. Exit onto SR-150 and go east for 2 miles, then south for 2 miles, follow signs. 918-799-5843. *GPS*: 35.33306, -95.5

Broken Cove: Apr-Oct, 73 sites with electric (some 50amp) hookups, some pull thrus, $18. *Amenities*: Drinking water, dump station, restrooms, showers, boat ramp, fishing, playground, swimming, hiking, marina. *Directions*: Located on Eufaula Lake near the dam. From Enterprise, OK, travel 5 miles north on SR-71, follow signs. 918-799-5843. *GPS*: 35.29028,-95.3844

Dam Site East: All year, 10 sites with electric, non-reservable, $12. *Amenities*: Drinking water, restrooms. *Directions*: Located on the northeast side below the dam. 918-484-5135.

Dam Site South: Apr-Sep, 42 sites with electric hookups and 15 basic sites, $11–$20. *Amenities*: Drinking water, dump station, restrooms, showers, boat ramp, playground, hiking, fishing, swimming. *Directions*: Located near the dam. From Enterprise, OK, travel 6 miles north on SR-71, follow signs. 918-799-5843. *GPS*: 35.29417, -95.3675

Elm Point: All year, 14 sites with electric, 3 basic sites, non-reservable, $8-$12. *Amenities*: Drinking water, dump station, restrooms, boat ramp, boat dock. *Directions*: From McAlester follow SR-31 northeast for 13 miles. 918-484-5135.

Gentry Creek: Apr-Sep, 15 sites with electric hookups, 10 basic sites, $13-$18. *Amenities*: Drinking water, restrooms, showers, boat ramp, fishing, hiking. *Directions*: From Checotah, OK, travel 9 miles west on US-266, follow signs. 918-799-5843. *GPS*: 35.4954, -95.6709

Highway 9 Landing: Apr-Sep, 65 sites with electric hookups, 15 basic sites, some pull thrus, $8-$20. *Amenities*: Drinking water, dump station, restrooms, showers, boat ramp, fishing, playground, swimming. *Directions*: From Eufaula, go 7 miles east on SR-9. 918-799-5843. *GPS*: 35.24, -95.49222

Mill Creek Bay: Apr-Oct, 12 sites, no hookups, non-reservable, $8. *Amenities*: Drinking water, restrooms, boat ramp. *Directions*: From Eufaula, go 6 miles west on SR-9, then 2 miles south. 918-484-5135.

Oak Ridge: Mar-Oct, 8 sites with electric, 5 basic sites, non-reservable, $8-$12. *Amenities*: Drinking water, restrooms, boat ramp, boat dock. *Directions*: From Eufaula, go south 6 miles on US-69, then northeast on SR-9A. 918-484-5135.

Porum Landing: Apr-Sep, 49 sites with electric hookups, some pull thrus, $18. *Amenities*: Drinking water, dump station, restrooms, showers, boat ramp, fishing, hiking, playground, swimming, marina. *Directions*: From Porum, OK, travel 7 miles west on Texanna Rd, follow signs. 918-799-5843. *GPS*: 35.35083, -95.38306

5) Fort Gibson Lake

U.S. Army Corps of Engineers
8568 SR-251A
Fort Gibson, OK 74434
Phone: 918-682-4314
District: Tulsa

Fort Gibson Lake is located on the Grand Neosho River about 5 miles northwest of historic Fort Gibson and north of Muskogee. From I-40 Exit 286, take Muskogee Turnpike north to the Tahlequah/Fort Gibson exit. Travel east on US-62 to the town of Fort Gibson, then take Hwy-80 north about 7 miles to the dam. The project office is on the hill on the west side of the dam. Information and maps are available. Dam tours are given.

The lake draws its name from historic Fort Gibson which played a prominent part in the military history of early day Oklahoma. A reconstructed log stockade stands on the site of the first log fort. Volunteers reenact the lifestyle of the late 1800's for various events during the year.

The lake is 7 miles above the confluence of the Neosho and Arkansas Rivers and is noted for its fishing where sportsmen will find bass, crappie and several varieties of catfish and panfish. A marina is located at Flat Rock Creek. Bird watchers enjoy the various migratory birds that pass through the area.

RV Camping

Blue Bill Point: Apr-Sep, 40 sites with electric (some 50amp) hookups, 3 basic sites, $18–$20. The campground sits along the banks of Flat Rock Bay. *Amenities*: Drinking water, dump station, restrooms, showers, boat ramp, dock, fishing, hunting. *Directions*: From Wagoner, OK, travel north on US-69 for 5 miles, follow signs. 918-476-6638. *GPS*: 36.0425, -95.33444

Dam Site: Apr-Sep, 48 sites with electric hookups, $18. *Amenities*: Drinking water, dump station, restrooms, showers, boat ramp, fishing, hunting, birding. *Directions*: From Okay, OK, travel 6 miles east on SR-251A. 918-683-6618. *GPS*: 35.86778, -95.23361

Flat Rock Creek: Apr-Sep, 30 sites with electric hookups and 3 non-reservable basic sites, $18. The campground sits along the banks of Flat Rock Bay. *Amenities*: Drinking water, dump station, restrooms, showers, boat ramp, fishing, hunting, birding. *Directions*: From Wagoner, OK, travel north on US-69 for 5 miles, then 3 miles east and 1 mile south and follow signs. 918-476-6766. *GPS*: 36.04556, -95.32694

Rocky Point: Apr-Sep, 48 sites with electric (some 50amp) hookups, $18–$20. *Amenities*: Drinking water, dump station, restrooms, showers, dock, boat ramp, fishing, hunting, birding, swimming. *Directions*: From Wagoner, go north 4 miles on US-69 then east 3 miles on Whitehorn Cove Rd. Follow signs into the campground. 918-462-3492. *GPS*: 36.03306, -95.31639

Taylor Ferry: Apr-Sep, 89 sites with electric (some 50amp) hookups, 6 basic sites, $18–$20. *Amenities*: Drinking water, dump station, restrooms, showers, boat ramp, fishing, hunting. *Directions*: From Wagoner, go 5 miles east on SR-51. 34179 Marina Dr, Wagoner, OK 74467 / 918-485-4792. *GPS*: 35.94083, -95.27611

Wildwood: Apr-Sep, 30 sites with electric (some 50amp) & water hookups, $18-$20. The serene campground is located along Fourteen Mile Creek and provides excellent lake access. *Amenities*: Drinking water, dump station, restrooms, showers, boat ramp, fishing, hunting. *Directions*: From Fort Gibson Dam, follow SR-80 north approximately 8 miles. 918-682-4314. *GPS*: 35.91806, -95.21444

6) Fort Supply Lake

U.S. Army Corps of Engineers
RR 1 Box 175
Fort Supply, OK 73841
Phone: 580-766-2701
District: Tulsa

The Fort Supply project is located in northwestern Oklahoma in Woodward County near the panhandle. It consists of 6,369 land acres, 1,786 water acres and 26 shoreline miles. From Woodward, Oklahoma, travel 11 miles northwest on US-183 then west 2 miles to dam. The Visitor Center at the project office has displays of animals native to the area, arrowheads and historic artifacts. Fishing is popular for crappie, walleye, white bass, hybrid bass and catfish. There is plenty of open shore line for bank fishing as well as piers. Boat ramps are available throughout.

A swim beach and sand dunes are on the east side of the lake. Places of interest in the area include the Fort Supply site and museum, Pioneer Museum & Art Center in Woodward and Boiling Springs State Park, just north of Woodward.

RV Camping

Beaver Point: All year, 16 sites, no hookups, non-reservable, $11. *Amenities*: Restrooms, boat ramp. *Directions*: Located near the dam. 580-766-2701.

Supply Park: All year, 114 sites, most with electric (some 50amp), some pull thrus, $15–$22. *Amenities*: Drinking water, dump station, restrooms, showers, boat ramp, playground, swimming, hunting. *Directions*: From Woodward, OK, travel 9 miles northwest on US-270 to the Fort Supply Lake sign. Turn west and follow for 3 miles, crossing the Fort Supply Dam, continue .75 mile to the 4-way stop. Then left and follow access road. 580-766-2001. *GPS*: 36.5, -99.58333

7) Heyburn Lake

U.S. Army Corps of Engineers
27349 West Heyburn Lake Rd
Kellyville, OK 74039
Phone: 918-247-6391
District: Tulsa

Located south of Tulsa in the Sandstone Hills of the Osage Section central lowlands, the Heyburn project encompasses 6,344 land acres, 920 water acres and 50 shoreline miles. From I-44 Exit 196 (Bristow), travel north and east on SR-66 for 9 miles to 257th West Ave, then north on paved road 2 miles to Heyburn Lake Road.

RV Camping

Heyburn Park: Apr-Oct, 46 sites with water and electric (some 50amp) hookups, some pull thrus, $14–$16. **Amenities**: Drinking water, dump station, restrooms, showers, boat ramp, dock, playground, swimming. **Directions**: From I-44 Exit 196, follow SR-66 north and east for 9 miles, turn north onto 257th West Ave for 2 miles then west 1.5 miles on Lake Heyburn Rd. 918-247-6601. **GPS**: 35.9448, -96.3075

Sheppard Point: All year, 21 sites with electric and water hookups ($14-$16), 17 tent sites ($10). **Amenities**: Drinking water, dump station, restrooms, showers, playground, boat ramp, dock, equestrian sites and horseback riding trails, swimming, hiking. **Directions**: Campground is on the north side of the lake. From I-44 Exit 211, follow SR-33 west for 8 miles then go south 2.2 miles on 305th Ave then go east 1.2 miles on 141st St. 918-247-4551. **GPS**: 35.9553, -96.3136

Sunset Bay: All year, 14 sites, no hookups, non-reservable, $7. **Amenities**: Drinking water, dump station, restrooms, boat ramp, swimming beach. **Directions**: From I-44 Exit 196, follow SR-66 north and east for 9 miles, turn north onto 257th West Ave for 2 miles then west 1/2 mile on Lake Heyburn Rd. 918-247-6391. **GPS**: 35.9512, -96.2894

8) Hugo Lake

U.S. Army Corps of Engineers
P.O. Box 99
Sawyer, OK 74756
Phone: 580-326-3345
District: Tulsa

Located in southeastern Oklahoma near the Texas state line, the project has 28,608 land acres, 13,250 water acres and 110 shoreline miles. Hugo Lake is on the Kiamichi River about 7 miles east of Hugo and 30 miles north of Paris, Texas. The project office is on the east side of US-70 in Hugo.

Sportsmen find a wide variety of fish including bass, crappie, catfish, bluegill, sunfish, carp and drum. Speedboats and water skiers enjoy some 8,000 acres of open water.

RV Camping

Kiamichi Park: Mar-Dec, 86 sites, 20 with electric hookups, 66 with electric and water, $15–$22, 9 horse stalls for equestrian campers. **Amenities**: Drinking water, dump station, restrooms, showers, boat ramp, fishing, horseback riding trail, hiking, hunting, playground, swimming, marina. **Directions**: From Hugo, follow US-70 east for 5 miles. 580-326-9650. **GPS**: 34.0156, -95.4086

Rattan Landing: All year, 13 sites with electric, some pull thrus, $14. Reservations not accepted. **Amenities**: Drinking water, restrooms, boat ramp. **Directions**: From Antlers, follow SR-3 east for 7.6 miles. 580-326-3345. **GPS**: 34.2004, -95.4832

Virgil Point: All year, 52 sites with electric and water hookups, $18-$22. **Amenities**: Drinking water, dump station, restrooms, showers, boat ramp, fishing, hiking, hunting, biking, water skiing, wildlife viewing. **Directions**: From Hugo, follow US-70 east for 7 miles then go north 2.6 miles on SR-147. 580-326-0173. **GPS**: 34.0497, -95.3777

9) Kaw Lake

U.S. Army Corps of Engineers
9400 Lake Rd
Ponca City, OK 74604
Phone: 580-762-5611
District: Tulsa

Located in north-central Oklahoma about 25 miles east of I-35, the Kaw Lake project encompasses 33,075 land acres, 17,040 water acres and 168 shoreline miles. It is on the Arkansas River about 8 miles east of Ponca City. Maps and information are available at the project office located on the west end of the dam.

Kaw Lake and the Arkansas River are noted for producing some of the state's largest catfish. In winter, the area has one of the largest populations of Bald Eagles. Hikers and horseback riders are attracted to the beautiful trails along Kaw Lake's eastern shore. The Eagle View Hiking Trail, about 12 miles long, runs between Osage Cove and Burbank Landing. The Five Fingers Equestrian Trail extends from Burbank Landing to the Sarge Creek Cove area. Off-road vehicle trails are at Sarge Creek. Designated swimming areas are at Pioneer Park and Sandy Park.

RV CAMPING

Bear Creek Cove: May-Nov, 22 sites with electric hookups, $15. **Amenities**: Drinking water, dump station, restrooms, showers, boat ramp, fishing, wildlife viewing. **Directions**: From Newkirk, go east on East River Rd for 8 miles, then 3 miles south on Bear Creek Rd. 580-762-5611. **GPS**: 36.8397, -96.9061

Coon Creek: Mar-Nov, 54 sites with electric hookups, $16-$18. **Amenities**: Drinking water, dump station, restrooms, showers, boat ramp, fishing, hiking. **Directions**: From Ponca City follow US-77 north for 4 miles then go east 7 miles on John B Hayes Rd and then go north 1 mile on Rocky Ridge Rd. 580-762-5611. **GPS**: 36.78492, -86.92297

McFadden Cove: Mar-Nov, 15 sites with electric hookups, $12. Reservations not accepted. **Amenities**: Drinking water, restrooms, marina, boat ramp, dock. **Directions**: From Ponca City, go east on Lake Rd for 8 miles to park entrance. 580-762-5611. **GPS**: 36.7008, -96.9340

Osage Cove: Mar-Nov, 94 sites with electric hookups, some pull-thrus, $18. **Amenities**: Drinking water, dump station, restrooms, showers, playground, boat ramp, fishing, hiking. **Directions**: From Ponca City, go east on US-60 for 9.8 miles then north on Kaw Dam Rd .4 miles, turn right and continue north on Osage Cove Rd for 1.7 miles. 580-762-5611. **GPS**: 36.7134, -96.8880

Sandy: Apr-Oct, 12 sites with electric hookups, $12. Reservations not accepted. **Amenities**: Drinking water, restrooms, boat ramp, swimming. **Directions**: From Ponca City, follow US-60 east for 9.3 miles then turn north .5 mile onto 11 Mile Rd; continue west 1 mile on Sandy Park Rd. 580-762-5611. **GPS**: 36.6984, -96.9216

Sarge Creek: Mar-Nov, 51 sites with electric hookups, 7 sites are available for equestrian campers with horse pens provided, $18. **Amenities**: Drinking water, dump station, restrooms, showers, boat ramp, fishing, hunting, equestrian trail, playground. **Directions**: From Ponca City, follow SR-11 east for 14 miles. 580-762-5611. **GPS**: 36.7667, -96.8081

Washunga Bay: Mar-Nov, 24 sites with electric & water hookups, $16-18. **Amenities**: Drinking water, dump station, restrooms, showers, boat ramp, fishing, boating, wildlife viewing. **Directions**: From Kaw City, go east about 3.5 miles on SR-11, then north on the county road for about 1 mile, then west on county road for 3.3 miles. 580-762-5611. **GPS**: 36.7921, -96.8453

10) Keystone Lake

U.S. Army Corps of Engineers
23115 West Wekiwa Rd
Sand Springs, OK 74063
Phone: 918-865-2621
District: Tulsa

Noted for its blue-green water, Keystone Lake has 23,610 water acres and 330 shoreline miles. The project is on the Arkansas River and is surrounded by 59,580 acres of public land. From Tulsa, travel 14 miles west on US-64/412. Look for signs to Keystone and go south on SR-151 toward the lake. Before crossing over the dam, turn left on West Wekiwa Road to the project office; information and maps are available.

The project features 11 boat ramps throughout, three marinas, miles of sandy beaches, two ORV areas and five short distance trails. A wildlife refuge provides extensive wildlife viewing opportunities. Keystone Lake is noted for several varieties of bass, crappie and catfish. Boat rentals are available at the marinas. Off road vehicle trails are at the Appalachia Bay camping area.

RV CAMPING

Nearby Keystone State Park and Walnut Creek State Park offer camping and rental cabins.

Appalachia Bay: All year, 18 sites with water hookups, $8. Reservations not accepted. **Amenities**: Drinking water, restrooms, swimming, boat ramp, ATV trail. **Directions**: From Sand Springs, go 10.1 miles west on US-64 and take the Bears Glen exit. Campground is on the west side of US-64. 918-243-7822. **GPS**: 36.1873, -96.2912

Brush Creek: All year, 20 sites with electric and water hookups, $15-$20. Reservations not accepted. **Amenities**: Drinking water, restrooms, boat ramp, swimming beach, ATV trail. **Directions**: From Sand Springs, OK, travel 8 miles west on US-64. Campground is below the dam on the north side of the spillway. 918-865-2621. **GPS**: 36.1509, -96.2469

Salt Creek North: All year, 112 sites with electric hookups and 12 basic sites, $10–$17. *Amenities*: Drinking water, dump station, restrooms, showers, boat ramp, dock, fishing, playground, swimming, amphitheater. *Directions*: From Tulsa, follow US-412 west 14 miles then go south 2.6 miles on SR-151 and then go west 3 miles on SR-51. 918-865-2845. *GPS*: 36.1294, -96.3215

Washington Irving: All year, 38 sites with electric hookups, 2 sites without hookups, $10–$17. There is heavy tree cover and low hanging limbs in some areas. *Amenities*: Drinking water, dump station, restrooms, showers, playground, swimming, hiking trail, boat ramp, fishing. *Directions*: From Tulsa, follow US-412 west for 17 miles to Bears Glen exit. Turn left at the stop sign onto Frontage Rd and drive 1 block. Turn right at the first paved road and follow 1 mile. 918-865-2621. *GPS*: 36.1979, -96.2600

11) Lake Texoma

U.S. Army Corps of Engineers
351 Corps Rd
Denison, TX 75020
Phone: 903-465-4990
District: Tulsa

This project is in south-central Oklahoma on the Texas state line. It has 102,968 land acres, 88,000 water acres and 680 shoreline miles. From Denison, Texas, go 5 miles northwest on TX-91. Before the dam, turn right onto Corps Road to the project office.

Cross Timbers is a popular hiking trail that wends for 14 miles above the lake on rocky ledges and through the woodland. Also available are 40 miles of equestrian trails. Texoma is known as the "Striper Capitol of the World," one of the few reservoirs in the nation where striped bass reproduce naturally.

Swimming beaches are at Burns Run East and West and Caney Creek. Boat ramps and fishing piers are conveniently located throughout. Marinas can be found at Johnson Creek, Lakeside and Platter Flats campgrounds. Overnight accommodations, boat rentals, slip rentals and supplies are available at many of the 23 concessions located adjacent to the lake. There are two state parks and two wildlife refuges at Texoma.

RV Camping

Buncomb Creek: Apr-Oct, 54 sites with electric & water hookups, $20. Gates close at 10pm. *Amenities*: Drinking water, dump station, restrooms, showers, boat ramp. *Directions*: From Madill, OK, travel south on SR-99 for 17 miles to Willis, then east for 1 mile on paved access road. 15824 West Buncomb Creek Rd, Kingston, OK 73439 / 580-564-2901. *GPS*: 33.89806, -96.81306

Burns Run East: Apr-Oct, 14 full hookup sites, 26 with electric-only, 9 basic sites, $15–$24. Gates close at 10pm. *Amenities*: Drinking water, dump station, restrooms, showers, playground, swimming, boat ramp. *Directions*: From US-75 in Denison, TX, take Exit 72 to SR-91, travel north on 91 across Denison Dam 5 miles, take the first exit left. 525 E. Burns Rd, Cartwright, OK 74731 / 903-465-4990. *GPS*: 33.85139, -96.57472

Burns Run West: Apr-Oct, 105 sites with electric (some 50amp) & water hookups, some pull thrus, $15–$24. Gates close at 10pm. *Amenities*: Drinking water, dump station, restrooms, showers, playground, boat ramp, swimming. *Directions*: From Denison, TX, take US-75 Exit 72 to SR-91, travel north on SR-91 across Denison Dam 5 miles, take the second left, follow signs for about 1.5 miles. 825 West Burns Rd, Cartwright, OK 74731 / 903-465-4990. *GPS*: 33.85556, -96.59111

Caney Creek: Apr-Oct, 41 sites with electric (some 50amp) & water hookups, 10 basic sites, $15–$22. *Amenities*: Drinking water, dump station, restrooms, showers, boat ramp, hiking, playground. *Directions*: From SR-32 in Kingston, OK, take Donahoo Rd south 6 miles on access road, follow signs. 580-564-2632. *GPS*: 33.92806, -96.70167

Johnson Creek: Apr-Oct, 54 sites with electric (some 50amp) & water hookups, $20-$22. Gates close at 10pm. *Amenities*: Drinking water, dump station, restrooms, showers, boat ramp. *Directions*: From Durant, OK, travel 11 miles west on SR-70. Exit off SR-70 to the north, the park entrance is 300 yards ahead. 903-465-4990. *GPS*: 33.99917, -96.56944

Lakeside: Apr-Oct, 127 sites with electric (some 50amp) & water hookups, $20–$22. Gates close at 10pm. Most sites are near the water. *Amenities*: Drinking water, dump station, restrooms, showers, boat ramp, horseback riding trail. *Directions*: From Durant, OK, travel 10 miles west on SR-70 to Streetman Rd. Turn south on Streetman and go 4 miles to the park. 580-920-0176. *GPS*: 33.9375, -96.55056

Platter Flats: All year, 26 sites with electric and water hookups, 37 equestrian sites with electric & 20 equestrian basic sites, $12–$16. Gates close at 10pm. *Amenities*: Drinking water, dump station, restrooms, showers, boat ramp, horseback riding trails. *Directions*: From Colbert, OK, travel 5 miles north on US-75, turn west 5 miles, follow signs. *GPS*: 33.92167, -96.54472

12) Locks & Dams - Arkansas River

    a. Newt Graham
    b. Chouteau
    c. Webbers Falls

The Locks & Dams are part of the Arkansas River Navigation System. All are administered by the Tulsa District, Army Corps of Engineers. The waterway and pools (lakes) formed by the dams provide good areas for recreation, particularly fishing, swimming, camping and picnics in the park. Some Locks & Dams located along about 150 miles of shoreline southeast of Tulsa near the Muskogee Turnpike have camping areas.

12a) Newt Graham Lock & Dam

Fort Gibson, OK
Phene: 918-682-4314

RV CAMPING

Bluff Landing: All year, 25 sites with electric & water, 14 basic sites, $14-$20. Reservations not accepted. *Amenities*: Drinking water, dump station, restrooms, showers, boat ramp. *Directions*: From Broken Arrow, OK, go 12 miles east on 71st St, follow signs. 918-775-4475.

12b) Chouteau Lock & Dam

Muskogee, OK
Phone: 918-682-4314

RV CAMPING

Afton Landing: All year, 20 sites with electric & water hookups, 2 basic sites, $18–$20. *Amenities*: Drinking water, dump station, restrooms, showers, boat ramp, picnic area. *Directions*: From Wagoner, OK, at junction of US-69 & SR-51, go 5 miles west on SR-51. 918-489-5541.

12c) Webbers Falls Lock & Dam

Gore, OK
Phone: 918-487-5252

Note: The Visitor Center at Webbers Falls features a platform where visitors can watch the lockage of barges and view a large area of the lake.

RV CAMPING

Brewers Bend: All year, 34 sites with electric & water hookups, 8 basic sites, some pull thrus, non-reservable, $10–$18. *Amenities*: Dump station, restrooms, showers, boat ramp. *Directions*: From Webbers Falls, travel 2 miles west on US-64, then about 5 miles north on Road N4410, follow signs. 918-489-5541.

Spaniard Creek: All year, 35 sites with electric & water hookups, non-reservable, $15–$18. *Amenities*: Dump station, restrooms, showers, boat ramp. *Directions*: From Muskogee, travel 10 miles south on US 64 and then east 5 miles on Elm Grove Rd, follow signs. 918-489-5541.

13) Oologah Lake

U.S. Army Corps of Engineers
P.O. Box 700
Oologah, OK 74053
Phone: 918-443-2250
District: Tulsa

From Tulsa, go 30 miles north on US-169, then east on OK-88. Before going over the dam, turn at the project office sign. A popular sailing destination, Oologah Lake has 29,460 water acres and 209 shoreline miles. There are 36,735 acres of public land. Several Corps-managed camping areas are located around the lake. Restaurants, shopping and sightseeing are available in the area. A nearby attraction is Dog Iron Ranch, the birthplace of Will Rogers.

RV CAMPING

Big Creek Ramp: All year, 16 sites, no hookups, non-reservables, free. *Amenities*: Restrooms, boat ramp. *Directions*: From Nowata, 5.1 miles east on US-60, then 2 miles north. 918-443-2250.

Blue Creek: Apr-Sep, 28 sites with electric hookups, 37 basic sites, $14–$18. The campground includes a loop of equestrian sites. *Amenities*: Drinking water, dump station, restrooms, showers, boat ramp, fishing, playground, hiking, horseback riding trails, swimming, water skiing. *Directions*: Campground is 12 miles north and east of the city of Oologah via county roads, follow signs. 13400 E 390 Rd, Claremore, OK 74017 / 918-341-4244 or 918-443-2250. *GPS*: 36.45222, -95.5925

Hawthorn Bluff: Apr-Sep, 44 sites with electric hookups, 15 basic sites, $16–$20. *Amenities*: Drinking water, dump station, restrooms, showers, boat ramp, dock, fishing, playground, swimming, hiking, birding, water skiing. *Directions*: From Oologah, OK, travel 2 miles east on SR-88, follow signs. 8377 E. Hwy 88, Oologah, OK 74053 / 918-443-2319. *GPS*: 36.43222, -95.68083

Redbud Bay: Apr-Oct, 12 sites with electric, non-reservables, $16. *Amenities*: Boat ramp, restrooms. *Directions*: From Oologah go 3.2 miles east on SR-88 to the east side of the dam. 918-443-2250.

Spencer Creek: Apr-Sep, 29 sites with electric hookups, 22 basic sites, $14–$18. *Amenities*: Drinking water, dump station, restrooms, showers, playground, swimming, boat ramp, fishing, sailing, water skiing. *Directions*: Located 15 miles from Oologah via county roads, follow signs. 6998 S 4180 Rd, Claremore, OK 74017 / 918-341-3690 or 918-443-2250. *GPS*: 36.51083, -95.56111

Verdigris River: Apr-Oct, 8 sites, no hookups, non-reservables, $12. *Amenities*: Drinking water, restrooms, boat ramp. *Directions*: From US-169 in Oologah, take SR-88 east for 3.1 miles to the camping area below the dam. 918-443-2250.

14) Pine Creek Lake

U.S. Army Corps of Engineers
Route 1, Box 400
Valliant, OK 74764
Phone: 580-933-4239
District: Tulsa

Located on Little River in McCurtain County, the project encompasses 21,559 land acres, 4,880 water acres and 74 shoreline miles. From Idabel, Oklahoma, go 18 miles west on US-70 to Valliant, then 1.5 miles north on county road (Dalton Street), follow brown signs to the project office.

RV CAMPING

Little River Park: Mar-Nov, 12 full hookup sites (50amp), 19 electric-only and 25 basic sites, $12–$18. Park gates close at 10pm. *Amenities*: Drinking water, dump station, restrooms, showers, boat ramp, playground, hiking trail, swimming. *Directions*: From Broken Bow, OK, take SR-3 west for 28 miles, follow signs. 580-876-3720. *GPS*: 34.16667, -95.125

Lost Rapids: All year, 18 sites with electric hookups, 13 basic sites, $10–$15. *Amenities*: Drinking water, restrooms, dump station, boat ramp. *Directions*: From Broken Bow, travel

west on SR-3 for 22 miles, follow signs. 580-876-3720. *GPS*: 34.17639, -95.10833

Pine Creek Cove: Mar-Nov, 41 sites with electric (some 50amp) hookups, $18–$22. *Amenities*: Drinking water, dump station, restrooms, showers, boat ramp, playground, swimming. *Directions*: From Valliant, OK, travel north on Pine Creek Rd for 7 miles to the access road, follow signs. 580-933-4215. *GPS*: 34.10694, -95.0875

Turkey Creek: All year, 8 sites with electric hookups, 22 basic sites, $10–$12. *Amenities*: Drinking water, dump station, restrooms, showers, boat ramp, playground, swimming, wildlife viewing. *Directions*: From Broken Bow, travel west on SR-3 for 28 miles, follow signs. 580-876-3720. *GPS*: 34.21503, -95.12522

15) Robert S. Kerr Lock & Dam

U.S. Army Corps of Engineers
R.S. Kerr Navigation Office
HC 61 Box 238
Sallisaw, OK 74955
Phone: 918-775-4475 or 918-489-5541
District: Tulsa

From I-40 Exit 307, travel 8 miles south on US-59. The navigation office is near the powerhouse. Drive past the convenience store and look for the brown sign for the office, turn right. The project consists of 21,913 land acres, 42,000 water acres and 260 shoreline miles.

RV CAMPING

Applegate Cove: May-Sep, 28 sites with electric hookups, $15. *Amenities*: Drinking water, dump station, restrooms, showers, boat ramp, marina, swimming. *Directions*: From Sallisaw, OK, travel 8 miles south on US-59, then 3 miles west on the paved county road, follow signs. 918-775-4475. *GPS*: 35.36194, -94.82306

Cowlington Point: May-Sep, 32 sites with electric & water hookups, $15. *Amenities*: Drinking water, dump station, restrooms, showers, boat ramp, swimming. *Directions*: From Sallisaw, OK, travel 12 miles south on US-59, then 4 miles west on the paved county road, follow signs. 918-775-4475. *GPS*: 35.30333, -94.82833

Short Mountain Cove: May-Sep, 32 sites with electric & water hookups, $15. *Amenities*: Drinking water, dump station, restrooms, showers, boat ramp, hiking. *Directions*: From Sallisaw, OK, travel 12 miles south on US-59, then 2 miles west on the paved county road, follow signs. 918-775-4475. *GPS*: 35.32, -94.78306

16) Sardis Lake

U.S. Army Corps of Engineers
HC 60 Box 175
Clayton, OK 74536
Phone: 918-569-4131
District: Tulsa

Located in southeastern Oklahoma, 5 miles north of Clayton, the lake covers 14,360 water acres and has 117 miles of shoreline. From McAlester, go 36 miles southeast on SR-1, then 15 miles south on SR-2. The project office is on SR-2 about a mile past the parks. Maps are available. The project is situated at the western tip of the Ouachita Mountain Range. Fishing is a popular activity providing excellent opportunities to catch crappie, catfish and walleye.

RV Camping

Potato Hills Central: Apr-Sep, 82 sites with electric, $18. Campground gates close at 10pm. *Amenities*: Drinking water, dump station, restrooms, showers, playground, hiking, fishing dock. *Directions*: From McAlester, OK, go southeast on SR-1 for 31 miles then go south 11.6 miles on SR-2. 918-569-4131. *GPS* 34.6706, -95.3233

Potato Hills South: Apr-Oct, 18 sites, no hookups, $10. *Amenities*: Restrooms, drinking water, swimming beach, playground, boat ramp, hiking trail. *Directions*: From Clayton, OK, follow SR-2 north for 6 miles. 918-569-4131. *GPS*: 34.6593, -95.3284

Sardis Cove: Apr-Oct, 22 sites with electric hookups and 23 basic sites, all non-reservable, $10-$15. *Amenities*: Drinking water, dump station, restrooms, boat ramp and boat dock. *Directions*: From Clayton, follow SR-2 north for 5.4 miles then go west 8.7 miles on SR-43. 918-569-4637. *GPS*: 34.6449, -95.4539

17) Skiatook Lake

U.S. Army Corps of Engineers
HCR 67 Box 135
Skiatook, OK 74070
Phone: 918-396-3170
District: Tulsa

Located in Osage County, about 25 miles northwest of Tulsa, Skiatook has 10,190 water acres, 100 miles of shoreline and 10,130 land acres. The lake is on Hominy Creek about 5 miles west of the town of Skiatook. From Tulsa, take SR-11 northwest for about 20 miles into Skiatook, then west on OK-20, travel through the town of Skiatook and continue another 4 miles to Lake Road. Travel south on Lake Road for 2 miles to the project office, where maps and information are available.

Sport fishing is a primary activity at the lake. A sand beach and swimming area is located at Tall Chief Cove. Boat rentals and supplies are available at the marina. Golf is nearby.

RV Camping

Bull Creek Peninsula: All year, 41 sites, no hookups, all non-reservable, $8. *Amenities*: Restrooms, boat ramp, picnic area. *Directions*: From Skiatook, OK, follow SR-20 west for 14 miles then go north 3.6 miles on CR-2535 and then east 1 mile on CR-2130. 918-396-2444. *GPS*: 36.4213, -96.2191

Tall Chief Cove: Apr-Oct, 50 sites with 50amp electric hookups, $20-$30. *Amenities*: Drinking water, dump station, restrooms, showers, boat ramp, fishing, boating, dock, playground, swimming. *Directions*: From Skiatook, OK, follow SR-20 west for 6 miles then go south on Lake Rd for 5 miles. 918-288-6820. *GPS*: 36.3197, -96.1139

Twin Points: Apr-Oct, 49 sites with 50amp electric hookups, $20. *Amenities*: Drinking water, dump station, restrooms, showers, boat ramp, fishing, hiking, hunting, playground, swimming. *Directions*: From Skiatook, OK, follow SR-20 west for 13.4 miles. 918-396-1376. *GPS*: 36.3844, -96.2161

18) Tenkiller Ferry Lake

U.S. Army Corps of Engineers
Route 1, Box 259
Gore, OK 74435
Phone: 918-487-5252
District: Tulsa

Nestled in the Cookson Hills of eastern Oklahoma, the Tenkiller project has 17,734 land acres, 12,800 water acres and 130 shoreline miles. From Muskogee, Oklahoma, travel 21 miles southeast on OK-10, then 7 miles east on OK-10A to Hwy-100. Turn left on Hwy-100 and go 1 mile to the project office on the right.

The lake is known as Oklahoma's Clear Water Wonderland.

Attractions at the lake include marinas, golf, three floating restaurants and many islands to explore. Nearby attractions include Sequoyah National Wildlife Refuge, the Nature Center at Tenkiller State Park and the historic city of Tahlequah.

Fishing, boating and scuba diving are popular. Three nature trails vary in length from 1.25 to over 2 miles. Spectacular vistas, rock formations and many species of wildlife can be observed.

RV CAMPING

Camping may be found at the many Corps-managed facilities around the lake as well as Tenkiller State Park and Cherokee Landing State Park.

Carters Landing: All year, 10 sites with electric & water hookups, 15 basic sites, non-reservable, $7–$11. *Amenities*: Restrooms, boat ramp. *Directions*: From Tahlequah, OK, go 4 miles southeast on US-62, then 6.6 miles south on SR-82, then 2 miles northeast on the access road. 918-487-5252.

Chicken Creek: Jan-Sep, 103 sites with electric hookups, $16. *Amenities*: Drinking water, dump station, restrooms, showers, boat ramp, playground, swimming. *Directions*: From Gore, OK, go 17.5 miles northeast on Hwy-100, then turn left and go 1.75 miles northwest on the paved access road, follow signs. 918-487-5252. *GPS*: 35.68167, -94.96278

Cookson Bend: Jan-Sep, 64 sites with electric (some 50amp) hookups, and 43 basic sites, $10–$18. *Amenities*: Drinking water, dump station, restrooms, showers, boat ramp, boat dock, playground, swimming beach, marina concession at the entrance to the park. *Directions*: From Tahlequah, OK, go 17.5 miles southeast on Hwy-82, then right for 2 miles on the paved access road, follow signs. *GPS*: 35.70667, -94.96

Elk Creek Landing: Jan-Sep, 17 sites with electric hookups, 25 basic sites, $10–$15. *Amenities*: Drinking water, dump station, restrooms, showers, boat ramp, public marina. *Directions*: From Tahlequah, OK, go 14.5 miles southeast on Hwy-82, then right on the paved access road, follow signs. 918-487-5252. *GPS*: 35.75139, -94.9025

Pettit Bay: Jan-Sep, 7 full hookup sites, 67 sites with electric (some 50amp) and 15 basic sites, $10–$20. *Amenities*: Drinking water, dump station, restrooms, showers, boat ramp, playground, swimming, public marina. *Directions*: From

Tahlequah, OK, go 8.5 miles south on Hwy-82, then right on Indian Rd 2 miles south, then left for 1 mile on paved access road, follow signs. 918-487-5252. *GPS*: 35.75361, -94.94778

Snake Creek: Jan-Sep, 110 sites with electric (some 50amp) and 7 full hookup sites, $16–$25. *Amenities*: Drinking water, dump station, restrooms, showers, boat ramp, playground, swimming, public marina, group camping area. *Directions*: From Gore, OK, go 15 miles northeast on Hwy-100, then turn left and go .5 mile west on the paved access road, follow signs. 918-487-5252. *GPS*: 35.6475, -94.97222

Strayhorn Landing: Jan-Sep, 43 sites with electric hookups, two are full hookup, $16–$20. *Amenities*: Drinking water, dump station, restrooms, showers, boat ramp, playground, marina, swimming, hiking trail. *Directions*: From Gore, OK, go 6 miles northeast on Hwy-100, then north on Hwy-10A for 1.5 miles, then east on the paved access road, follow signs. 918-487-5252. *GPS*: 35.61611, -95.05694

19) Waurika Lake

U.S. Army Corps of Engineers
Route 1, Box 68
Waurika, OK 73573
Phone: 580-963-2111
District: Tulsa

Located on Beaver Creek, a tributary of the Red River, the project has 12,505 land acres, 10,100 water acres and 80 shoreline miles. The town of Waurika is near the junction of US-70 & US-81. Go left on US-70 for 1.5 miles to Main Street in Waurika. Turn right onto Main Street (at the Waurika Quick Mart), stay on Main Street (turns into Hwy-5) for 6 miles. At the brown Waurika Lake sign, turn right to the project office. Maps are available. Fishing, boating and water skiing are popular activities.

RV CAMPING

Chisholm Trail Ridge: May-Sep, 95 sites with electric hookups, $14–$16. *Amenities*: Drinking water, dump station, restrooms, showers, boat ramp, fishing dock, playground, swimming. *Directions*: From the city of Waurika, go 5 miles northwest on SR-5, then 3 miles north on Advent Rd and 1 mile west on county road. 580-439-8040. *GPS*: 34.25917, -98.035

Kiowa Park: Apr-Oct, 166 sites with electric hookups, some pull thrus, $14–$16. *Amenities*: Drinking water, dump station, restrooms, showers, boat ramp, fishing dock, playground, swimming beach, group camping area, hunting. *Directions*:

From Waurika, travel 8 miles northwest on SR-5, then 3 miles north on the county road to the park entrance. 580-963-9031. *GPS*: 34.0, -98.08333

Moneka North: Mar-Oct, 38 sites, no hookups, non-reservable, $8. *Amenities*: Drinking water, restrooms, hiking nature trail. *Directions*: From Hastings, go 3.7 miles east on SR-5, then north for .8 mile. 580-963-2111.

Wichita Ridge: All year, 10 sites with electric hookups, 16 basic sites, non-reservable, $8–$12. *Amenities*: Drinking water, restrooms, dump station, boat ramp, hiking nature trail, equestrian trail, picnic area. *Directions*: From Hastings, go 1.2 miles east on SR-5, then 3 miles north, 1 mile west and 2.1 miles north. 580-963-2111.

Oregon

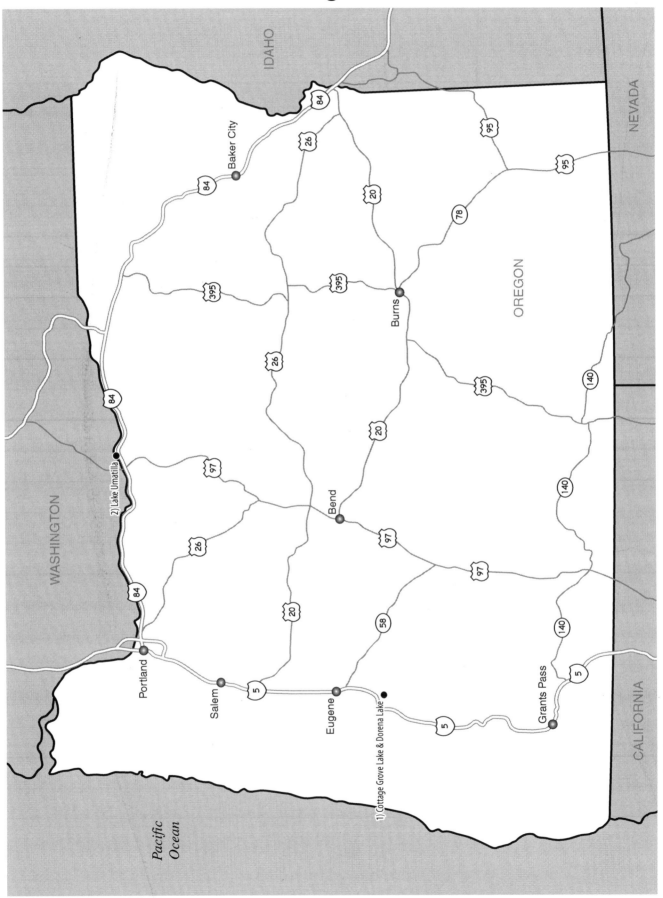

Activities

	Auto Touring	Biking	Boating	Climbing	Cultural / Historic Sites	Educational Programs	Fishing	Groceries / Supplies	Hiking	Horseback Riding	Hunting	Lodging	Off Highway Vehicles	Visitor Center
1) Cottage Grove Lake & Dorena Lake		◆	◆				◆		◆					◆
2) Lake Umatilla			◆				◆		◆					◆

Oregon Projects

1) Cottage Grove Lake & Dorena Lake

U.S. Army Corps of Engineers
75819 Shortridge Hill Rd
Cottage Grove, OR 97424
Phone: 541-942-5631
District: Portland

Cottage Grove and Dorena Lakes are both set in the Willamette Valley, about 20 miles south of Eugene and on the east side of I-5. The lakes are nestled in the valley's rolling, wooded hill country. The area is managed to provide a habitat for a wide variety of wildlife species of birds and animals. Cottage Grove is accessed from I-5 Exit 172 and Dorena from I-5 Exit 174. Corps-managed camping areas are located at both lakes.

RV Camping

Pine Meadows: May-Sep, 95 sites, no hookups, $12-$16. **Amenities**: Drinking water, dump station, restrooms, showers, amphitheater, birding, boating, fishing, playground, swimming. **Directions**: At Cottage Grove Lake. From I-5 Exit 172, turn left on London Rd for about 3 miles, then turn left on Cottage Grove Reservoir Rd, 3 miles to the campground. 75166 Cottage Grove Reservoir Rd, Cottage Grove, OR 97424 / 541-942-8657. **GPS**: 43.70028, -123.0575

Schwarz Park: Apr-Sep, 69 sites, no hookups, $14. **Amenities**: Drinking water, dump station, restrooms, showers, playground, interpretive trail, 12-mile bike path nearby. **Directions**: At Dorena Lake. From I-5 Exit 174, turn left on Row River Rd and travel 5 miles to the campground on the left. 34909 Shoreview Dr, Cottage Grove, OR 97424 / 541-942-5631. **GPS**: 43.78889, -122.96667

2) Lake Umatilla

U.S. Army Corps of Engineers
P.O. Box 564
The Dalles, OR 97058
Phone: 541-296-1181
District: Portland

John Day Dam is 216 miles upstream from the mouth of the Columbia River and is located at I-84 Exit 109 in northern Oregon. The project consists of a navigation lock, spillway, powerhouse and fish passage facilities on both shores of the 76-mile long lake. The Visitor Center has a fish viewing window and self-guided tours. Water recreation is plentiful on the John Day River and along the lake.

RV Camping

Note: The Cliffs and Plymouth camping areas are on the Washington side of Lake Umatilla and are listed in the Washington section of this guide.

LePage Park: Apr-Oct, 22 sites with electric hookups, 20 tent sites, $14-$20, some pull thrus. **Amenities**: Drinking water, dump station, restrooms, showers, boat ramp, fishing, fish cleaning station, swimming, water skiing. **Directions**: From I-84 Exit 114, the campground is located on the eastbound side of the interstate. Westbound travelers must go under the roadway, follow signs. 541-506-7816. **GPS**: 45.7284, -120.65126

Pennsylvania

NEW JERSEY

95

Philadelphia

476

476

DE

84

380

78

Scranton

81

81

6

76

Harrisburg

220

83

80

Williamsport

180

522

MARYLAND

15

22

220

81

6) Raystown Lake

76

4) Tioga-Hammond Lake

522

NEW YORK

PENNSYLVANIA

3) East Branch Clarion River Lake

70

22

6

Smethport

99

80

WV

219

Brookville

119

2) Crooked Creek Lake

22

219

9) Youghiogheny River Lake

8) Tionesta Lake

5) Loyalhanna Lake

62

70
76

422

76

80

70

6

Pittsburgh

WEST VIRGINIA

Lake Erie

Erie

79

79

90

7) Shenango River Lake

79

76

70

Activities

	Auto Touring	Biking	Boating	Climbing	Cultural / Historic Sites	Educational Programs	Fishing	Groceries / Supplies	Hiking	Horseback Riding	Hunting	Lodging	Off Highway Vehicles	Visitor Center
1) Cowanesque Lake			♦				♦	♦	♦		♦			
2) Crooked Creek Lake	♦	♦	♦		♦	♦	♦		♦	♦	♦			
3) East Branch Clarion River Lake	♦		♦				♦		♦		♦			
4) Loyalhanna Lake		♦	♦			♦	♦		♦		♦			
5) Raystown Lake		♦	♦				♦	♦	♦					
6) Shenango River Lake	♦	♦	♦		♦		♦		♦				♦	
7) Tioga-Hammond Lakes		♦	♦				♦	♦	♦		♦			♦
8) Tionesta Lake	♦		♦		♦	♦	♦		♦		♦			
9) Youghiogheny River Lake		♦	♦		♦	♦	♦	♦	♦		♦			

Pennsylvania Projects

1) Cowanesque Lake

U.S. Army Corps of Engineers
RR1 Box 65
Tioga, PA 16946
Phone: 570-835-5281
District: Baltimore

Located north of the town of Tioga and near the New York state line, the project consists of 2,212 land acres, 1,085 water acres and 17 shoreline miles. It is off US-15, between PA-49 and CR-58052. Cowanesque Lake is popular for fishing, boating, hiking and hunting.

RV Camping

The campground is on the north side of the lake and many sites are shoreline. Tompkins has two scenic overlooks and two downstream fishing access points. Ranger programs are presented at the campground in season. Other activities include water skiing, baseball, swimming and a playground.

Tompkins: May-Sep, 35 full hookup sites, 34 sites with electric (some 50amp) and water hookups and 40 basic sites, $18-$30. **Amenities**: Drinking water, dump station, restrooms, showers, laundry, boat ramp, interpretive trail, fish cleaning station. **Directions**: Travel on US-15 north to the Cowanesque River Bridge in Lawrenceville, PA. Turn west on Bliss Rd, travel 1.5 miles. 570-835-5281. **GPS**: 41.98194, -77.1875

2) Crooked Creek Lake

U.S. Army Corps of Engineers
RD3 Box 323A
114 Park Main Rd
Ford City, PA 16226
Phone: 724-763-3161
District: Pittsburgh

The project has 2,511 land acres, 400 water acres and 15 shoreline miles. The lake is located about 48 miles southeast of Pittsburgh and just south of Kittanning. From Kittanning, Pennsylvania, travel 7 miles south on SR-66, then east on SR-2019 to the park management office.

Crooked Creek Rangers developed the Corps' first Auto Tour Trail that takes in the local history of Armstrong County and local townships. Visitors learn about the one-room schools of 1867, the first water-powered sawmill and depreciation lands awarded soldiers of the American Revolutionary War. Ranger interpretive programs are presented in season at the campground.

RV Camping

Crooked Creek: May-Sep, 50 sites, no hookups, all non-reservable, $10. **Amenities**: Drinking water, dump station, restrooms, playground, group camping area, public boat launch at the lake. **Directions**: From Ford City, PA, go south for 5 miles on SR-66, then .1 mile east on SR-2019/W.T. Heilman Rd, follow signs. 724-763-3161.

3) East Branch Clarion River Lake

U.S. Army Corps of Engineers
631 East Branch Dam Rd
Wilcox, PA 15870
Phone: 814-965-2065
District: Pittsburgh

This 1,160-acre lake is situated in scenic northeast Pennsylvania, 14 miles northeast of Johnsburg. From I-80 Exit 97, travel north 36 miles on US-219 into Wilcox, turn right at the sign and go 2 miles, continue to follow signs. The lake has 20 shoreline miles and is surrounded by 424 land acres. Popular activities include fishing, boating and water skiing. The self-guided Shady Ridge Nature Trail offers hiking opportunities. Elk State Park is also located at the lake.

RV Camping

East Branch: Apr-Oct, 16 sites with electric hookups, 16 basic sites, 9 tent sites, all non-reservable, $12–$15. *Amenities*: Drinking water, dump station, restrooms, showers. *Directions*: From Wilcox, follow signs. 631 East Branch Dam Rd, Wilcox, PA 15870 / 814-965-2065.

4) Loyalhanna Lake

U.S. Army Corps of Engineers
440 Loyalhanna Dam Rd
Saltsburg, PA 15681
Phone: 724-639-9013
District: Pittsburgh

The 400-acre lake, located 32 miles east of Pittsburgh, is 4 miles long. The project is .75 mile south of Saltsburg on PA-981. From Pittsburgh go east on US-22 to PA-981, then north and follow signs.

There are numerous biking and hiking trails at the lake as well as the Black Willow Water Trail, a unique self-guided boating trail. Brochures and trail maps are available at the ranger booth at the Bush Recreation Area. Fishing is popular from inlet coves and backwater areas. The lake contains plentiful crappie, bullhead, catfish, bluegill, bass and carp.

RV Camping

Bush: May-Sep, 44 wooded sites, some with electric & water hookups, all non-reservable, $16-$22. *Amenities*: Drinking water, dump station, restrooms, showers (fee), boat ramp, group camping area, playground, volleyball. *Directions*: From Saltsburg, go south on SR-981 past the dam, then 1 mile on Bush Rd. 724-639-9013.

5) Raystown Lake

U.S. Army Corps of Engineers
RD1 Box 222
Hesston, PA 16647
Phone: 814-658-3405
District: Baltimore

The lake is located in south-central Pennsylvania, east of Altoona and north of the Pennsylvania Turnpike. From US-22 in Huntington, Pennsylvania, travel south on PA-26 to Hesston. The park headquarters is 2 miles east of PA-26 at Hesston. Raystown Lake, the largest entirely within the state of Pennsylvania, extends 27 miles and covers 8,300 acres.

There is a full service marina at the lake. Ranger programs are presented in season at Seven Points. Other amenities include ball fields, playgrounds and swimming beaches. Golf is nearby. Other local attractions include the Lincoln and Indian Caverns, Altoona Railroad Museum and the Swigart Antique Car Museum.

RV Camping

Seven Points: Mar-Oct, 56 sites with electric (some 50amp) and water hookups, 193 sites with electric only (some 50amp), 6 tent sites, $21-$30. *Amenities*: Drinking water, dump station, restrooms, showers, boat ramp, boat rentals, marina, interpretive trail. *Directions*: From the PA Turnpike travel US-30 to PA-26. Take PA-26 to Saxton and continue north for 17.5 miles to the turnoff for Hesston and Seven Points, then 4 miles to the campground. 814-658-3405. *GPS*: 40.38306, -78.07833

Susquehannock: May-Sep, 45 basic sites and 17 tent sites, no hookups, $12-$15. *Amenities*: Drinking water, restrooms, laundry, fishing, boating, mountain biking, hiking trail. *Directions*: From Huntington, PA, take PA-26 south for 6 miles, then east on unmarked Rt-3011 (Hesston Rd). Travel 3 miles and turn left onto Bakers Hollow Rd, 3 miles to the campground. 814-658-6806. *GPS*: 40.3875, -78.05

6) Shenango River Lake

U.S. Army Corps of Engineers
2442 Kelly Rd
Hermitage, PA 16148
Phone: 724-962-7746
District: Pittsburgh

Located in the Shenango River Valley, the lake is 21 miles northeast of Youngstown, Ohio, near the PA/OH state line. From I-80 Exit 4B, go north on SR-18 for about 7 miles. Take the Birchwood Drive exit and go south on SR-18 for about .25 mile and turn right onto West Lake Drive, follow signs. The project covers 15,071 acres and the lake is 11 miles long.

History buffs will enjoy exploring the remnants of the Erie Extension Canal, sections of which are on project property. Other local attractions include the Kidd Mill Covered Bridge and the Great Blue Heron Sanctuary. Fishing enthusiasts will find bass, walleye and a variety of panfish in the lake.

RV Camping

Shenango: May-Sep, 111 sites with electric (some 50amp) hookups, 214 basic sites, $17-$22. *Amenities*: Drinking water, dump station, restrooms, showers, laundry, boat ramp, marina, playground, swimming, volleyball, horseshoes, interpretive trail. *Directions*: Located on the north shore of the lake. From I-80 Exit 4b, take SR-18 north about 6 miles until crossing the causeway. (The park is on the left side of the divided highway.) Continue north on SR-18 about 1/4 mile. Exit right at Birchwood Drive to the turnaround to SR-18 south. Before crossing the causeway again, turn right onto West Lake Rd. 724-646-1124. *GPS*: 41.28889, -80.43833

7) Tioga-Hammond Lakes

U.S. Army Corps of Engineers
RR1 Box 65
Tioga, PA 16946
Phone: 570-835-5281
District: Baltimore

Hammond Lake is located south of the town of Tioga and west of US-15. It is north of Wellsboro on PA-287 which is accessible from US-15. The lake has 685 surface acres of water. Boating, sailing and fishing are popular activities.

In the Endless Mountains of north-central Pennsylvania, the area offers excellent wildlife viewing. Display gardens are located near the Visitor Information Center. There is a mile-long Archery Trail with targets and two tree stands. Other activities include water skiing, swimming and ball fields.

RV Camping

The campground is located on the east shore of the lake. Ranger programs are presented in season at the amphitheater.

Ives Run: May-Oct, 81 full hookup sites (50amp), 55 sites with electric (some 50amp) and 56 basic sites, $20-$40. *Amenities*: Drinking water, dump station, restrooms, showers, laundry, boat launch, fishing, interpretive trail, playground. *Directions*: From Tioga, travel south 5 miles on SR-287 and exit east at the sign. 710 Ives Run Lane, Tioga, PA 16946 / 570-835-5281. *GPS*: 41.88083, -77.2

8) Tionesta Lake

U.S. Army Corps of Engineers
P.O. Box 539
Tionesta, PA 16353
Phone: 814-755-3512
District: Pittsburgh

Tionesta Lake winds through the rugged hills of northwestern Pennsylvania. It is situated in Forest County where nearly half the county is public land. From Tionesta, travel 1.5 miles south on PA-36 to the 3,184-acre project. The lake is 6.3 miles in length.

The Tionesta Indian Festival is held annually in August. The Forest County History Center in nearby Tionesta is open daily, May to October. Areas nearby include Allegheny National Forest and Cooks Forest State Park. Ranger programs are presented in season at the campgrounds.

RV Camping

Kellettville: Apr-Oct, 20 sites, no hookups, non-reservable, $10. *Amenities*: Drinking water, dump station, restrooms. *Directions*: From Kellettville, PA, take Forest Rd 127 southwest across the bridge. 814-755-3512.

Outflow: All year, 39 sites, no hookups, non-reservable, $12. *Amenities*: Drinking water, dump station, restrooms, picnic area. **Directions**: From Tionesta, PA, go .5 mile south on SR-36, follow signs. 814-755-3512.

Tionesta Recreation Area: May-Sep, 78 full hookup sites (some 50amp), $28. **Amenities**: Dump station, restrooms, showers, boat ramp, playground, hiking trail, public marina. **Directions**: From Tionesta, PA, go .5 mile south on SR-36, follow signs. 814-755-3512 or 814-755-3592. **GPS**: 41.48431, -79.4491

9) Youghiogheny River Lake

U.S. Army Corps of Engineers
497 Flanigan Rd
Confluence, PA 15424
Phone: 814-395-3242
District: Pittsburgh

In the heart of the Laurel Highlands and spanning the Mason-Dixon Line between Pennsylvania and Maryland, the lake is 16 miles long. It is located southeast of Uniontown, Pennsylvania, and just south of the town of Confluence. The project office is .5 mile south of Confluence on PA-281. Nearby Ohiopyle State Park is noted for some of the best whitewater in the east.

RV CAMPING

Of the three Corps-managed campgrounds, one (Mill Run) is in Maryland, two are in Pennsylvania. Ranger programs are presented in season in the campground amphitheater.

Mill Run: All year, 30 sites, no hookups, non-reservables, $12. Located in Maryland at the far southern end of the project and subject to low water conditions; it is advisable to call ahead. **Amenities**: Drinking water, dump station, restrooms, boat ramp, swimming area. **Directions**: From Friendsville, go north about 4 miles on Friendsville-Addison Rd, then west 1 mile on Mill Run Rd. 814-395-3242.

Outflow: All year, 36 sites with electric hookups (some 50amp), 15 basic sites, 10 tent-only, $10-$22. **Amenities**: Drinking water, dump station, restrooms, showers, fishing pier, hiking, biking, playground. **Directions**: From Confluence, PA, travel south on SR-281 and go over the Casselman and Youghioghney Rivers. Make an immediate left into the campground. From US-40 in Maryland, take US-281 north for 7 miles to just past the Youghioghney River entrance. Turn right into the campground. 814-395-3242. **GPS**: 39.805, -79.36694

Tub Run: May-Sep, 4 full hookup sites, 33 sites with electric (some 50amp) hookups, 26 basic sites, $18-$22. **Amenities**: Drinking water, dump station, restrooms, showers, laundry, boat ramp, playground, swimming, amphitheater. **Directions**: From Confluence, PA, travel south over the Casselman and Youghioghney Rivers. Go 4 miles and turn left on Tub Run Rd. 814-395-3242. **GPS**: 39.77083, -79.40194

South Carolina

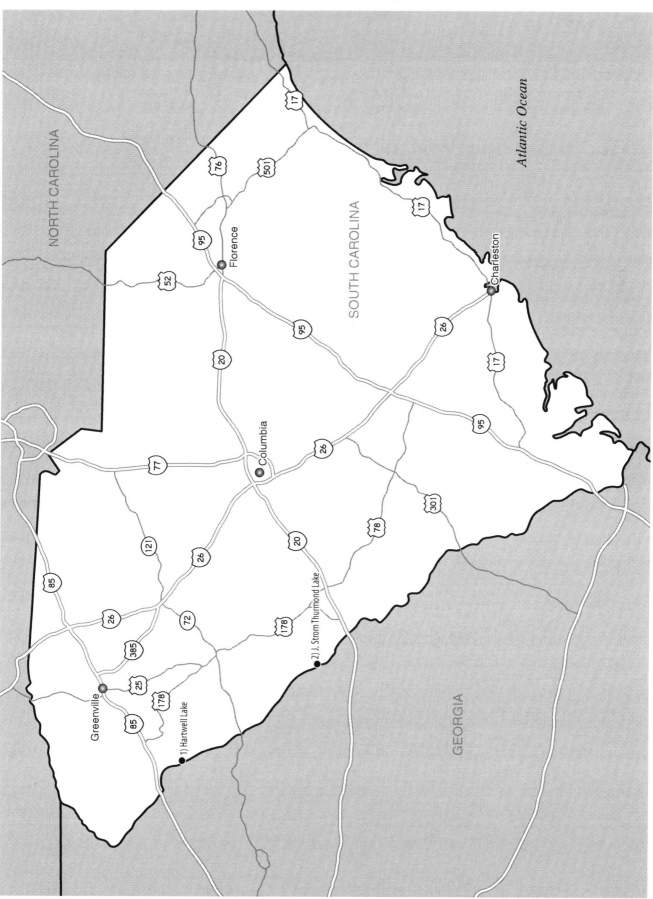

Activities

	Auto Touring	Biking	Boating	Climbing	Cultural / Historic Sites	Educational Programs	Fishing	Groceries / Supplies	Hiking	Horseback Riding	Hunting	Lodging	Off Highway Vehicles	Visitor Center
1) Hartwell Lake	♦		♦			♦	♦		♦		♦			♦
2) J. Strom Thurmond Lake	♦		♦		♦	♦	♦	♦	♦		♦	♦		♦

South Carolina Projects

1) Hartwell Lake

U.S. Army Corps of Engineers
5625 Anderson Hwy (US-29)
Hartwell, GA 30643
Phone: 706-856-0300
District: Savannah

Hartwell is one of the most popular Corps lakes in the nation. The dam is located just off US-29 on the SC/GA border. The Hartwell Visitor Center is located 1 mile past the dam on the Georgia side (5 miles north of Hartwell, Georgia). Guided tours of the dam and power plant are offered. Many lake access areas can be reached from I-85. Hartwell Lake comprises 56,000 acres of water with a shoreline of 962 miles. Over 20,000 acres of public land surround the lake.

Boat ramps are located around the lake. A private marina provides boating services and supplies. Swimming areas are provided at all campgrounds. Sailing is a popular activity at the lake. Boating safety courses are offered annually. The Anderson Jockey Lot, the largest flea market in the south, is nearby.

RV CAMPING

Four Corps-managed camping areas are located on the South Carolina side of the lake. See the Georgia section for additional project campgrounds.

Coneross Park: May-Oct, 94 sites with 50amp electric & water hookups and 12 basic sites, $18-$22. Gates close at 10pm. **Amenities**: Drinking water, dump station, restrooms, showers, boat ramp, birding, boating, fishing, playground, swimming. **Directions**: From I-85 in SC, take Exit 11 to Hwy-24 toward Townville. Go 1.5 miles past Townville and turn right onto Coneross Creek Rd, follow signs. 699 Coneross Park Rd, Townville, SC 29689 / 888-893-0678. **GPS**: 34.59111, -82.89722

Oconee Point: May-Sep, 70 waterfront sites with 50amp electric hookups, $24. All sites are waterfront. **Amenities**: Drinking water, dump station, restrooms, showers, boat ramp, fishing, swimming, playground. **Directions**: From I-85 Exit 11 in SC, take SR-24 toward Townville, South Carolina, and continue 1.5 miles past Townville. Turn right on Coneross Creek Rd and go 2.5 miles, turn south on South Friendship Rd, 3 miles. 200 Oconee Point Rd, Seneca, SC 28678 / 888-893-0678. **GPS**: 34.60167, -82.87083

Springfield: Apr-Sep, 79 sites with 50amp electric & water hookups, most sites are waterfront, $24. **Amenities**: Drinking water, dump station, restrooms, showers, boat ramp, birding, fishing, swimming, playground. **Directions**: From I-85 Exit 14, take SR-187 to Providence Church Rd, follow signs. 1915 Providence Church Rd, Anderson, SC 29625 / 888-893-0678. **GPS**: 34.44639, -82.82167

Twin Lakes: Mar-Nov, 99 sites with 50amp electric & water hookups, $22-$24. Most sites are waterfront. **Amenities**: Drinking water, dump station, restrooms, showers, dock, boat ramp, fishing, swimming, marina, playground. **Directions**: Located 5 miles from Clemson. From I-85 Exit 14, take SR-187 north toward Pendleton. Immediately after passing Clemson Research Center, turn left on Fants Grove Rd, follow signs. 140 Winnebago Trail, Pendleton, SC 29670 / 888-893-0678. **GPS**: 34.62806, -82.86556

2) J. Strom Thurmond Lake

U.S. Army Corps of Engineers
510 Clarks Hill Hwy
Clarks Hill, SC 29821
Phone: 864-333-1100 or 800-533-3478
District: Savannah

Thurmond Lake is a long, relatively narrow body of water that extends from the dam (just north of Augusta, GA) to 29 miles up the Savannah River, 46 miles up the Little River and 6 miles up the Broad River. It is one of the most visited Corps lakes in the nation.

With a shoreline of 1,200 miles and 71,000 acres of water, it straddles the SC/GA border. The Visitor Center (open 7 days a week, excluding Thanksgiving, Christmas & New Years Day) is located on the South Carolina side of the dam. Corps rangers are on duty throughout the year at the lake. From I-20 Exit 183 (in Georgia), the dam is north on US-221.

Fish species include bass, bream, crappie and catfish. Fishing piers and bank fishing areas are numerous. Navigational maps are available at area stores and marinas. On the north segment of the waterway, Hawe Creek campground is five miles from historic McCormick which offers sightseeing, shopping and restaurants. It is near two state parks and golf is also nearby. Mount Carmel, north of McCormick, is in the Old Ninety-Six tourism area. Modoc is in the south end near the dam and features a swimming area.

RV Camping

The Corps manages 13 campgrounds at the Thurmond Project; of these, four are located in South Carolina. See the Georgia section for additional project campgrounds. All the campgrounds have easy access to boat ramps and fishing.

Hawe Creek: Apr-Sep, 34 sites with electric (50amp) & water hookups, some pull thrus, $20–$24. *Amenities*: Dump station, restrooms, showers, marina, boat ramp, fishing, hunting, boating. *Directions*: Located one mile from the Dorn Sportfishing facility. From McCormick, go southwest on US-378 then south 4 miles on Park Rd. 1505 Chamberlains Ferry Rd, McCormick, SC 29835 / 864-443-5441. *GPS*: 33.83611, -82.33861

Leroys Ferry: All year, 10 sites, no hookups, non-reservables, $6. *Amenities*: Drinking water, boat ramp. *Directions*: From McCormick, follow SR-28 north 6.2 miles then SR-81 northwest for 5.6 miles and turn left onto the frontage road. Continue northwest .5 mile on SR-S-33-196 then turn left and follow Willington Academy Dr for 1.6 miles then continue south 2 miles on Leroys Ferry Rd. 864-333-1100. *GPS*: 33.9208, -82.4901

Mt. Carmel: Apr-Sep, 39 sites with electric (50amp) hookups, 5 tent sites, some pull thrus, $18–$22. A quiet, remote campground with many sites near the shoreline. 30-foot RV length limit. *Amenities*: Dump station, restrooms, showers, boat ramp, dock. *Directions*: From McCormick, go northwest on Hwy-28 to Hwy-81 into Mt. Carmel, follow signs. 2926 Fort Charlotte Rd, Mt Carmel, SC 29840 / 864-391-2711. *GPS*: 33.95833, -82.53944

Modoc: Apr-Nov, 49 sites with electric (50amp) and water hookups, some pull thrus, $22–$24. Many waterfront sites, beautiful views. *Amenities*: Dump station, restrooms, showers, laundry, boat ramp, playground, hiking. *Directions*: From I-20 Exit 200 (in GA), River Watch Pkwy, turn right and go 2 miles to Hwy-28 west (Furys Ferry Rd), turn right and go 13 miles to Clarks Hill, SC. Continue northwest on Hwy-221 for 4 miles. 296 Modoc Camp Rd, Modoc, SC 29838 / 864-333-2272. *GPS*: 33.71917, -82.22417

South Dakota

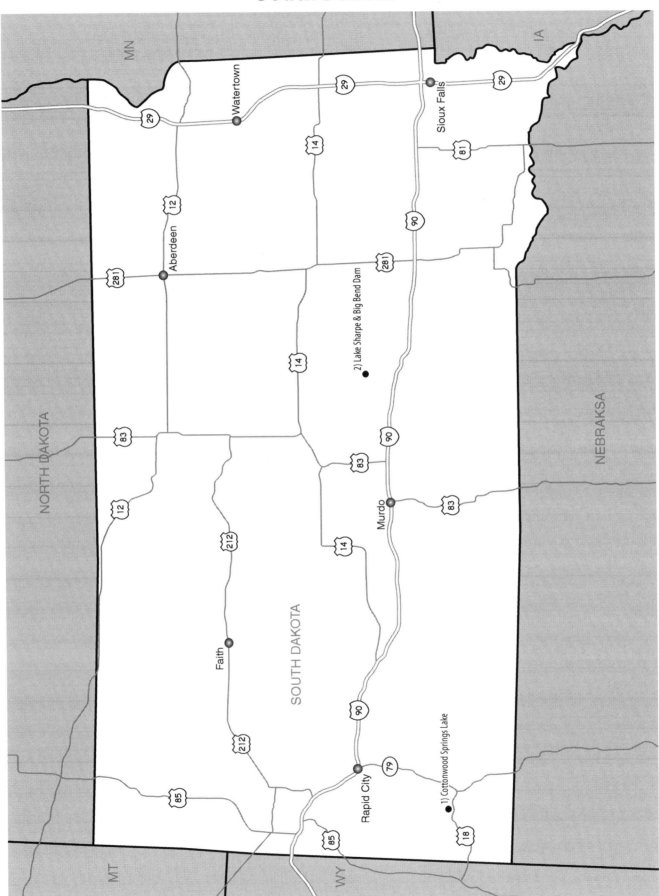

Activities

		Auto Touring	Biking	Boating	Climbing	Cultural / Historic Sites	Educational Programs	Fishing	Groceries / Supplies	Hiking	Horseback Riding	Hunting	Lodging	Off Highway Vehicles	Visitor Center
1)	Cottonwood Springs Lake			♦				♦		♦		♦			
2)	Lake Sharpe & Big Bend Dam			♦		♦		♦		♦		♦			

South Dakota Projects

1) Cottonwood Springs Lake

U.S. Army Corps of Engineers
HC 69 Box 74
Chamberlain, SD 57325
Phone: 605-745-5476
District: Omaha

The project is located in the southwestern corner of South Dakota on Cottonwood Creek, 3.5 miles west of Hot Springs. The lake is nestled in the rugged hills and evergreen trees of the southern Black Hills. It is a popular off-the-beaten-path destination for nature lovers. The most frequent recreational activities include hiking, fishing and boating (electric motors only). There is excellent wildlife viewing from the campground, so bring your binoculars.

RV Camping

Cottonwood Springs: May-Sep, 18 rustic sites in a hillside setting, no hookups, non-reservable, $5. 35-foot RV length limit. **Amenities**: Drinking water, restrooms. **Directions**: On the south end of Hot Springs along US-385/18, turn west on US-18 truck bypass, go 1.5 miles on the bypass to the stop sign, turn west on US-18 for 3.5 miles, follow signs. Turn right onto CR-17 (gravel) for 1.2 miles to the Cottonwood access road. 605-745-5476.

2) Lake Sharpe & Big Bend Dam

U.S. Army Corps of Engineers
Big Bend Project
HC 69, Box 74
33573 N. Shore Rd
Chamberlain, SD 57325
Phone: 605-245-2255
District: Omaha

Lake Sharpe has 56,000 water acres and 200 miles of shoreline. It is located in the heart of South Dakota's "Indian Country." The project office is at the dam near the North Shore camping area. From Sioux Falls, travel west on I-90 to Reliance (Exit 248), then northwest on SD-47 to the dam.

Big Bend takes its name from the unique bend in the Missouri River, 7 miles upstream from the dam, where the river makes almost a complete loop before returning south. There are 19 recreation areas -- varying from primitive to highly developed -- at Lake Sharpe.

RV Camping

The Corps manages 3 camping areas at the lake; all sites are nonreservable, first come first serve. Call the project office for more information.

Left Tailrace: Apr-Sep, 81 sites with electric hookups, non-reservables, some pull thrus, $14. **Amenities**: Drinking water, dump station, restrooms, showers, boat ramp, fish cleaning station. **Directions**: From Reliance, SD, (west of Chamberlain, which is on the Missouri River), travel on SD-47 north for 14 miles. Take the highway across the powerhouse structure and take the first turn right (about 1/4 mile). Located below the dam on the south side of the spillway. 605-245-2255.

North Shore: May-Sep, 24 sites, no hookups, non-reservable, free. **Amenities**: Swimming beach, playground. **Directions**: Two miles from Fort Thompson. Go across the crest of the dam, take the second left. (Sign says Administration – North Shore Area.) 605-245-2255.

Old Fort Thompson: May-Sep, 13 sites, no hookups, non-reservable, free. **Amenities**: Drinking water, dump station, restrooms, showers, boat ramp, playground. **Directions**: Located below the dam on the east side of the spillway, one-half mile to Fort Thompson. 605-245-2555.

Tennessee

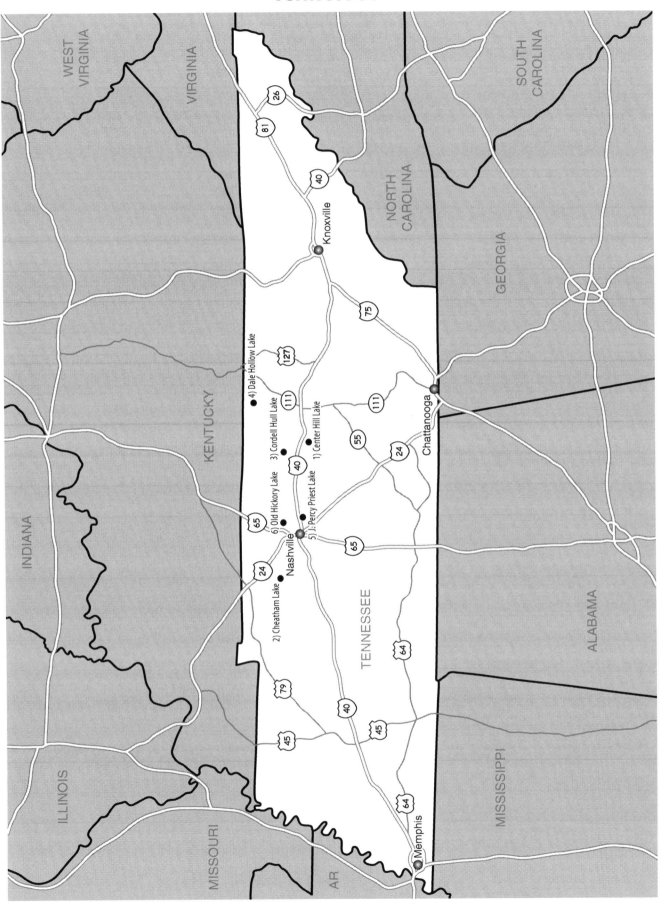

Activities

	Auto Touring	Biking	Boating	Climbing	Cultural/Historic Sites	Educational Programs	Fishing	Groceries/Supplies	Hiking	Horseback Riding	Hunting	Lodging	Off Highway Vehicles	Visitor Center
1) Center Hill Lake			♦		♦	♦	♦		♦		♦			♦
2) Cheatham Lake	♦		♦		♦		♦		♦		♦			
3) Cordell Hull Lake		♦	♦		♦		♦	♦	♦	♦	♦	♦		♦
4) Dale Hollow Lake		♦	♦			♦	♦		♦	♦	♦			♦
5) J. Percy Priest Lake	♦		♦		♦		♦		♦	♦	♦			♦
6) Old Hickory Lake	♦		♦		♦	♦	♦		♦		♦			♦

Tennessee Projects

1) Center Hill Lake

U.S. Army Corps of Engineers
158 Resource Ln
Lancaster, TN 38569
Phone: 931-858-3125
District: Nashville

Center Hill Lake is a popular fishing destination. Due to cooler water temperatures released from the dam, the Carney Fork River downstream is one of the most productive trout fisheries in the state. The lake also offers exceptional crappie, bass and walleye fishing. The 18,220-acre lake is located about 60 miles east of Nashville. Its 415 shoreline miles provide much opportunity for recreational activities. From I-40 Exit 268, go 5 miles south on TN-96, follow signs to the Resource Manager's Office where the Information Center features a pictorial history of the construction of the dam and a wildlife exhibit focusing on birds and animals of the area.

There are several commercial marinas at the lake. Rangers conduct boating and water safety programs. Facilities of interest at the lake include: Edgar Evins State Park, the Evins Appalachian Center for Crafts, Burgess Falls State Natural Area and Rock Island State Park.

RV Camping

Floating Mill: Apr-Oct, 57 sites with electric (some 50amp) hookups, 2 full hookup sites, 15 basic sites, 39 tent sites with electric, some pull thrus, $18-$24. *Amenities*: Drinking water, dump station, restrooms, showers, laundry, boat ramp, fish cleaning station, interpretive trail, playground, swimming, water skiing. *Directions*: From I-40 Exit 273, take US-56 for 5 miles to Hurricane Dock Rd. At the store turn right, follow signs. 430 Floating Mill Lane, Silver Point, TN 38582 / 931-858-4845. *GPS*: 36.04489, -85.76347

Long Branch: Apr-Oct, 3 full hookup sites (50amp), 58 sites with electric (some 50amp) hookups, $20-$24. *Amenities*: Drinking water, dump station, restrooms, showers, laundry, boat ramp, canoeing, boating, playground, fish cleaning station, good trout fishing below the dam. *Directions*: From I-40 Exit 268, follow US-96 west for 5 miles to the end of Center Hill Dam on SR-141, follow signs to the Long Branch Recreation Area. 615-548-8002. *GPS*: 36.09903, -85.83176

Ragland Bottom: Apr-Oct, 20 sites with electric (some 50amp) hookups, 9 full hookup, 16 basic tent sites and 10 tent sites with electric & water, $20-$22. *Amenities*: Drinking water, dump station, restrooms, showers, laundry, boat ramp, fishing, interpretive trail, playground, swimming. *Directions*: From Smithville, TN, take US-70 northeast for 8 miles, turn on Ragland Bottom Rd, follow signs. The campground is located 1 mile from Slego Bridge. 1410 Ragland Bottom Rd, Sparta, TN 38583 / 931-761-3616. *GPS*: 35.9774,-85.72087

2) Cheatham Lake

U.S. Army Corps of Engineers
1798 Cheatham Dam Rd
Ashland City, TN 37015
Phone: 615-792-5697
District: Nashville

Cheatham Lake is part of the Cumberland River located about 35 miles west of Nashville on SR-12/ Ashland City Hwy. The lake has 320 shoreline miles.

From Nashville, take SR-12 west through Ashland City, then another 12 miles to Cheap Hill. Turn left onto Cheatham Dam Road, follow brown signs. The project office is located on the right just before the dam. Maps and information are available.

Canoe rentals are available at Narrows of the Harpeth State Park. Riverfront Park in Nashville is popular for summertime concerts and festivals.

RV Camping

Two Corps-managed camping areas include Lock A, close to the lock & dam on the lake and on the Cumberland River, and Harpeth River Bridge, situated where SR-49 crosses the scenic Harpeth River. Camping elsewhere on public lands along the shoreline is prohibited.

Harpeth River Bridge: Apr-Oct, 15 sites with electric & water hookups, $12. Reservations not accepted. **Amenities**: Drinking water, restrooms, showers, boat ramp, courtesy float, playground. **Directions**: From Ashland City, TN, go west on SR-49 for 6 miles to the bridge. 615-792-4195.

Lock A: Apr-Oct, 45 sites with 50amp electric hookups including 7 tent sites, $19. **Amenities**: Drinking water, dump station, restrooms, showers, boat ramp, interpretive trails, horseshoe pit, basketball, volleyball and tennis courts, playground. **Directions**: From Ashland City, TN, take SR-12 west for 12 miles to Cheap Hill. Turn left on Cheatham Dam Rd, travel west for 4 miles. 615-792-3715. **GPS**: 36.31583, -87.18694

3) Cordell Hull Lake

U.S. Army Corps of Engineers
71 Corps Ln
Carthage, TN 37030
Phone: 615-735-1034
District: Nashville

The lake, located 50 miles east of Nashville, has 11,960 water acres and 381 shoreline miles. From I-40 Exit 258, travel north on TN-53 to Carthage, then SR-25 and SR-263; follow signs to the Resource Manager's Office & Visitor Center where information and maps are available.

Two commercial marinas have boating supplies and services and restaurants. The Bluegrass Festival held annually in June is nearby.

RV Camping

Defeated Creek: Apr-Sep, 63 full hookup sites (some 50amp), 92 sites with electric (some 50amp) & water hookups, $15-$25. **Amenities**: Drinking water, dump station, restrooms, showers, laundry, boat ramp, fishing, marina, playground, swimming, tennis courts, trailhead nearby. **Directions**: From Carthage, TN, go 4 miles west on SR-25, then north on US-80 and east on SR-85, follow signs. 140 Marina Ln, Carthage, TN 37030 / 615-774-3141. **GPS**: 36.29972, -85.90889

Salt Lick Creek: May-Sep, 31 full hookup sites, 119 sites with electric & water hookups, some pull thrus, $15-$26. **Amenities**: Drinking water, dump station, restrooms, showers, laundry, boat ramp, fishing, playground, swimming, horseback riding trails. **Directions**: From Carthage, TN, go 4 miles west on SR-25, then north on US-80, then east on SR-85 to Gladice, turn right on Smith Bend Rd, follow signs. 520 Salt Lick Park Ln, Gainesboro, TN 38562 / 931-678-4718. **GPS**: 36.32278, -85.80861

4) Dale Hollow Lake

U.S. Army Corps of Engineers
540 Dale Hollow Dam Rd
Celina, TN 38551
Phone: 931-243-3136
District: Nashville

The Dale Hollow project is located northeast of Nashville near the Kentucky state line. The 27,700-acre lake, with its 620 miles of shoreline, is 4 miles east of the town of Celina. The Dale Hollow National Fishery, located just below the dam, is open to visitors daily from 7am to 3:30pm. It features a Visitor Center, aquarium and various displays and exhibits. From I-40 Exit 280, travel 17 miles north on TN-56, then 23 miles north on TN-53 to Celina, follow signs. Dale Hollow Lake is a popular destination for scuba divers.

RV Camping

Camping is available at these four Corps-managed areas as well as Dale Hollow State Park.

Dale Hollow Damsite: Apr-Oct, 79 sites with 50amp electric (13 also have water hookups), $21-$24. **Amenities**: Drinking water, dump station, restrooms, showers, laundry, fishing dock, fish cleaning station, biking & hiking trails, volleyball & basketball courts, playground, amphitheater. *Directions*: From Celina, take TN-53 for 2 miles northwest. Turn right on Dale Hollow Dam Rd, then second right onto the campground road, follow signs. 931-243-3554. *GPS*: 36.53778, -85.45694

Lillydale: Apr-Sep, 33 sites with electric & water hookups, 43 electric-only sites (some 50amp), 29 tent sites (some with hookups) and 14 basic sites, many waterfront sites, $10-$24. *Amenities*: Drinking water, dump station, restrooms, showers, laundry, fishing, hiking, swimming, playground, volleyball & basketball courts, amphitheater. *Directions*: From I-40 Exit 288, take SR-111 north. At about 3.5 miles north of Livingston, go north on CR-294 (Willow Grove Rd) for 13.3 miles. Turn right onto Lillydale Rd, follow signs. 985 Lillydale Rd, Allons, TN 38541 / 931-823-4155. *GPS*: 36.60444, -85.3025

Obey River: Apr-Oct, 70 sites with electric (some 50amp) hookups, 32 basic sites and 24 tent sites, some sites also have water hookups, some pull thrus, $15-$24. *Amenities*: Drinking water, dump station, restrooms, showers, laundry, boat ramp, fishing, biking, birding, hiking, largest swimming beach on the lake, ball courts, amphitheater. *Directions*: From I-40 Exit 288, travel north on SR-111; about 15 miles past Livingston, follow signs to campground. 100 Obey Park Rd, Monroe, TN 38573 / 931-864-6388. *GPS*: 36.53136, -85.16764

Willow Grove: May-Sep, 63 sites with electric (some 50amp) & some have water hookups, 21 tent sites, $15-$24. *Amenities*: Drinking water, dump station, restrooms, showers, laundry, boat ramp, fishing, biking, birding, hiking, swimming, playground, volleyball, water skiing, amphitheater. *Directions*: From I-40 Exit 288, north on SR-111. About 3.5 miles north of Livingston, take CR-294 (Willow Grove Rd) north for 16 miles, follow signs. 11038 Willow Grove Rd, Allona, TN 38541 / 931-823-4285. *GPS*: 36.58733, -85.34212

5) J. Percy Priest Lake

U.S. Army Corps of Engineers
3737 Bell Rd
Nashville, TN 37214
Phone: 615-889-1975
District: Nashville

The project is located 10 miles east of Nashville. The Visitor Center, on the west side of the dam, is open on weekdays. From I-40 Exit 219 (Stewarts Ferry Pike) go right to the first stop light, then left on Bell Road and take the second right at the Visitor Center sign.

There are four commercial marinas and the Nashville Shores Water Park is at the lake. Nearby points of interest include The Hermitage, Opreyland and the Grand Ole Opry, Opry Mills shopping area and the Nashville Speedway.

RV Camping

Anderson Road: Apr-Sep, 37 sites, no hookups, $12-$14. *Amenities*: Drinking water, dump station, restrooms, showers, laundry, boat ramp, fishing, swimming, playground. *Directions*: From I-40 Exit 219 (Stewarts Ferry Pike), turn right on Stewarts Ferry Pike and go straight on Bell Rd 5 miles, then left on Smith Springs Rd. Go 1 mile and turn left on Anderson Rd for 1 mile. 4010 Anderson Rd, Nashville, TN 37217 / 615-361-1980. *GPS*: 36.10611, -86.60389

Poole Knobs: May-Oct, 56 sites with electric (some 50amp) and water hookups, 39 basic sites and 7 tent sites, $14-$24, some pull thrus. *Amenities*: Drinking water, dump station, restrooms, showers, laundry, boat ramp, fishing, canoeing, group camping. *Directions*: From I-24 Exit 66B, go right on Sam Ridley Pkwy for 3 miles, exit right onto Hwy-41 north (Murfreesboro Pike) 1.5 miles, then right on Fergus Rd for 2 miles, then right on Jones Mill Rd for 4 miles, follow signs. 493 Jones Mill Rd, Lavergne, TN, 37086 / 615-459-6948. *GPS*: 36.05083, -86.51028

Seven Points: Apr-Oct, 60 sites with electric (some 50amp) & water hookups, $20-$24. *Amenities*: Drinking water, dump station, restrooms, showers, laundry, boat ramp, canoeing, fishing, swimming. *Directions*: From I-40 Exit 221B, go right on Old Hickory Blvd, then left on Bell Rd, right on New Hope Rd for 1 mile, then left on Stewarts Ferry Pike for 1 mile, follow signs. 1810 Stewarts Ferry Pike, Hermitage, TN 37076 / 615-889-5198. *GPS*: 36.13306, -86.57028

6) Old Hickory Lake

U.S. Army Corps of Engineers
No. 5 Power Plant Rd
Hendersonville, TN 37075
Phone: 615-822-4846
District: Nashville

Located 10 miles northeast of metropolitan Nashville, the lake has 22,500 acres of water. The Visitor Center is in the Rockland Recreation Area in Hendersonville. From I-65 (north of Nashville) exit onto Vietnam Veterans Blvd, travel to Exit 3, proceed to the town of Hendersonville and get into the right lane. Turn right at the traffic light onto Rockland Road, follow signs. The Center features displays, exhibits and video programs. Maps and information are available. A display narrated by a country and western star depicts the history and development of the Cumberland River.

Old Hickory Lake is conveniently close to Opreyland USA. Many parks and recreation areas are located along the large waterway. The Old Hickory Nature Trail on the south side of the dam is part of the National Trail System. Wildlife viewing is excellent.

RV Camping

Cages Bend: Apr-Oct, 42 sites with electric (some 50amp) hookups, $20-$24. **Amenities**: Drinking water, dump station, restrooms, showers, laundry, boat ramp, fishing, playground. **Directions**: From I-65, north of Nashville, exit onto Vietnam Veterans Blvd East and follow until it joins Gallatin Rd/Hwy-31E, then right on Cages Bend Rd South, then left onto Benders Ferry Rd, follow signs. 1125 Benders Ferry Rd, Gallatin, TN 37066 / 615-824-4989. **GPS**: 36.30389, -86.51528

Cedar Creek: Apr-Oct, 59 sites with electric (some 50amp) & water hookups, $19-$23. **Amenities**: Drinking water, dump station, restrooms, showers, laundry, boat ramp, playground, swimming. **Directions**: From I-40, east of Nashville, exit onto Old Hickory Blvd North. Turn right on Lebanon Rd, then left onto Andrew Jackson Pkwy to the first red light, continue straight on Saundersville Rd for 10 miles, follow signs. 9264 Saundersville Rd, Mt Juliet, TN 37122 / 615-754-4947. **GPS**: 36.27861, -85.50861

Texas

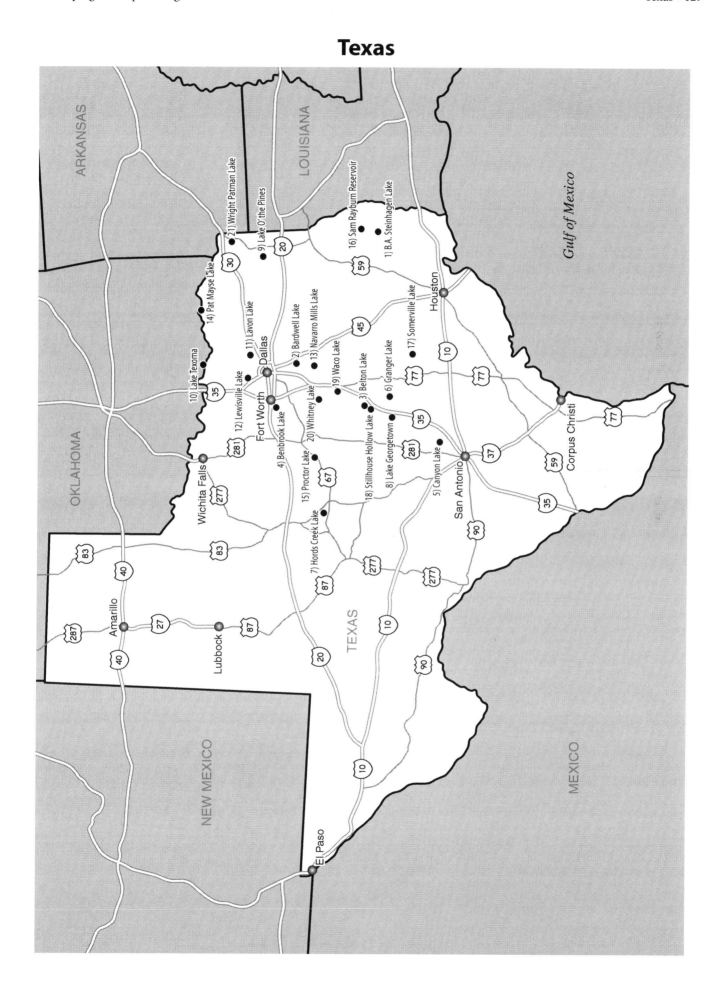

Activities

	Auto Touring	Biking	Boating	Climbing	Cultural / Historic Sites	Educational Programs	Fishing	Groceries / Supplies	Hiking	Horseback Riding	Hunting	Lodging	Off Highway Vehicles	Visitor Center
1) B.A. Steinhagen Lake		♦	♦				♦	♦	♦		♦	♦		
2) Bardwell Lake	♦		♦		♦		♦		♦	♦	♦			
3) Belton Lake	♦	♦	♦		♦		♦		♦		♦	♦		♦
4) Benbrook Lake	♦		♦		♦		♦		♦	♦	♦			
5) Canyon Lake	♦	♦	♦			♦	♦		♦	♦	♦	♦		
6) Granger Lake	♦	♦	♦				♦		♦	♦	♦	♦		
7) Hords Creek Lake			♦				♦		♦		♦	♦		
8) Lake Georgetown	♦	♦	♦				♦		♦		♦			
9) Lake O' The Pines	♦		♦				♦		♦		♦	♦		
10) Lake Texoma		♦	♦				♦		♦	♦	♦			
11) Lavon Lake	♦		♦		♦		♦		♦	♦	♦			
12) Lewisville Lake	♦		♦		♦		♦		♦		♦			
13) Navarro Mills Lake	♦		♦				♦	♦	♦		♦			
14) Pat Mayse Lake	♦		♦				♦		♦		♦			
15) Proctor Lake			♦				♦		♦		♦	♦		
16) Sam Rayburn Reservoir	♦		♦				♦	♦	♦	♦	♦	♦		
17) Somerville Lake	♦		♦				♦		♦		♦	♦	♦	
18) Stillhouse Hollow Lake	♦	♦	♦		♦		♦		♦	♦	♦			♦
19) Waco Lake	♦	♦	♦		♦	♦	♦		♦	♦	♦	♦		
20) Whitney Lake	♦		♦				♦	♦	♦	♦	♦	♦		
21) Wright Patman Lake	♦	♦	♦		♦		♦		♦		♦			♦

Texas Projects

1) B.A. Steinhagen Lake

U.S. Army Corps of Engineers
890 FM-92
Woodville, TX 75979
Phone: 409-429-3491
District: Fort Worth

Located in east-central Texas about 75 miles north of Beaumont, Steinhagen Lake has 13,800 water acres. From Jasper, Texas, go 15 miles west on US-190, then 5 miles south on FM-92 to the project office.

RV Camping

RV camping can also be found at Hen House Ridge and Walnut Ridge areas of Dies State Park.

Magnolia Ridge: All year, 32 sites with electric & water hookups, 8 basic sites, some pull thrus, $10-$16. **Amenities**: Drinking water, dump station, restrooms, showers, boat ramp, fishing dock, hiking, hunting, playground. **Directions**: On the northwest side of the lake. From Woodville, TX, go east on US-190 for 11 miles to FM-92 (caution light), turn north on FM-92 and travel 1.5 miles. 1376 Magnolia One, Woodville, TX 75979 / 409-283-5493. **GPS**: 30.86667, -97.2375

Sandy Creek: All year, 54 sites with electric (some 50amp) & water hookups, 6 basic sites, some pull thrus, some non-reservables, $10-$18. **Amenities**: Drinking water, dump station, restrooms, showers, boat ramp, fishing, birding, biking, canoeing, hiking, playground, volleyball, hunting. *Directions*: From Jasper, TX, go west on US-190 for 10 miles, then south on FM-777 for 2 miles, then west on CR-155 for 2.5 miles, follow signs. 114 Pivate Rd, Jasper, TX 75951 / 409-429-3491 or 409-384-6166. *GPS*: 30.80833, -94.15833

2) Bardwell Lake

U.S. Army Corps of Engineers
4000 Observation Dr
Ennis, TX 75119
Phone: 972-875-5711
District: Fort Worth

Located 35 miles southeast of Dallas in north-central Texas, the lake is 5.4 miles long and 1.2 miles wide. It covers 3,500 water acres. From Dallas take I-45 south to Exit 247, then US-287 north/Barton Pkwy toward Waxahachie. Travel north 3.4 miles to Ensign Road. Turn left and go 1.5 miles to Observation Dr. Turn right and go 1.5 miles to the lake headquarters.

The Corps manages three camping areas and three swimming beaches. A private marina is located at the lake. Local attractions include the Texas Motorplex Drag Racing facility, Railroad and Cultural Heritage Museum, the Old Train Depot and the oldest mapped Blue Bonnet Trails known in Texas. The National Polka Festival, featuring dancing and Czech cuisine, is held annually during Memorial Day weekend in Ennis.

RV Camping

High View Park: All year, 39 sites with electric (some 50amp) hookups, $14-$16. Gates close at 10pm. *Amenities*: Drinking water, dump station, restrooms, showers, boat ramp, swimming, marina. *Directions*: From Ennis, TX, I-45 Exit 247, exit onto the US-287 bypass. Travel 4.5 miles and exit at Bardwell Lake sign. Turn left onto Hwy-34 and go 2.5 miles southwest. Turn left immediately past the Fina Station onto High View Park Rd. Travel .2 mile to the entrance. 260 High View Rd, Ennis, TX 75119 / 972-875-5711. *GPS*: 32.27139, -96.66778

Mott Park: Apr-Sep, 33 sites with electric hookups and 7 tent sites, pull thrus, $14-$16. Gates close at 10pm. *Amenities*: Drinking water, dump station, restrooms, showers, boat ramp, fishing, courtesy dock, swimming. *Directions*: Campground is on the western shore. From Ennis, TX, I-45 Exit 247, exit onto the US-287 bypass. Travel 4.5 miles and exit at Bardwell Lake sign. Turn left onto Hwy-34 and go 3.5 miles southwest, then

left onto FM-985 and go 1.6 miles southeast. 957 FM-985, Ennis, TX 75119 / 972-875-5711. *GPS*: 32.25444, -96.66694

Waxahachie: All year, 49 sites with electric, 4 equestrian electric, 2 basic RV sites and 14 tent sites (10 have electric), $16-$18. *Amenities*: Drinking water, dump station, restrooms, showers, boat ramp, fishing, nature trail, equestrian trail. *Directions*: On the western shore. From I-45 Exit 247, exit onto the US-287 bypass. Travel 4.5 miles and exit at Bardwell Lake sign. Turn left onto Hwy-34 and go 3 miles southwest to Bozek Rd, turn right 1.5 miles to the campground. 930 Bozek Rd, Ennis, TX 75119 / 972-875-5711. *GPS*: 32.29306, -96.69389

3) Belton Lake

U.S. Army Corps of Engineers
3110 FM-2271
Belton, TX 76513
Phone: 254-939-2461
District: Fort Worth

The project office is located south of the lake (1 mile south of US-190 on FM-1670 in Belton). The 12,300-acre lake is adjacent to Fort Hood army base. From Belton go 3 miles north on TX-317, then 2 miles west on FM-439 and 1 mile north on FM-2271.

The Miller Springs Nature Area, located below the dam, includes a hiking trail along the Leon River, a restored historic bridge and several wildlife viewing areas. A mural painted on the spillway wall of Belton Dam depicts the history of the Bell County area.

RV Camping

Camping is also available at the Fort Hood Recreation area.

Cedar Ridge: All year, 56 sites with electric (some 50amp) hookups, 8 overnight shelters with electric, 3 tent sites, some pull thrus, $20-$30. *Amenities*: Drinking water, dump station, restrooms, showers, laundry, boat ramp, dock, marina, playground, swimming, basketball. *Directions*: From I-35 Exit 299 in Temple, TX, take SR-36 west toward Gatesville. Turn left on Cedar Ridge Park Rd. 3790 Cedar Ridge Park Rd, Temple, TX 76502 / 254-986-1404. *GPS*: 31.16964, -97.44363

Iron Bridge: All year, 5 sites, no hookups, non-reservable, free. *Amenities*: Restrooms, boat ramp. *Directions*: From I-35 go west on SR-36 for about 11 miles, then north on Iron Bridge Rd. 254-939-2461.

Live Oak Ridge: All year, 48 shaded sites with electric (some 50amp) hookups, $18-$20. *Amenities*: Drinking water, dump station, restrooms, showers, laundry, boat ramp, hiking, birding, playground. *Directions*: From I-35 Exit 299 in Temple, TX, exit to FM-2305, travel west to FM-2271 and turn left 1.5 miles. 254-780-1738. *GPS*: 31.11639, -97.47389

Westcliff: All year, 27 sites with electric & water hookups, some pull thrus, 4 tent-only sites, $10-$20. *Amenities*: Drinking water, dump station, restrooms, showers, boat ramp, playground, swimming. *Directions*: From I-35 Exit 294 in Belton, TX, exit onto 6th Ave/FM-93 west. Turn north onto 317 (Main St) for 2 miles. Turn west on FM-439 (Lake Rd) for 4 miles. Turn right on Sparta Rd and then right on Westcliff Park Rd. 254-939-9828. *GPS*: 31.12167, -97.51917

White Flint: All year, 13 sites with 50amp electric & water hookups, some pull thrus, $20. *Amenities*: Drinking water, dump station, restrooms, boat ramp, dock. *Directions*: From I-35 Exit 299 in Temple, TX, take SR-36 west about 11 miles and cross the bridge to the north side. 254-939-2461. *GPS*: 31.23111, -97.47222

Winkler: Mar-Oct, 14 paved sites with water hookups, no electric, $12. *Amenities*: Drinking water, restrooms, showers, biking, birding, wildlife viewing. A popular fishing camp. *Directions*: From I-35 Exit 299 go west on SR-36 for about 12 miles. Exit to the right 2 miles past White Flint. 11740 Winkler Park Rd, Moody, TX 76557 / 254-986-1579 or 3419. *GPS*: 31.25111, -97.47306

4) Benbrook Lake

U.S. Army Corps of Engineers
7001 Lakeside Dr
Fort Worth, TX 76132
Phone: 817-292-2400
District: Fort Worth

The 3,770-acre lake is 12 miles southwest of Fort Worth on the south side of Benbrook and just south of I-20. It is on the Clear Fork of the Trinity River and is situated partially within the city limits of Fort Worth. From I-20 Exit 429A, take US-377 for 2.5 miles southwest to the lake. The Corps office is then 2 miles east on Winscott Road and Lakeside Drive.

A 7-mile horseback and hiking trail, located on the west side of the lake, is part of the National Trail System. There is a model airplane field at Mustang Park. Sightseeing and special events all year long are found at nearby Fort Worth, known as the city "Where the West Begins."

RV Camping

Bear Creek: All year, 40 sites with electric (some 50amp) hookups, $20. *Amenities*: Drinking water, dump station, restrooms, showers, boat ramp, fishing, wildlife viewing. *Directions*: From I-20 take Exit 429A for Hwy 377 and go south for 6 miles. Turn left onto Ben Ray-Murrin Rd, continue for 1.5 miles to the campground. *GPS*: 32.59972, -97.5

Holiday Park: All year, 79 sites with electric (some 50amp) hookups, 24 basic sites, $10-$20. *Amenities*: Drinking water, dump station, restrooms, showers, boat ramp, fishing dock, birding, hiking, horseback riding trails. *Directions*: From I-20 Exit 429A, take US-377 to Granbury. Go southwest for 5.7 miles, then east onto Pearl Ranch Dr, go 2 miles. 817-292-2400. *GPS*: 32.61833, -97.4975

Mustang: All year, 100 basic sites, $10, *Amenities*: Drinking water, dump station, restrooms, boat ramp, fishing, swimming, water skiing. *Directions*: From I-20 Exit 429A, take US-377 south for 6 miles, then 1 mile east on FM-1187, then north on CR-1025 (Ben Day-Murrin Rd) for 1.5 miles, follow signs. 817-292-2400. *GPS*: 32.59278, -97.48

Rocky Creek: Apr-Sep, 11 sites, no hookups, $10. *Amenities*: Drinking water, dump station, restrooms, boat ramp, hiking & horseback riding trails. *Directions*: From I-20 Exit 429A, take US-377 south, then southeast on FM-1187 for 7 miles, then north on CR-1089 for 3.6 miles. At junction CR-1150 exit south to the park. 5800 Rocky Creek Park Rd, Crowley, TX 76036 / 817-292-2400. *GPS*: 32.60611, -97.45222

5) Canyon Lake

U.S. Army Corps of Engineers
601 C.O.E. Rd
Canyon Lake, TX 78133
Phone: 830-964-3341
District: Fort Worth

The 8,240-acre lake is located northeast of San Antonio on the Guadalupe River in Comal County. From I-35 Exit 191 take FM-306 northwest 14 miles and turn left onto Lake Access Road. The road to the dam, scenic overlook and lake office is less than one mile on the right.

Interpretive programs are presented by rangers at Potters Creek, the largest campground located on the north shore of the lake. Scuba diving is a popular activity at the lake. There are several private resorts and state recreation areas surrounding the lake. Hill

Country sightseeing, restaurants and shopping are nearby.

RV Camping

Canyon Park: Apr-Sep, 150 sites, no hookups, non-reservable, $8-$12. Gates close at 10pm. *Amenities*: Restrooms, water fountains, dock, boat ramp, 8 miles of trails. *Directions*: Located on the north shore of the lake near Hancock. From I-35 Exit 191 (north of New Braunfels), go west on Canyon Park Rd for 17.5 miles. 830-964-3341.

Cranes Mills: Mar-Sep, 30 RV sites, 34 tent sites, electric hookups throughout, non-reservable, $8-$12. Gates close at 10pm. *Amenities*: Drinking water, dump station, restrooms, showers, boat ramp. *Directions*: From I-35 Exit 191, go west on FM-306 for about 14 miles. Turn left on FM-2673 just after the Guadalupe River crossing. The park is located at the westernmost end of FM-2673 and South Cranes Mill Rd. 830-964-3341.

North Park: Apr-Sep, 19 campsites, no hookups, all non-reservables, $8-$12. Gates close at 10pm. *Amenities*: Drinking water, dump station, restrooms. Popular scuba diving area. *Directions*: Located on the north side of the lake. From I-35 Exit 191, take FM-306 west for 18.5 miles. 830-964-3341.

Potters Creek: All year, 109 sites with electric (some 50amp) hookups, 7 overnight shelters with electric, 7 tent sites with electric, many lakefront sites, $18-$40. Gates close at 10pm. *Amenities*: Drinking water, dump station, restrooms, showers, boat ramp, boat dock, fishing, hiking, biking, birding, swimming, water skiing, jet skiing. *Directions*: The campground is on the north side of the lake. From I-35 Exit 191, take Canyon Park Rd (FM-306) west for 21 miles; turn left on Potters Creek Rd for 2.7 miles. 830-964-3341. *GPS*: 29.90472, -98.27306

6) Granger Lake

U.S. Army Corps of Engineers
3100 Granger Dam Rd
Granger, TX 76530
Phone: 512-859-2668
District: Fort Worth

The 4,400-acre lake is located 35 miles northeast of Austin. From I-35 (at Round Rock) take US-79 east to SR-95 in Taylor. Take SR-95 north through Taylor to Circleville, then north to Granger. The dam is located 7 miles east of Granger via FM-971 on the San Gabriel River. The lake is known as one of the top five crappie/white bass fishing spots in Central Texas. The bike and hike trail is popular and there is an equestrian trail. Wildlife viewing is excellent at the project.

RV Camping

Taylor: Mar-Sep, 48 sites with electric hookups, $18-$22. Gates close at 10pm. *Amenities*: Drinking water, dump station, restrooms, showers, boat ramp, fishing, hiking, biking, birding, swimming, playground, water skiing, wildlife viewing. *Directions*: From I-35 go east on US-79, then north on SR-95 north, then east on FM-1331 for 5 miles. 4801 FM 1331, Taylor, TX 76574 / 512-859-2668. *GPS*: 30.66417, -97.36444

Willis Creek: All year, 27 sites with electric hookups, $18-$22. Gates close at 10pm. An equestrian camping area (non-reservable) is located directly across from Willis Creek Park. *Amenities*: Drinking water, dump station, restrooms, showers, boat ramp, fishing, horseback riding, swimming, sailing, water skiing. *Directions*: From I-35 go east on US-79, then north on SR-95, turn right on CR-346 and go 4 miles. 2900 CR 249, Granger, TX 76530 / 512-859-2668. *GPS*: 30.69583, -97.40139

Wilson H. Fox: All year, 58 sites with electric (a few 50amp) hookups, $14-$26. Gates close at 10pm. *Amenities*: Drinking water, dump station, restrooms, showers, boat ramp, fishing dock, swimming, playground. *Directions*: From I-35, take US-79 east, then SR-95 north to FM-1331, east on FM-1331 for about 7 miles. 512-859-2668. *GPS*: 30.68006, -97.34227

7) Hords Creek Lake

U.S. Army Corps of Engineers
230 Friendship Park Rd
Coleman, TX 76834
Phone: 325-625-2322
District: Fort Worth

The 510-acre lake is located in Coleman County in the northern portion of the Texas Hill Country, 55 miles south of Abilene. From Coleman, go west for 8 miles on FM-153. Hords Creek is a popular fishing destination.

RV Camping

Lakeside: All year, 30 full hookup and 15 sites with electric (some 50amp), 6 overnight shelters with electric, some pull thrus, $16-$26. *Amenities*: Drinking water, dump station, restrooms, showers, boat ramp, fishing dock, swimming. *Directions*: From Coleman, TX, take Hwy-153 west for 8 miles to the lake, follow signs. 325-625-2322 ext 15. *GPS*: 31.84667, -97.57944

Flat Rock: May-Oct, 58 sites with electric (some 50amp) hookups, 6 overnight shelters with electric, some pull thrus, $16-$40. *Amenities*: Drinking water, dump station, restrooms, showers, boat ramp, fishing dock, swimming. *Directions*: From Coleman, TX, go 8.7 miles west on Hwy-153, go south across the dam, then west to the park, follow signs. 325-625-2322 ext 15. *GPS*: 31.82611, -97.56583

8) Lake Georgetown

U.S. Army Corps of Engineers
500 Lake Overlook Dr
Georgetown, TX 78628
Phone: 512-930-5253
District: Fort Worth

The 1,310-acre lake is located 25 miles north of Austin, west of I-35 in the Texas Hill Country. From I-35 (Georgetown) travel west on Williams Drive about 3.5 miles to D.B. Wood, turn left to the project entrance.

A 16-mile hiking trail features varied scenery and there is a challenging mountain biking trail. A washed pebble beach is located at Russell Park.

RV Camping

Cedar Breaks: All year, 58 sites with electric (some 50amp) hookups, $24. Gates close at 10pm. *Amenities*: Drinking water, dump station, restrooms, showers, boat ramp, dock, fishing, hiking, hunting. *Directions*: Campground is on the south side of the lake. From I-35, take FM-2338 west for 3.5 miles to Cedar Breaks Rd, then south 2 miles, follow signs. 500 Cedar Breaks Rd, Georgetown, TX 78633 / 512-930-5253 or 512-819-9046. *GPS*: 30.68167, -97.73306

Jim Hogg Park: All year, 137 sites with electric hookups, 5 overnight shelters with electric, $24-$30. Gates close at 10pm. *Amenities*: Drinking water, dump station, restrooms, showers, boat ramp, fishing, hiking, hunting. *Directions*: From I-35, take FM-2338 west for 6 miles to Jim Hogg Rd, then south 2 miles. 512-930-5253 or 512-819-9046. *GPS*: 30.68167, -97.73306

9) Lake O' The Pines

U.S. Army Corps of Engineers
2669 FM-726
Jefferson, TX 75657
Phone: 903-665-2336
District: Fort Worth

Located in the Piney Woods of northeast Texas, 9 miles south of Jefferson, the project includes 18,700 water acres and 9,000 land acres. It is situated between I-30 to the north and I-20 to the south. From Texarkana, Texas, take US-59 south to Jefferson, then west on SR-49 for 4 miles to FM-726, then west 2 miles to the project office near the dam.

There are 11 boat ramps located throughout the project. Restaurants, shopping and sightseeing are nearby. Many festivals are held in local towns. Antique shopping is popular.

RV Camping

Private campgrounds around the lake also have full service camping.

Alley Creek: Mar-Sep, 30 sites with electric (some 50amp) hookups and 30 tent-only sites, $16-$28. *Amenities*: Drinking water, dump station, restrooms, showers, boat ramp, fishing, playground, swimming, water skiing, group camping area for RVs. *Directions*: From Jefferson, TX, travel 4 miles northwest on SR-49, then turn left on FM-729 and travel 12 miles west to the park entrance. Route 1 Box 2282, Jefferson, TX 75657 / 903-755-2637 or 903-755-2336. *GPS*: 32.79944, -94.59194

Brushy Creek: All year, 39 sites with electric (some 50amp) hookups, some pull thrus, 37 tent-only sites, $14-$28. *Amenities*: Drinking water, dump station, restrooms, showers, boat ramp, fishing, playground, swimming, water skiing. *Directions*: From Jefferson, TX, go 4 miles northwest on SR-49, then 3.5 miles west on FM-729, then south 4.8 miles on FM-726 past the dam, follow signs. 903-777-3491. *GPS*: 32.74278, -94.53583

Buckhorn Creek: Mar-Sep, 39 sites with electric (some 50amp) hookups and 38 tent-only sites, some pull thrus, $16-$26. *Amenities*: Drinking water, dump station, restrooms, showers, boat ramp, fishing, hiking, playground, swimming, water skiing. *Directions*: From Jefferson, TX, travel 4 miles northwest on SR-49, then turn left on FM-729 and 3.5 miles west, then turn left on FM-726 and travel 2.4 miles south to the park. 903-665-8261. *GPS*: 32.75528, -94.49444

Johnson Creek: All year, 31 sites with electric (some 50amp) hookups, some pull thrus, 22 tent-only sites, $16-$28. *Amenities*: Drinking water, dump station, restrooms, showers, boat ramp, dock, fishing, playground, swimming, group camping area for RVs. *Directions*: From Jefferson, TX, travel 4 miles northwest on SR-49, then left on FM-729 for 8.5 miles west to the park entrance. 903-755-2435 or 903-665-2336. *GPS*: 32.78667, -94.55056

10) Lake Texoma

U.S. Army Corps of Engineers
351 Corps Rd
Denison, TX 75020
Phone: 903-465-4990
District: Tulsa

This project is on the Texas/Oklahoma state line. It has 102,968 land acres, 88,000 water acres and 680 shoreline miles. From Denison, Texas, go 5 miles northwest on TX-91. Before the dam, turn right onto Corps Road to the project office.

Cross Timbers is a popular hiking trail that wends for 14 miles above the lake on rocky ledges and through the woodland. Accomodations, boat rentals and supplies are available at the many marinas located at the lake. Wildlife viewing within the project is excellent.

RV Camping

Of the 15 Corps-managed campgrounds, the 3 that are located in Texas are listed below. See the Oklahoma section of this guide for additional campgrounds at Lake Texoma.

Dam Site: All year, 20 sites with electric & water hookups, $10-$16. **Amenities**: Dump station, restrooms, showers. **Directions**: The camping area is on the south side of the dam. From Denison, TX, travel 5 miles north on SR-91. 903-463-6455.

Juniper Point: Apr-Oct, 44 sites with electric (some 50amp) hookups, 25 tent sites, $15-$22. **Amenities**: Drinking water, dump station, restrooms, showers, boat ramp, hiking. **Directions**: From Whitesboro, TX, travel 13 miles north on Hwy-377. The campground is on both sides of the highway as the highway enters the Willis Bridge crossing into Oklahoma. 903-523-4022. **GPS**: 33.85972, -96.83194

Preston Bend: Apr-Oct, 26 sites with electric hookups and 12 tent sites, $15-$20. **Amenities**: Dump station, restrooms, showers, boat ramp. **Directions**: From Pottsboro, TX, travel 9 miles north on Hwy-120, follow signs. 129 Preston Bend Rd, Pottsboro, TX 75076 / 903-786-8408. **GPS**: 33.87833, -96.64722.

11) Lavon Lake

U.S. Army Corps of Engineers
3375 Skyview Dr
Wylie, TX 75098
Phone: 972-442-3141
District: Fort Worth

The 21,400-acre lake is located 30 miles northeast of Dallas. From Wylie, go 3 miles east on TX-78, then 1 mile north on CR-434 to the park headquarters.

The project features hiking, equestrian and bike trails operated by the county. The Heard Natural Science Museum & Wildlife Sanctuary in nearby McKinney, Texas, features natural history exhibits and nature trails.

RV Camping

Clear Lake: Mar-Sep, 23 full hookup sites, $20. **Amenities**: Dump station, restrooms, showers, boat ramp, fishing dock. **Directions**: From Princeton, go 9 miles south on FM-982 (changes to CR-735). Watch for Clear Lake signs. Take FM-436 and follow to dead end. 8199 County Road 436, Princeton, TX 75098 / 972-442-3014. **GPS**: 33.05528, -96.48194

East Fork: All year, 50 sites with electric (50amp) & water hookups (includes 10 equestrian sites with hookups and portable horse stalls in a separate Equestrian Loop) and 12 tent-only sites, some pull thrus, $10-$18. **Amenities**: Drinking water, dump station, restrooms, showers, horse trail, public marina, boat ramp. **Directions**: From Wylie, TX, take Hwy-78 east to FM-389 (Eubanks). Go north on FM-389, stay to the right at the fork and continue on FM-389 to the park. 972-442-3014. **GPS**: 33.03889, -96.51028

Lavonia: All year, 31 full hookup sites and 15 basic sites, $10-$20. Gates locked at 10pm. **Amenities**: Drinking water, dump station, restrooms, showers, boat ramp, fishing, swimming. **Directions**: From Wylie, take Hwy-78 east to CR-486 (Lake Rd), follow signs. 1301 CR-486, Lavon, TX 75166 / 972-442-3141. **GPS**: 33.03778, -96.44556

12) Lewisville Lake

U.S. Army Corps of Engineers
1801 North Mill St
Lewisville, TX 75057
Phone: 469-645-9100
District: Fort Worth

The 28,980-acre lake is adjacent to Interstate 35E at Exit 457A northwest of Dallas. The project office located on Mill Street is open on weekdays.

Three hiking and equestrian trails are on project land. Golf is nearby. Boat rentals are available at the marina. In the heart of the Dallas-Fort Worth Metroplex, there are many sightseeing, shopping and restaurant opportunities in the area.

RV Camping

There is one Corps-managed campground as well as a private campground.

Hickory Creek: All year, 121 sites with electric (some 50amp) hookups and 10 primitive tent sites, $10-$20. *Amenities*: Drinking water, dump station, restrooms, showers, fishing, boating, hiking, swimming, playground. *Directions*: From I-35 Exit 457B, follow the service road to the overpass leading to the southbound access service road and follow to Turbeville Rd, then right to Point Vista Rd. Turn left for 1 mile to the park. 469-645-9100.

13) Navarro Mills Lake

U.S. Army Corps of Engineers
1175 FM-667
Purdon, TX 76679
Phone: 254-578-1431
District: Fort Worth

The 5,070-acre lake is 71 miles south of Dallas and 18 miles west of Corsicana, Texas. From Corsicana, go 20 miles southwest on TX-31 then 1 mile north on FM-667.

Points of interest in Corsicana, the Fruit Cake Capital, include Collin Street Bakery, Pioneer Village and an Indian art and crafts exhibit at the Gooch Library.

RV Camping

Liberty Hill: All year, 14 full hookup sites, 75 sites with electric (some 50amp), 3 basic sites, $18-$32, some pull thrus. *Amenities*: Drinking water, dump station, restrooms, showers, boat ramp, fishing dock, swimming, playground, convenience store, public marina. *Directions*: From Dawson, travel north on FM-709 for 4 miles. 254-578-1431. *GPS*: 31.94615, -96.71671

Oak: All year, 5 full hookup sites and 43 sites with electric (some 50amp) hookups, $18-$22. *Amenities*: Drinking water, dump station, restrooms, showers, boat ramp, fishing, playground, interpretive trail, swimming, general store. *Directions*: From Corsicana, follow SR-31 southwest 15.6 miles to FM-667, turn right and follow 1.4 miles to park. 254-578-1431. *GPS*: 31.9642, -96.6882

Pecan Point Park: Apr-Sep, 5 sites with electric (some 50amp) hookups and 30 basic sites, $10-$12. Some lakefront sites. *Amenities*: Drinking water, dump station, restrooms, boat ramp, fishing, hiking, biking, jet skiing, water skiing. *Directions*: From Corsicana, follow FM-744 southwest 16.6 miles; turn left onto FM-1578 for 2 miles; turn right onto CR-3360 for .3 miles to park entrance. 254-578-1431. *GPS*: 31.9662, -96.7415

Wolf Creek: Apr-Sep, 50 sites with electric hookups, 22 basic sites, $14-$16. *Amenities*: Drinking water, dump station, restrooms, showers, boat ramp, general store, marina. *Directions*: From Corsicana, follow SR-31 south 15.6 miles; turn right on FM-667 3.1 miles; turn left on FM-639 1.6 miles. *GPS*: 31.9744, -96.7261

14) Pat Mayse Lake

U.S. Army Corps of Engineers
1679 Farm Rd 906 West
P.O. Box 129
Powderly, TX 75473
Phone: 903-732-3020
District: Tulsa District

The 5,990-acre lake is located in the Red River Basin in Lamar County. The damsite is on Sanders Creek, a tributary of the Red River, about 12 miles north of Paris, Texas. From Paris, take US-271 north for 15 miles, then FM-906 west for 3 miles to the lake.

A few miles north of the project area are the famed Red River Bottoms where waterfowl congregate in great numbers.

RV Camping

Pat Mayse East & West: All year, 83 sites with electric hookups and 5 basic sites, $10-$15. Gates close at 10pm. Sites at Pat Mayse East are non-reservable. *Amenities*: Dump station, restrooms, showers, boat ramp, swimming. *Directions*: From Paris, TX, follow US-271 north for 12 miles to FM-906 west, then 4 miles to FM-197. Turn west for 3 miles to CR-35810, turn left 1 mile to CR-35800, turn left into the park. 903-732-4955 or 903-732-3020. *GPS*: 33.84778, -95.60694

Sanders Cove: All year, 85 sites with electric hookups, $18. Gates close at 10pm. *Amenities*: Drinking water, dump station, restrooms, showers, boat ramp, swimming. *Directions*: From Paris, TX, take US-271 north for 12 miles to FM-906 west, then 1 mile to CR-35920, follow signs. 903-732-4956 or 903-732-3020. *GPS*: 33.84083, -95.53417

15) Proctor Lake

U.S. Army Corps of Engineers
2180 FM-2861
Comanche, TX 76442
Phone: 254-879-2424
District: Fort Worth

The 4,610-acre lake is located 97 miles southwest of Fort Worth in the historic territory of the Comanche Indians. From Comanche, Texas, go 5 miles east on US-377, then 2 miles north on FM-2861. Proctor Lake is a popular destination for sportsmen, birders and naturalists. The lake is a popular fishing destination for Hybrid Striper and Crappie.

RV Camping

Copperas Creek: All year, 24 full hookup (50amp) sites, 45 sites with electric hookups, $16-$26. *Amenities*: Drinking water, dump station, restrooms, showers, boat ramp, fishing, hiking, hunting. *Directions*: From Comanche, TX, take US-67/377 northeast for 5 miles, then left on FM-2861 for 2.5 miles. 254-879-2498 or 254-879-2424. *GPS*: 31.96667, -98.50417

Promontory: Apr-Sep, 52 sites with electric (some 50amp), 4 overnight shelters and 30 basic sites, $16-$28. *Amenities*: Drinking water, dump station, restrooms, showers, boat ramp, fishing, hiking, hunting, swimming, horseback riding trails. *Directions*: From Comanche, take SR-16 north for 12 miles to the town of Downing, turn right on FM-2318 for 5 miles. 254-893-7545. *GPS*: 31.98, -98.49

Sowell Creek: All year, 14 full hookup sites (50amp) and 47 sites with electric (some 50amp), $16-$28. *Amenities*: Drinking water, dump station, restrooms, showers, boat ramp, dock, fishing, hiking, swimming. *Directions*: From Comanche, take US-67/377 east for 12 miles to the town of Proctor, then left on FM-1476 west for 2 miles to RR-6, turn left .5 mile. 254-879-2322. *GPS*: 31.99, -98.46

16) Sam Rayburn Reservoir

U.S. Army Corps of Engineers
Rt-3 Box 486
Jasper, TX 75951
Phone: 409-384-5716
District: Fort Worth

Sam Rayburn Lake is the largest body of water within the State of Texas. It is in the Piney Woods, 18 miles north of Jasper. With 114,500 surface acres and 750 miles of shoreline, the project spans five counties. From Jasper, Texas, go 15 miles northwest on TX-63, then east on TX-255 and follow signs to the project office located next to Overlook Park.

A 28-mile hiking trail is in nearby Sabine National Forest. Restaurants, shopping and sightseeing can be found in local towns. 16 boat ramps are located conveniently throughout.

RV Camping

Ebenezer: This area caters best to equestrian campers and tent campers. All year, 23 equestrian sites with electric and 17 tent-only sites, $14-$28. *Amenities*: Drinking water, dump station, restrooms, fishing, swimming, birding, horseback riding trails. *Directions*: From Jasper, follow US-96 north 9.6 miles; go west 9.4 miles on Hwy-255. 409-384-5716. *GPS*: 31.07028, -94.12472

Hanks Creek: All year, 47 sites with electric (some 50amp) hookups, 8 overnight shelters with electric, $16-$38. *Amenities*: Drinking water, dump station, restrooms, showers, boat ramp, fishing, mountain biking, swimming, group camping, volleyball, horseshoes. *Directions*: From Zavalla, TX, take SR-147 northeast for .25 mile, then north on FM-2109 for 8 miles to FM-2801. Turn right (east) on FM-2801 for 2 miles. 409-384-5716. *GPS*: 31.27194, -94.40306

Mill Creek: All year, 110 sites with electric (some 50amp) hookups, $26-$28. *Amenities*: Drinking water, dump station, restrooms, showers, boat ramp, fishing, swimming, playground, wildlife viewing. *Directions*: From Jasper, follow US-96 north 15.1 miles; turn left onto SR-149 Loop 1.2 miles; turn left onto SR-165 Spur .7 miles. 409-384-5716. *GPS*: 31.15139, -94.00639

Rayburn: All year, 24 sites with electric (some 50amp) hookups, 22 basic sites, $14-$28, some pull thrus. *Amenities*: Drinking water, dump station, restrooms, showers, boat ramp, fishing, playground, swimming. *Directions*: From Pineland, TX, take FM-83 west for 10 miles, then south on FM-705 for 11 miles, then west on FM-3127 for 1.5 miles. 409-384-5716. *GPS*: 31.10667, -97.10722

San Augustine: All year, 100 sites with electric hookups, $16-$18. *Amenities*: Drinking water, dump station, restrooms, showers, boat ramp, fishing, interpretive trail, swimming beach, playground, volleyball, basketball, horseshoes. *Directions*: From Pineland, TX, take FM-83 west 6 miles, then south on FM-1751 for 4 miles. 409-384-5716. *GPS*: 31.19917, -94.07889

Twin Dikes: All year, 6 full hookup sites (some 50amp), 14 sites with electric (some 50amp) hookups, 24 basic sites, $14-$28. *Amenities*: Drinking water, dump station, restrooms, showers, boat ramp, fishing, swimming. *Directions*: From Jasper, TX, take US-96 north for 13 miles, then west on Recreation Rd (FM-255) for 5 miles. 409-384-5716. *GPS*: 31.0725, -94.05944

17) Somerville Lake

U.S. Army Corps of Engineers
6500 Thornberry Dr
Somerville, TX 77879
Phone: 979-596-1622
District: Fort Worth

Located 84 miles east of Austin and northwest of Houston, the project consists of 11,000 water acres and 19,000 land acres. From Austin, Texas, take US-290 east to Brenham, then SR-36 north for about 11.5 miles to FM-1948. Turn left, cross the railroad tracks and turn right, follow the road for about 4 miles across the dam and turn left into the office complex to the project office where information is available.

RV Camping

Rocky Creek: All year, 193 sites with electric (some 50amp) hookups, $26-$28. *Amenities*: Drinking water, dump station, restrooms, showers, boat ramp, fishing, boating, playground. *Directions*: From Austin, take US-290 east, then SR-36 north for 11.5 miles, then left on FM-1948 for 5 miles, follow signs. 979-596-1622. *GPS*: 30.29861, -96.56806

Yequa Creek: All year, 65 sites with electric (most 50amp) and 17 basic sites, $28. *Amenities*: Drinking water, dump station, restrooms, showers, 2 boat ramps, fishing, interpretive trails, playground. *Directions*: From Austin, take US-290 east to Brenham, then SR-36 north for 11.5 miles, then left on FM-1948 for 2.5 miles, follow signs. 979-596-1622. *GPS*: 30.30278, -96.54472

18) Stillhouse Hollow Lake

U.S. Army Corps of Engineers
3740 FM-1670
Belton, TX 76513
Phone: 254-939-2461
District: Fort Worth

The 6,430-acre lake is located near Fort Hood, about 80 miles north of Austin. From Belton, follow US-190 west for 2 miles; go south 3.4 miles on FM-1670. The Clark Falls Environmental Center is located below the dam and includes a hiking trail along the Lampasas River, a spring-fed creek with a waterfall and several wildlife viewing points. There are hiking, biking and equestrian trails at the lake.

Swimming is available at both campgrounds and at Stillhouse Park. Boat ramps, fishing docks and fish cleaning stations are conveniently located. Nearby historic sites include the Stage Coach Inn in Salado.

RV Camping

Dana Peak: All year, 26 sites with electric (some 50amp) hookups (including some tent sites) and 8 primitive sites, $16-$20, most sites are close to the shoreline. *Amenities*: Drinking water, dump station, restrooms, showers, boat ramp, fishing, interpretive trails, fishing dock, horseback riding, playground, swimming. *Directions*: From I-35 in Belton, TX, take US-190 west to Simmons Rd exit. Cross under the highway and turn west on FM-2410, then south on Commanche Gap Rd, 5 miles, follow signs. 3800 Comanche Gap Rd, Harker Heights, TX 76548 / 254-698-4282. *GPS*: 31.02889, -97.61306

Union Grove: All year, 40 sites with electric (some 50amp) hookups (including tent sites and screened shelters), some pull thrus, some double sites, $16-$30. *Amenities*: Drinking water, dump station, restrooms, showers, boat ramp, crabbing, fishing dock, playground, birding, swimming. *Directions*: From I-35 in Salado, take FM-2484 exit and travel west about 5 miles. 8680 Union Grove Rd, Salado, TX 76571 / 254-947-0072. *GPS*: 31.00833, -97.62111

19) Waco Lake

U.S. Army Corps of Engineers
3801 Zoo Park Dr
Waco, TX 76708
Phone: 254-756-5359
District: Fort Worth

The 7,270-acre lake is on the northwest side of Waco. In McLennan County, the project is entirely within the city limits of Waco. From I-35 Exit 330, go west on TX-6, exit at Twin Bridges, follow signs.

Free educational programs and live exhibits are presented every Saturday night during the summer at the amphitheater in Reynolds Creek Park. Dogs on leashes are permitted on the six-mile hiking and biking trail.

The Waco Marina features a floating restaurant. Nearby Cameron Park is the largest municipal park in the country. The nation's oldest suspension bridge (1870) still in operation is located in Waco. Golf is nearby.

RV Camping

Camping is also available at Waco Marina.

Airport: All year, 17 full hookup and 25 sites with electric (some 50amp), 6 overnight shelters with electric, 20 basic sites, some pull thrus, $20-$30. *Amenities*: Dump station, restrooms, showers, boat ramp, fishing, boating, dock. *Directions*: Located on the north shore of the lake 1/4 mile west of the dam. From I-35 take Exit 339 (Lake Shore Dr.) and exit west, travel to Airport Rd, then right for 2 miles, follow signs. 4600 Skeet Eason Rd, Waco, TX 76708 / 254-756-5359. *GPS*: 31.59722, -97.23694

Midway: All year, 12 full hookup and 22 electric hookup sites (a few 50amp), 5 basic sites, $20-$24. *Amenities*: Drinking water, dump station, restrooms, showers, boat ramp, fishing, hiking, playground, swimming. *Directions*: Located on the east shore of the South Bosque River. From I-35 Exit 330, take SR-6 about 5 miles and take the Midway Park exit. Circle under the bridge .5 mile on the service road. 2332 W. Highway 6, Waco, TX 76708 / 254-756-5359. *GPS*: 31.5, -97.20833

Reynolds Creek: All year, 31 sites with electric hookups (includes 10 equestrian sites) and 6 tent sites, $12-$20. *Amenities*: Dump station, restrooms, showers, boat ramp, fishing, hiking, horseback riding trails, playground. *Directions*: From I-35 Exit 330, take SR-6 north for 7 miles to Speegleville Rd, exit right and go 1 mile to the stop sign, go straight and curve left, 1 mile to the entrance, follow signs. 2885 Speegleville Rd, Waco, TX 76708 / 254-756-5359. *GPS*: 31.54972, -92.25

20) Whitney Lake

U.S. Army Corps of Engineers
285 Corps Rd 3602
Clifton, TX 76634
Phone: 254-694-3189
District: Fort Worth

The 23,560-acre lake, located in the Prairies and Lakes region of Texas, is 65 miles south of Fort Worth and 35 miles north of Waco on the Brazos River. From I-35 Exit 368 take SR-22 west 12 miles to Whitney, continue on SR-22 and follow signs to the dam.

Boat ramps are conveniently located around the lake. There is excellent wildlife viewing throughout the project.

RV Camping

Seven Corps-managed parks are suitable for RVs. Additional camping can be found at private parks and a state park on the lake.

Cedar Creek: All year, 20 sites, non-reservable, free. *Amenities*: Drinking water, restrooms, boat ramp, fishing, general store. *Directions*: From Whitney Lake Dam, take SR-22 east to the city of Whitney, then FM-993 north about 5 miles, turn left on CR-2604 and follow signs. 100 Cedar Creek Park Rd, Whitney, TX 76692 / 254-694-3189. *GPS*: 31.99472, -97.36944

Cedron Creek: Apr-Sep, 46 sites with electric (some 50amp) hookups, $16-$20. *Amenities*: Drinking water, dump station, restrooms, showers, boat ramp, fishing, playground, swimming, convenience store. *Directions*: From I-35 Exit 368 (Hillsboro), take SR-22 west for 12 miles into Whitney, then Hwy-933 north for 3 miles, then left on FM-1713 and cross the bridge over the lake. Turn at the first road on the left and follow signs. 557 FM 1713, Morgan, TX 76671 / 254-694-3189. *GPS*: 31.96444, -97.41417

Kimball Bend: All year, 34 sites with 50amp electric hookups, $20. *Amenities*: Drinking water, restrooms, dump station, showers, boat ramp, fishing, hiking, fitness trails, swimming, water skiing. *Directions*: From Kopperl, go north on Hwy-56 for about 2.5 miles, then right onto Hwy-174 about 2.3 miles, then left into park (just before the bridge). 3351 Highway 174, Kopperl, TX 76652 / 254-694-3189. *GPS*: 32.12333, -97.49806

Lofers Bend East & West Areas: All year, 117 sites with electric (some 50amp) hookups and 29 basic sites, some pull thrus, $12-$20. Gates close at 10pm. *Amenities*: Drinking water, dump station, restrooms, showers, boat ramp, playground, swimming. *Directions*: From I-35 Exit 368 (Hillsboro), take SR-22 west for 12 miles into Whitney, continue 7 miles and turn right before the dam. Follow the park road to the 4-way stop. Turn left to West Lofers or turn right to East Lofers. 254-694-3189. *GPS*: 31.88528, -97.3611

McCown Valley: All year, 52 RV sites, 38 equestrian sites and 3 overnight shelters, all have electric (some 50amp), some pull thrus, $16-$24. *Amenities*: Drinking water, dump station, restrooms, showers, boat ramp, biking, hiking, playground, horseshoes, swimming. *Directions*: From I-35 Exit 368, take SR-22 west and go 12 miles into Whitney, exit at FM-933 north for 2.5 miles, then FM-1713 for 6 miles west, follow signs. 283 McCown Valley Park Rd, Whitney, TX 76692 / 254-694-3189. *GPS*: 31.95, -97.38306

Plowman Creek: All year, 22 RV sites and 10 equestrian sites with electric (some 50amp) and 12 primitive tent sites, $12-$16. *Amenities*: Dump station, restrooms, showers, boat ramp, fishing, hiking, horseback riding, biking, playground, basketball. *Directions*: From Kopperl, TX, travel 1 mile south on FM-56, follow signs. 15188 FM 56, Kopperl, TX 76652 / 254-694-3189. *GPS*: 32.07, -97.49333

Steele Creek: All year, 21 sites, no hookups, non-reservable, free. *Amenities*: Drinking water, restrooms, boat ramp. *Directions*: From FM-927, go 1 mile east on FM-56, then northeast on the gravel road. 254-622-3332.

21) Wright Patman Lake

U.S. Army Corps of Engineers
P.O. Box 1817
64 Clear Springs Park
Texarkana, TX 75501
Phone: 903-838-8781
District: Fort Worth

Located on the Sulphur River, 9 miles southwest of Texarkana, the lake covers about 33,000 water acres. From Texarkana, go south on US-59 for 9 miles, then west on FM-2148 to the lake entrance. The project is nestled in the southern pine woods near the Arkansas border.

A trail system connects Rocky Point and Piney Point campgrounds. Swimming beaches are located at North Shore area and at Atlanta State Park. Restaurants, shopping, sightseeing and riverboat gaming are nearby. Wildlife viewing is excellent, especially in winter when many migratory birds, including Bald Eagles, are in the area.

RV Camping

Clear Spring: All year, 41 full hookup and 60 electric-only sites (some 50amp) and 15 tent-only sites, $18-$22. *Amenities*: Drinking water, dump station, restrooms, showers, boat ramp, fishing, playground, volleyball & basketball courts,

horseshoes, hunting. *Directions*: From Texarkana, take US-59 south, then west on FM-2148 to the lake entrance, follow the park road west. 903-838-8781 or 903-838-8636. *GPS*: 33.35833, -94.19167

Malden Lake: All year, 39 sites with electric (some 50amp) hookups, $18-$20. *Amenities*: Drinking water, dump station, restrooms, showers, boat ramp, fishing, biking, birding, hunting, canoeing, wildlife viewing, waterfront sites, visitor center. *Directions*: Malden Park is on the north side of the lake. From I-30 Exit 201, travel on SR-8 south, through Maud, Texas, and continue south about 6 miles. 903-585-2497. *GPS*: 33.27472, -94.34778

Piney Point: Mar-Sep, 48 sites with electric (some 50amp) hookups, non-reservables, $18. *Amenities*: Drinking water, dump station, restrooms, showers, boat ramp, fishing, hunting, hiking trail, volleyball, water skiing. *Directions*: From Texarkana, take US-59 south for 12 miles. Take the first right past the Sulphur River Bridge, follow signs. 903-838-8781. *GPS*: 33.29861, -94.16806

Rocky Point: All year, 14 full hookup sites (some 50amp) and 111 sites with electric (some 50amp) hookups, many waterfront sites, $18-$22. *Amenities*: Drinking water, dump station, restrooms, showers, boat ramp, fishing, hunting, swimming, playground, interpretive trail. *Directions*: Located on the eastern shore of the lake. From Texarkana, take US-59 south to the lake. The park is just south of the dam on the right. 903-838-8781. *GPS*: 33.28694, -94.16583

Vermont

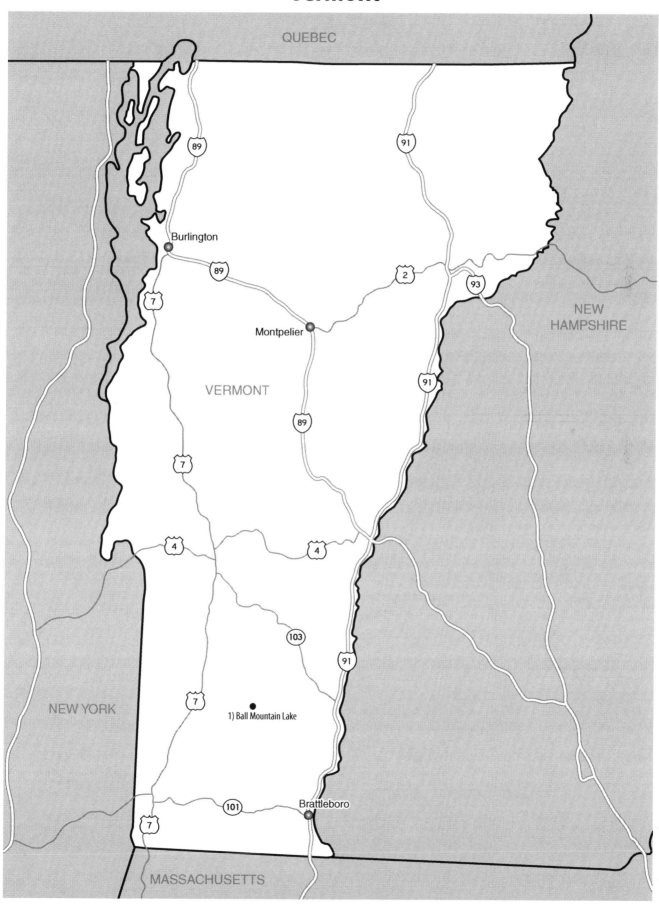

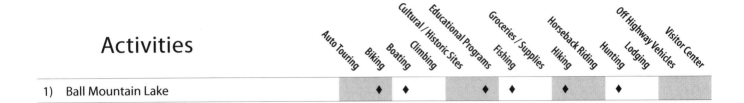

Activities	Auto Touring	Biking	Boating	Climbing	Cultural/Historic Sites	Educational Programs	Fishing	Groceries/Supplies	Hiking	Horseback Riding	Hunting	Off Highway Vehicles	Lodging	Visitor Center
1) Ball Mountain Lake		♦	♦			♦	♦		♦		♦			

Vermont Projects

1) Ball Mountain Lake

U.S. Army Corps of Engineers
88 Ball Mountain Ln
Jamaica, VT 05343
Phone: 802-874-4881
District: New England

The 75-acre lake surrounded by 965 land acres is located some 30 miles northwest of Brattleboro in southern Vermont. The project is a popular destination for outdoor recreation in summer and winter. From Brattleboro, travel north on SR-30 to the town of Jamaica and follow signs to the dam and project office.

On two weekends each year (in April and September) Ball Mountain Dam releases water for whitewater rafting, canoeing and kayaking. The camping area is nestled in the Green Mountains along the Winhall Brook. Interpretive programs are presented by park rangers in the campground amphitheater.

RV Camping

Winhall Brook: Apr-Oct, 25 sites with electric hookups and 86 basic sites, $18-$22. Most sites are streamside. **Amenities**: Drinking water, dump station, restrooms, showers, swimming, hiking trails, biking, fishing, hunting, amphitheater, educational programs, ball field, playground, volleyball and basketball courts. **Directions**: Located about 5 miles north of the Ball Mountain Dam. From Brattleboro, VT, take SR-30 north to Rt-100. Go 2.5 miles north on Rt-100 to Winhall Station Rd, then 1 mile to the campground. 919 Winhall Station Rd, South Londonderry, VT 05155 / 802-874-4881. **GPS**: 43.16333, -72.80972

Virginia

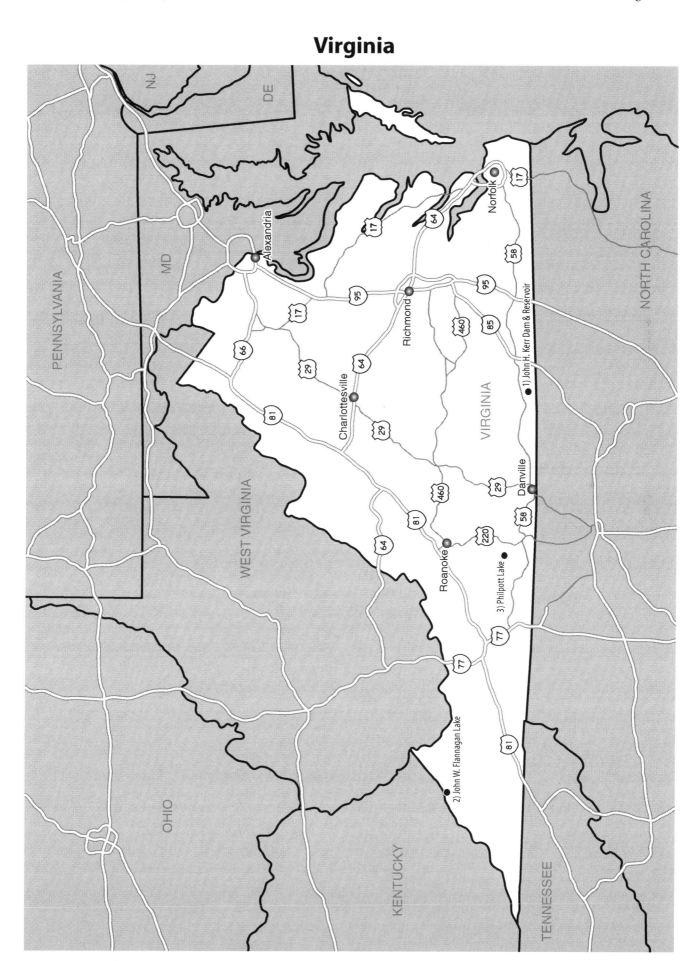

Activities

	Auto Touring	Biking	Boating	Climbing	Cultural/Historic Sites	Educational Programs	Fishing	Groceries/Supplies	Hiking	Horseback Riding	Hunting	Lodging	Off Highway Vehicles	Visitor Center
1) John H. Kerr Dam & Reservoir			♦	♦			♦	♦	♦		♦			♦
2) John W. Flannagan Lake				♦			♦		♦		♦			
3) Philpott Lake			♦	♦			♦		♦		♦			♦

Virginia Projects

1) John H. Kerr Dam & Reservoir

U.S. Army Corps of Engineers
1930 Mays Chapel Rd
Boydton, VA 23917
Phone: 434-738-6143
District: Wilmington

The project, with 50,000 water acres, 70,000 land acres and 900 miles of wooded, cove-studded shoreline, stretches across the VA/NC state line. The Visitor Center, adjacent to the dam next to North Bend Park, is open on weekdays. The Tanner Environmental Education Center is just down the road at the intersection of Mays Chapel Road & Route 4 (which leads across the dam). The Tanner Center is open Thursday to Sunday, Memorial Day through Labor Day. From Richmond, take I-85 south to Exit 12, then US-58 west to SR-4 south to the dam and Visitor Center.

There are 30 recreation areas at the project. The reservoir is widely known for bass fishing. Boat ramps and fishing piers are conveniently located throughout. Ranger programs are presented in season at North Bend campground.

RV CAMPING

Five Corps campgrounds as well as Virginia State Parks and North Carolina State Parks are available for RV camping.

Buffalo Park: May-Sep, 12 sites with 50amp hookups, $15. **Amenities**: Drinking water, dump station, restrooms, showers, boat ramp, fishing, playground, swimming. **Directions**: From Clarksville, VA, travel 8 miles west on US-58 to Buffalo Springs Rd (SR-1501) to Carters Point Rd. 434-738-6143. **GPS**: 36.66194, -78.63139

Longwood Park: Apr-Oct, 33 sites with electric (some 50amp) hookups and 33 basic sites, $18-$24. Gates close at 11pm. **Amenities**: Drinking water, dump station, restrooms, showers, boat ramp, swimming, playground. **Directions**: From Clarksville, VA, take US-15 south about 5 miles, follow signs. 13500 Hwy 15, Clarksville, VA 23927 / 434-738-6143 or 434-374-2711. **GPS**: 36.57722, -78.55139

North Bend: Apr-Oct, 138 sites with electric hookups and 107 basic sites, $18-$24. Gates close at 11pm. **Amenities**: Drinking water, dump station, restrooms, showers, fishing dock, boat ramp, fishing, hiking, interpretive trail, swimming, playground. **Directions**: From South Hill, VA, take US-58 west to SR-4 (Buggs Island Rd) and follow for 6 miles and bear right at the dam to the park entrance. 64 North Bend Dr, Boydton, VA 23917 / 434-738-0059. **GPS**: 36.58833, -78.32583

Rudds Creek: Apr-Oct, 74 sites with electric (50amp) hookups and 25 basic sites, $18-$24. Gates close at 11pm. **Amenities**: Drinking water, dump station, restrooms, showers, boat ramp, fishing, playground, interpretive trails, swimming. **Directions**: From Boydton, VA, travel 2 miles west on US-58 and follow signs into the recreation area. 160 Hwy 58, Boydton, VA 23917 / 434-738-6827 or 434-738-6143. **GPS**: 36.65528, -78.44028

2) John W. Flannagan Lake

U.S. Army Corps of Engineers
Rt 1 Box 268
Haysi, VA 24256
Phone: 276-835-9544
District: Huntington

Located in the Cumberland Mountains on the Kentucky state line, the 1,145 acre lake is northwest of the town of Haysi. The project lands adjoin the Jefferson National Forest. From US-460 take SR-80 into Haysi. Take VA-63, VA-614 and VA-739 (7 miles), to the dam, follow signs. The project office and Visitor Center are located at the dam.

Boat ramps are conveniently located and a marina has docking facilities and supplies.

RV CAMPING

Cranesnest: May-Sep, 25 sites with electric hookups, all non-reservables, $10-$12. **Amenities**: Drinking water, dump station, restrooms, showers, boat ramp, playground. **Directions**: From Clintwood go 2 miles southeast on SR-83, then north. 276-835-9544.

Lower Twin: May-Sep, 15 sites with electric hookups, 17 basic sites, all non-reservables, $10-$12. **Amenities**: Drinking water, dump station, restrooms, showers, boat ramp, playground, interpretive hiking trails, amphitheater. **Directions**: From SR-739, go 3 miles west on SR-611 and exit southeast on SR-683. 276-835-9544.

Pound River: May-Sep, 23 sites, with electric hookups, all non-reservables, $10-$12. **Amenities**: Drinking water, dump station, restrooms, showers, boat ramp, playground. **Directions**: From Clintwood go .2 mile west on SR-83, then 2 miles north on SR-631. 276-835-9544.

3) Philpott Lake

U.S. Army Corps of Engineers
1058 Philpott Dam Rd
Bassett, VA 24055
Phone: 276-629-2703
District: Wilmington

Philpott Lake is located south of Roanoke, northwest of Martinsville, and west of US-220. Over 6,000 acres of surrounding land, 3,000 acres of water and a power plant make up the Philpott project. From Roanoke, go south on US-220 to the Bassett, Virginia, exit. Travel west on VA-57 for about 6 miles to Philpott Dam Road. Look for the brown directional sign and turn right, 1 mile to the Visitor Assistance Center which is open daily 9-5, April to October. An overlook at Philpott Park gives visitors a spectacular view of the lake and the Blue Ridge Mountains.

RV CAMPING

Goose Point: Apr-Oct, 53 sites with electric (50amp) and 10 basic sites, some pull thrus, $18-$22. **Amenities**: Drinking water, dump station, restrooms, showers, boat ramp, fishing pier, swimming, playground, amphitheater. **Directions**: From US-220 take the Bassett, VA, exit onto VA-57 and go about 10 miles to Goose Point Rd (follow brown directional sign). Turn right and go 5 miles on the paved park road. 276-629-1847. **GPS**: 36.80389, -80.05722

Horseshoe Point: May-Sep, 15 sites with electric and 34 basic sites, some pull thrus, $20-$25. **Amenities**: Drinking water, dump station, restrooms, showers, boat ramp, swimming, playground. **Directions**: The park is located in a rural and sparsely populated part of Franklin County near the small community of Henry. From US-220, turn onto Henry Rd (SR-605) and go 8 miles. Turn left onto Horseshoe Point Rd, follow signs. 3950 Horseshoe Point Rd, Henry, VA 24102 / 540-365-7385. **GPS**: 36.83306, -80.06333

Jamison Mill: Apr-Oct, 5 sites with electric hookups and 4 basic sites, some pull thrus, non-reservable, $18-$21. **Amenities**: Drinking water, dump station, restrooms, showers, hiking. **Directions**: From Henry, VA, travel 5 miles northwest on CR-605, then 2 miles south on CR-778. 276-629-2703.

Salthouse Branch: Apr-Oct, 45 sites with electric (some 50amp) and 47 basic sites, $20-$25. **Amenities**: Drinking water, dump station, restrooms, showers, boat ramp, interpretive trail, swimming, playground, amphitheater. **Directions**: From US-220, turn onto Henry Rd (SR-605), go 6 miles, turn left onto Knob Church Rd, go 2 miles and turn left onto the Salthouse Branch access road. 620 Salthouse Branch Rd, Henry, VA 24102 / 540-365-7005. **GPS**: 36.81361, -80.04

Washington

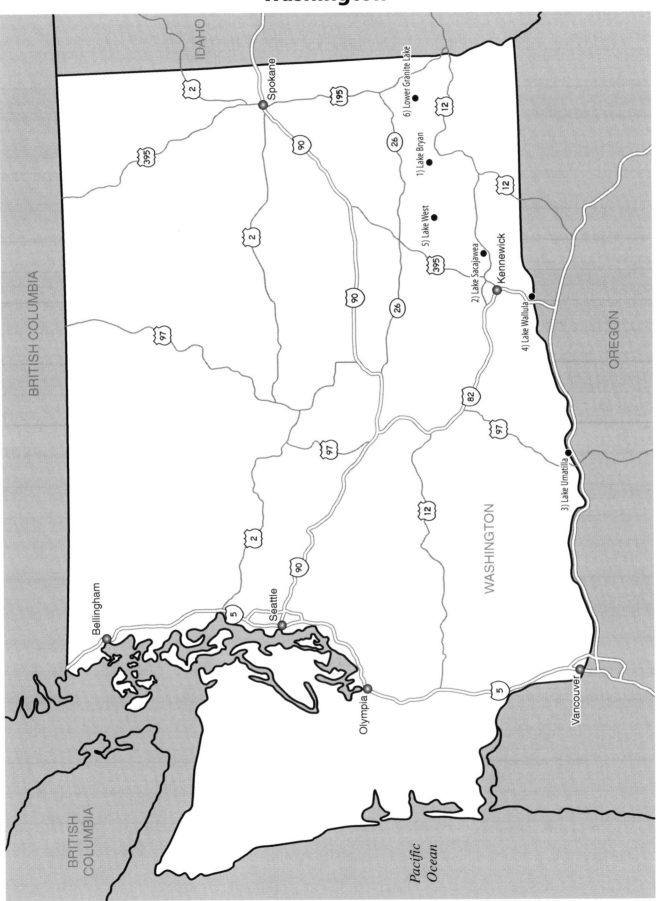

Activities

	Auto Touring	Biking	Boating	Climbing	Cultural / Historic Sites	Educational Programs	Fishing	Groceries / Supplies	Hiking	Horseback Riding	Hunting	Lodging	Off Highway Vehicles	Visitor Center
1) Lake Bryan			♦				♦		♦		♦	♦		♦
2) Lake Sacajawea			♦		♦	♦	♦	♦	♦		♦			♦
3) Lake Umatilla			♦				♦		♦					
4) Lake Wallula	♦		♦		♦	♦	♦		♦			♦		♦
5) Lake West			♦			♦	♦		♦		♦			♦
6) Lower Granite Lake	♦	♦	♦		♦	♦	♦		♦			♦		♦

Washington Projects

1) Lake Bryan

U.S. Army Corps of Engineers
100 Fair St
Clarkston, WA 99403
Phone: 509-751-0240
District: Walla Walla

Lake Bryan and Little Goose Dam are located just west of the Lower Granite area. The lake is in a remote part of the Lower Snake River and the landscape features steep canyon walls and few trees. The lake is 45 miles north of Walla Walla and 8 miles northeast of Starbuck. A Visitor Center is on the south end of the dam – follow the Little Goose Dam access road north out of the town of Starbuck. Lake Bryan is a popular destination for fishing and hunting and semi-primitive camping.

RV Camping

The three Corps-managed camping areas listed below are all primitive. Full-service campgrounds with RV hookups are at the nearby Boyer Park & Marina and Central Ferry State Park.

Illia Landing: All year, free primitive camping, non-reservable. *Amenities*: Drinking water, restrooms, fishing pier, boat ramp. *Directions*: From the Lower Granite Dam, go 3 miles west on Almota Ferry Rd. 509-751-0240.

Little Goose Landing: All year, free primitive camping, non-reservable. *Amenities*: Drinking water, restrooms, fishing pier, boat ramp. *Directions*: From the town of Starbuck, go 9 miles northeast on Little Goose Dam Rd. 509-751-0240.

Willow Landing: All year, free primitive camping, non-reservable. *Amenities*: Restrooms, dock, boat ramp. *Directions*: From Central Ferry State Park go 1 mile south on Hwy-127, then 4 miles east on Deadman Rd and 5 miles north on Hasting Hill Rd. 509-751-0240.

2) Lake Sacajawea

U.S. Army Corps of Engineers
2330 Monument Dr
Burbank, WA 99323
Phone: 509-547-2048 or 509-547-7781
District: Walla Walla

Lake Sacajawea is formed by the Ice Harbor Dam and is the first of the reservoir/lakes in the Lower Snake River Project in southeastern Washington. The lake stretches for 31 miles between the Ice Harbor Lock & Dam northward to the Lower Monumental Lock & Dam. To reach the Visitor Center from Burbank, travel east on SR-124 for 5.5 miles, then 2.5 miles north on Monument Dr. The Visitor Center is on the south end of the dam and features a fish viewing room and exhibits on the early inhabitants of the region. It is open daily April through October.

The lake has great appeal to boaters and anglers and the white sandy beaches are an attractive feature. Ranger programs are presented in season at the Charbonneau amphitheater.

RV Camping

Charbonneau: Apr-Oct, 15 full hookup and 39 sites with electric and some water hookups, $18-$28, some pull thrus. All sites are paved and shaded. *Amenities*: Drinking water, dump station, restrooms, showers, boat ramp, playground, swimming, volleyball courts, public marina. *Directions*: From

Pasco, WA, take US-12 east. After crossing the Snake River Bridge, take the next left onto SR-124. Travel east on 124 through Burbank WA and pass the turnoff to the Visitor Center, continue eastbound on SR-124 and turn left, heading north on Sun Harbor Dr. Follow Sun Harbor Dr for 1.5 miles, then turn left on Charbonneau Rd. 642 Campground Rd, Burbank, WA 99323 / 509-547-2048. *GPS*: 46.25556, -118.84472

Fishhook Park: May-Sep, 42 sites with electric & some with water hookups, 10 tent sites, $14-$22. *Amenities*: Drinking water, dump station, restrooms, showers, boat ramp, fishing, boating, swimming, playground. *Directions*: From Pasco, WA, take US-12 east and, after crossing the Snake River Bridge, go east on SR-124 for 19 miles, then left (north) on Fishhook Park Rd for 4 miles. 4562 Fishhook Park Rd, Prescott, WA 99348 / 509-547-2048. *GPS*: 46.315, -118.76611

Lake Emma: All year, free primitive camping, non-reservable. *Amenities*: No services, open for fishing and hunting. *Directions*: From Pasco, follow Pasco Kahlotus Rd northeast for 15.3 miles; turn right on Murphy Rd 3.7 miles. 509-547-2048.

Matthews: All year, free limited primitive camping area, non-reservable. *Amenities*: Restrooms, boat ramp, fishing pier. *Directions*: From Burbank, travel 26 miles east on Hwy-124, then 8.6 miles north on Lyons Ferry Rd to Clyde, 15.2 miles north (left) on Lower Monumental Rd, go left 1 mile before the dam, then east 1 mile. 509-547-2048.

Walker: All year, free limited primitive camping area, non-reservable. *Amenities*: No services, fishing, hunting, birding, wildlife viewing. *Directions*: From Burbank, travel 26 miles east on Hwy-124, then 8.6 miles north on Lyons Ferry Rd to Clyde, then 4 miles northwest (left) on Lower Monumental Rd, then 9.2 miles west on Wooden Rd. 509-547-2048.

3) Lake Umatilla

U.S. Army Corps of Engineers
P.O. Box 564
The Dalles, OR 97058
Phone: 541-296-1181
District: Portland

John Day Dam and Lake Umatilla is 216 miles upstream from the mouth of the Columbia River and is located at Exit 109 off I-84 in northern Oregon. The project consists of a navigation lock, spillway, powerhouse and fish passage facilities on both shores of the 76-mile long lake. Water recreation is plentiful on the John Day River and along the lake.

RV CAMPING

Corps-managed campgrounds are on both the Oregon and Washington sides of Lake Umatilla and are listed in their respective state sections of this guide.

Cliffs: All year, free primitive camping, non-reservable. *Amenities*: Restrooms, boat ramp. *Directions*: Park is located near the dam, 7 miles east of US-97 along SR-14. 541-296-1181.

Plymouth: Apr-Oct, 16 full hookup sites, 16 sites with electric (some 50amp) hookups, $18-$24. *Amenities*: Drinking water, dump station, restrooms, shower, laundry, boat launch, swimming, playground, fishing. *Directions*: The campground is nestled in the high desert along the Columbia River. From Kennewick, WA, go south on I-82 to Exit 131; west .7 mile on SR-14; south .7 mile on Plymouth Rd; west .3 mile on Christie Rd. 541-506-7816. *GPS*: 45.93167, -119.34833

4) Lake Wallula

U.S. Army Corps of Engineers
82925 Devore Rd
Umatilla, OR 97882
Phone: 509-547-2048
District: Walla Walla

Lake Wallula was formed by McNary Lock & Dam on the WA/OR border. It is located along the Columbia River in eastern Washington. The Visitor Center is 1 mile northeast of Umatilla and features interpretive displays and fish viewing rooms.

On the northern sector of the lake, near the junction of US-12 & US-730 is an area known as Wallula Gap, where the canyon narrows. The Gap is the site of colorful Indian lore and is a place where interesting natural phenomenon occurred during an ancient catastrophic event known as the Great Missoula Floods. Ranger programs in season are presented in the campground amphitheater. The campground is convenient to the Tri Cities where there are shopping malls and other activities. The McNary National Wildlife Refuge is next to Hood Park.

RV CAMPING

Hood Park: May-Sep, 68 paved and shady sites with electric (some 50amp) and some water hookups, $11-$22. *Amenities*: Drinking water, dump station, restrooms, showers, boat ramp, fishing, hiking, swimming, playground, horseshoes, basketball. *Directions*: From Pasco, WA, take US-12 east. After crossing the Snake River Bridge, take the next left at the junction of SR-124 to the park entrance. 592 Hood Circle, Burbank, WA 99323 / 509-547-2048. *GPS*: 46.21372, -119.013

5) Lake West

U.S. Army Corps of Engineers
5520 Devil's Canyon Rd
Kahlotus, WA 99335
Phone: 509-282-3219
District: Walla Walla

The second reservoir of the four major locks & dams of the Lower Snake River Project, Lake West consists of 6,590 water acres. It is nestled in a remote section of the river where visitors can enjoy the scenic surrounding countryside. A Visitor Center is on the northwest end of the dam. Travel 41.5 miles northeast of Pasco, Washington, on the Pasco-Kahlotus Hwy, go 6 miles south on Devil's Canyon Road. At the Lower Monumental Lock & Dam, visitors can watch barge traffic pass through the 100-foot tall navigation locks.

RV Camping

Primitive camping is offered at three Corps-managed areas. Full service camping is available at Lyons Ferry Marina.

Ayer Boat Basin: All year, free primitive camping, non-reservable. *Amenities*: Restrooms, boat ramp, fishing pier. *Directions*: From Burbank, travel 26 miles east on SR-124, then 24 miles north through Clyde and Pleasant View to Ayers, follow signs. 509-282-3219.

Devils Bench: All year, 6 primitive campsites, free, non-reservable. *Amenities*: Restrooms, boat ramp, fishing pier. *Directions*: From Kahlotus, go south on SR-263 for 6 miles. 509-282-3219.

Riparia: All year, free primitive camping area, non-reservable. *Amenities*: Restrooms. *Directions*: From Little Goose Dam, go 3 miles west on North Shore Rd. 509-282-3219.

6) Lower Granite Lake

U. S. Army Corps of Engineers
885 Almota Ferry Rd
Pomeroy, WA 99403
Phone: 509-843-1493
District: Walla Walla

Lower Granite Lake is located in deep southeastern Washington along the Lower Snake and Clearwater Rivers near the Washington/Idaho border at Clarkson, Washington, and Lewiston, Idaho. A Visitor Center at the dam features a fish viewing room that allows visitors an up-close look at the many species of fish in the Lower Snake River, as well as movies and interactive displays. To reach the dam from Pomeroy, go west on US-12 to SR-127 to Lower Deadman Road, then east to the dam. Maps and information about camping and area attractions are available. The dam and lake are in the heart of the Lewis & Clark expedition area. Nez Perce Historical Park is about 10 miles east of Lewiston on US-12.

The lake adjoins the towns of Clarkson, Washington, and Lewiston, Idaho, where a series of 22 levees have been designated as the Clearwater & Snake River National Recreation Trail for walking, bicycling and running. Sightseeing, shopping and restaurants are in the area. Golf is nearby.

RV Camping

The three Corps-managed camping areas listed here are all primitive camping areas and are managed by the Corps of Engineers Clarkston Resources Office, 100 Fair St, Clarkston, Washington. Sites with hookups for RVs can be found at Hells Gate State Park (on the Idaho side of the historic Lewis & Clark area) and at private RV parks on the Washington side.

Blyton Landing: All year, free primitive camping, non-reservable. *Amenities*: Restrooms, fishing pier, boat ramp. *Directions*: From Lewiston, Idaho, go 20 miles west on CR-9000 (North Shore Snake River Rd). 509-751-0240.

Chief Timothy Park: 25 full hookup and 9 electric-only sites (some 50amp), 28 basic sites, some pull thrus, 4 camping cabins with electric, $23-$29, $63 for cabins. *Amenities*: Drinking water, restrooms, dump station, showers, boating, canoeing, dock, fishing, kayaking, playground, swimming, volleyball, horseshoes, jet skiing, wind surfing. *Directions*: The campground is located at 13766 Highway 12, eight miles west of Clarkston. *GPS*: 46.41667, -117.1875

Nisqually John Landing: All year, free primitive camping, non-reservable. *Amenities*: Restrooms, fishing pier, boat ramp. *Directions*: From Lewiston, ID, go 15 miles west on CR-9000 (North Snake River Rd). 509-751-0240.

Wawawai Landing: All year, free primitive camping, non-reservable. *Amenities*: Restrooms, fishing pier, boat ramp. *Directions*: From Lewiston, ID, go 28 miles west on CR-9000 (North Snake River Rd) –or– 19 miles southwest of Pullman on Wawawai Rd. 509-751-0240.

West Virginia

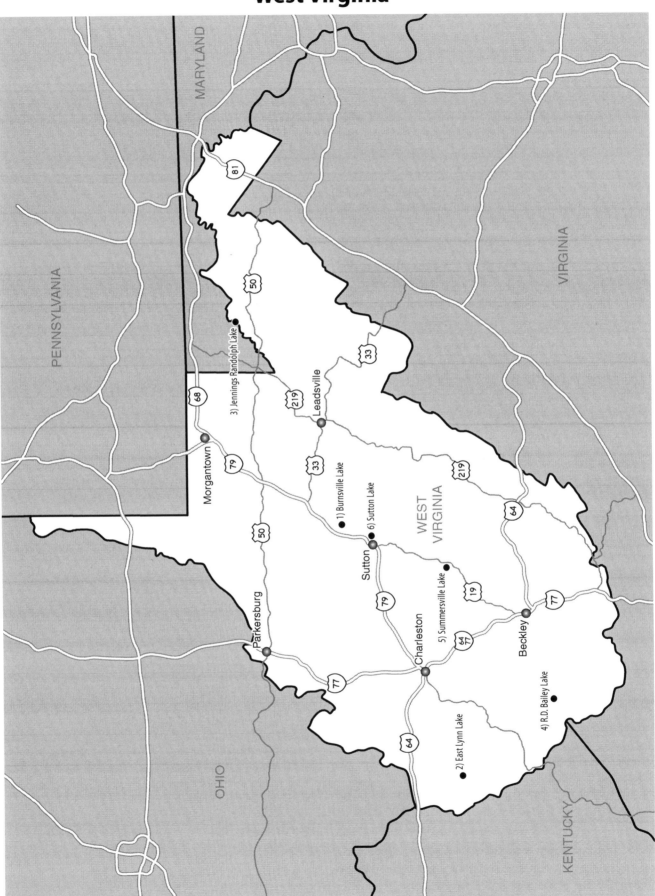

MARYLAND

PENNSYLVANIA

VIRGINIA

OHIO

KENTUCKY

WEST VIRGINIA

81

50

3) Jennings Randolph Lake

68

Morgantown

79

Leadsville

219

33

33

1) Burnsville Lake

6) Sutton Lake

Sutton

219

64

50

79

Parkersburg

Charleston

5) Summersville Lake

19

64
77

77

Beckley

77

4) R.D. Bailey Lake

64

2) East Lynn Lake

Activities

	Auto Touring	Biking	Boating	Climbing	Cultural / Historic Sites	Educational Programs	Fishing	Groceries / Supplies	Hiking	Horseback Riding	Hunting	Lodging	Off Highway Vehicles	Visitor Center
1) Burnsville Lake	♦		♦		♦		♦	♦	♦	♦	♦	♦		♦
2) East Lynn Lake	♦	♦	♦				♦		♦		♦		♦	♦
3) Jennings Randolph Lake	♦		♦		♦		♦	♦	♦		♦	♦		
4) R.D. Bailey Lake		♦	♦				♦		♦	♦	♦			♦
5) Summersville Lake	♦	♦	♦	♦	♦		♦		♦		♦	♦		
6) Sutton Lake	♦	♦	♦				♦		♦	♦	♦			♦

West Virginia Projects

1) Burnsville Lake

U.S. Army Corps of Engineers
HC 10 Box 24
Burnsville, WV 26335
Phone: 304-853-2371
District: Huntington

The 968-acre lake is located northeast of Charleston, just east of I-79 at Exit 79. It is on the Little Kanawha River three miles north of Burnsville. From I-79 Exit 79, follow CR-5 east 2.8 miles to the Visitor Center. Wildlife viewing is excellent at the project.

Boat rentals and supplies are available at the marina. The Bulltown Historical Village gives visitors a chance to see pioneer life during the Civil War era. Civil War re-enactments are held.

RV CAMPING

Bulltown: May-Sep, 124 full hookup and 71 electric-only sites, $22-$26. **Amenities**: Drinking water, dump station, restrooms, showers, boating, biking, hiking, hunting, horseback riding trails, wildlife viewing, interpretive trail, swimming, playground, horseshoes, basketball. **Directions**: From I-79 Exit 67 (Flatwoods), go north on US-19 for 10 miles and follow signs to the campground. 2550 South Main St, Burnsville, WV 26335 / 304-452-8006. **GPS**: 38.79167, -80.56639

Rifle Run: Apr-Nov, 54 full hookup sites and 6 primitive tent sites, $12-$26, all nonreservables. **Amenities**: Drinking water, restrooms, dump station, playground. Boat ramp and marina are located at the Rifle Run Day Use area. **Directions**: From I-79 Exit 79, go east on CR-5 for 3 miles. 304-853-2583 or 304-853-2371.

2) East Lynn Lake

U.S. Army Corps of Engineers
HC 85 Box 35-C
East Lynn, WV 25512
Phone: 304-849-2355
District: Huntington

The project, located south of Huntington near the Kentucky state line, covers 25,000 acres of land and water. The lake is on the Twelvepole Creek, 12 miles south of the town of Wayne. From Huntington, travel south on SR-152 to Wayne, then take SR-37 to the lake office and Visitor Center. Trail maps and information are available.

The Environmental Interpretive Center is located at the Overlook area. It features wildlife exhibits.

RV CAMPING

East Fork: May-Oct, 166 sites with electric hookups, $18-$22. **Amenities**: Drinking water, dump station, restrooms, showers, boat ramp, fishing dock, swimming, nature trail, horseshoes, basketball & volleyball courts, playground. **Directions**: From Huntington, I-64 Exit 8, go south on SR-152 to Wayne, then east on SR-37 for 19 miles, follow signs. 304-849-5000 or 304-849-2355. **GPS**: 38.09972, -82.31778

3) Jennings Randolph Lake

U.S. Army Corps of Engineers

P.O. Box 247
Elk Garden, WV 26717
Phone: 304-355-2346
District: Baltimore

The project, with a total of 4,500 acres of land and water, is located on the North Branch Potomac River in Garrett County, Maryland, on the West Virginia state line. From Cumberland, Maryland, travel south on US-220 then west on US-50, then north on WV-42 to WV-46 east, follow project signs.

There is an excellent trout stream at the project. Several whitewater releases are done each year when rafters put in to enjoy an 8-mile ride downstream. Along the way they pass through a wilderness area filled with history and natural beauty. A resident pair of Bald Eagles has been breeding at the lake since the late 1990's and they usually fledge two young a year.

RV Camping

Robert W. Craig Campground: Apr-Sep, 81 sites with electric hookups, $18-$22. **Amenities**: Drinking water, dump station, restrooms, showers, interpretive trail, playground, general store. **Directions**: From Cumberland, MD, take US-220 south to US-50 west to WV-42 north, then north to WV-46 east, follow signs. 304-355-2346. **GPS**: 39.41677, -79.11611

4) R.D. Bailey Lake

U.S. Army Corps of Engineers
Drawer 70 US Route 52
North Justice, WV 24851
Phone: 304-664-3229
District: Huntington

This beautiful 1,005-acre lake is in the rugged terrain of deep southwestern West Virginia. The dam is on the Guyandotte River near the town of Justice. From Justice go east on US-52 and turn left at the R.D. Bailey sign.

The Visitor Center overlooks the lake and provides a breathtaking view of the dam, lake and surrounding forest. Viewing telescopes are mounted on the observation deck. The Center is open on weekdays. A marina is at the lake. Golf is nearby.

RV Camping

Guyandotte: May-Sep, 94 sites with 50amp electric hookups, some pull thrus, non-reservable, $16-$14. Campsites are spread along a scenic 6-mile stretch of the Guyandotte River; the campground is divided into four sections. **Amenities**: Drinking water, restrooms, showers, laundry, boat ramp, playground. **Directions**: From Justice, go east 2.6 miles on US-52; turn left on SR-97 and follow for 5.4 miles. 304-664-3229 or 304-664-9587. **GPS**: 37.5910, -81.7170

5) Summersville Lake

U.S. Army Corps of Engineers
2981 Summersville Lake Rd
Summersville, WV 26651
Phone: 304-872-3412
District: Huntington

Summersville is the largest lake in central West Virginia. It is located 69 miles east of Charleston. From I-79 Exit 57, travel south on US-19. At Mount Nebo take SR-129 west for 3 miles to the project office at the dam.

The project is noted for its spectacular cliffs and whitewater on the river. Technical rock climbing and whitewater rafting are available year-round nearby, with whitewater releases below the dam on the Gauley River in September and October. A marine and dive shop is located on the lake. Shopping and restaurants are in Summersville. Civil War historic sites are nearby.

RV Camping

Battle Run: May-Oct, 107 sites with electric and some water hookups, 7 primitive tent sites, $16-$24. **Amenities**: Drinking water, dump station, restrooms, showers, laundry, boat ramp, fishing dock, swimming, playground, hiking and biking trails. **Directions**: Located 5 miles south of Summersville. From US-19 go 4 miles west on SR-129, follow signs. 304-872-3459. **GPS**: 38.22167, -80.90972

6) Sutton Lake

U.S. Army Corps of Engineers
P.O. Box 426
Sutton, WV 26601
Phone: 304-765-2816
District: Huntington

The project is located 70 miles north of Charleston in the wooded hills of central West Virginia. There are 1,440 water acres and 20,000 land acres. The lake winds 14 miles along the Elk River with many coves along the 45 miles of shoreline. From I-79 Exit 64, take the Sutton/Gassaway exit, go north on SR-4 and follow signs to Sutton Dam. The project office is at the dam, 1 mile east of Sutton.

Local attractions include a riding stable, canoe livery, outlet mall and bowling alley. There is a marina at the lake.

RV Camping

Bakers Run – Mill Creek: May-Oct, 79 sites with electric hookups, some pull thrus, non-reservable, $12-$14. **Amenities**: Drinking water, dump station, restrooms, showers, boat ramp, playground, swimming, hunting. **Directions**: From I-79 Exit 62, go 2 miles to Sutton, then 4 miles south on old US-19 (CR-19/40), then 12 miles east on CR-17. 304-765-2816 or 304-765-5631.

Bee Run: May-Dec, 12 sites, no hookups, all pull thrus, non-reservable, $5, 20-foot RV length limit. **Amenities**: Drinking water, restrooms. **Directions**: From I-79 Exit 67, go 1 mile east on SR-4, then 1.2 miles east on SR-15, turn right. 304-765-2816.

Gerald Freeman Campground: May-Dec, 74 sites with electric hookups and 85 basic sites (some have water hookups), $16-$22. **Amenities**: Drinking water, dump station, restrooms, showers, laundry, boat ramp, fishing, hiking, hunting, horseshoe pit, basketball courts, wildlife viewing, marina. **Directions**: From I-79 Exit 67, turn right on SR-4 and go 1 mile, then left on SR-15 and follow for 12 miles to the camping area. 304-765-2816 or 304-765-7756. **GPS**: 38.6766, -80.5473

Wisconsin

Activities

	Auto Touring	Biking	Boating	Climbing	Cultural / Historic Sites	Educational Programs	Fishing	Groceries / Supplies	Hiking	Horseback Riding	Hunting	Lodging	Off Highway Vehicles	Visitor Center
1) Eau Galle Reservoir	♦		♦				♦		♦	♦				
2) Mississippi River Camping	♦		♦				♦		♦					

Wisconsin Projects

1) Eau Galle Reservoir

U.S. Army Corps of Engineers
P.O. Box 190
W500 Eau Galle Dam Rd
Spring Valley, WI 54767
Phone: 715-778-5562
District: St. Paul

This 150-acre lake is surrounded by recreation areas including the campground, beach, hiking and equestrian trails and boat launches. The project is located just north of Spring Valley, Wisconsin, and 50 miles east of Minneapolis, Minnesota. Local attractions, sightseeing and shopping are nearby. Golf courses, gift stores and other attractions are nearby.

RV Camping

Highland Ridge: Apr-Dec, 33 sites with electric hookups, 10 basic sites and 10 non-electric equestrian sites, some pull thrus, $16-$24. *Amenities*: Drinking water, dump station, restrooms, showers (fee), boat ramp, fishing, hiking, interpretive trail, swimming, playground. *Directions*: From I-94 Exit 24, take CR-B south about 2 miles. Go east on CR-N for 2 miles, then south on CR-NN, follow signs. 715-778-5562. *GPS*: 44.8725, -92.2432

2) Mississippi River Camping
    a) DeSoto - Blackhawk Park
    b) Potosi - Grant River

U.S. Army Corps of Engineers
District: Rock Island (309-794-4522)
District: St. Paul (507-895-6341)

Of the 15 Corps-managed campgrounds that dot the shoreline along the upper Mississippi River, two are in Wisconsin: Grand River Campground in Potosi and Blackhawk Park in De Soto.

Fishing and boating are major attractions of Mississippi River camping. Watching river traffic is a popular pastime. Historic sites can be found along the river as well as scenic drives.

RV Camping

2a) De Soto - Blackhawk Park (COE Pool 9)

Blackhawk Park: Apr-Nov, 75 sites with electric (some 50amp) and 100 basic sites, $24. *Amenities*: Drinking water, dump station, restrooms, showers (coin-operated), interpretive trails, swimming, boat ramps, playground, volleyball, horseshoe pits. *Directions*: From LaCrosse, WI, go 25 miles south on Hwy-35 and turn right on CR-B1. E590 County Rd Bl, Desoto, WI 54624 / 507-895-6341. *GPS*: 43.46083, -91.22306

2b) Potosi - Grant River (COE Lock & Dam 11)

Grant River Campground: Apr-Oct, 63 sites with 50amp electric hookups and 10 tent sites, $10-$16. *Amenities*: Drinking water, dump station, restrooms, showers, boat ramp, playground. *Directions*: From Potosi, WI, go south for 2 miles on SR-133, turn left on River Lane, follow signs. 309-794-4522. *GPS*: 42.65944, -90.70972

Appendix A

About the Army Corps of Engineers

The U.S. Army Corps of Engineers is familiar to many of us from the Corps' involvement in dam construction to control river overflows, building lake reservoirs or producing hydroelectric power.

The Corps of Engineers is the steward of lands and waters at Corps water resource projects. It has responsibility for managing our nation's water resources infrastructure. The Corps systems for navigation, flood control and storm damage reduction, together with its efforts to restore aquatic ecosystems make an important contribution to the national welfare.

As a leading provider of outdoor recreation on federally-managed lands, the Corps recreation base is built primarily around the water. Consequently, the Corps has a dedicated focus on water safety. Rangers present water safety programs in season at many of the projects. Corps-developed water safety programs, materials and information are available from the Corps of Engineers at http://watersafety.usace.army.mil/

Part of the Army Corps of Engineers' charter is to open river and lakeside areas to the public and to provide recreational opportunities for fishing, boating and camping. Corps camping facilities are clean and well-maintained. The Corps operates 2,500 recreation areas at 463 projects (mostly lakes) and leases an additional 1,800 sites to state or local recreation authorities or private interests.

The Corps hosts about 360 million visits a year at its lakes, beaches and other areas and estimates that 25 million Americans (one in ten) visit a Corps project at least once a year. Supporting visitors to Corps recreation areas generates 600,000 jobs.

About Corps Projects

- Corps RV campsites generally have other basic amenities not mentioned in the individual listings such as picnic tables, lamp posts, fire rings and grills.

- Recreational opportunities are affected by high and low water marks that may impede shoreline access. Call the project office for information about current conditions.

- Fishing and hunting licenses are required in most states. Contact the state for information about hunting and fishing regulations, requirements, licensing and seasons.

- Directional signs to Corps projects are standard throughout the country. Look for the brown signs with white lettering.

- Camping fees listed are valid as of press time and are subject to change.

- Many Corps lakes have campgrounds that are not managed by the Corps, such as state parks and private concessionaires who lease space at the lake. These campgrounds generally do not accept Senior Pass or Access Pass discount cards, but it's always a good idea to ask.

- Corps campgrounds are subject to change without notice. New parks may be opened or existing parks closed or consigned to other agencies or concessionaires at any time.

- When a campground season of operation is listed as ending in September, it generally is the day after Labor Day.

Appendix B

General Rules for Corps Campgrounds

Camping

- If you are staying at a campground, you must camp only in those places specifically provided or marked.
- All vehicles, RVs and trailers must be parked on your campsite or driveway. Driving or parking off road is not permitted.
- Quiet hours are between 10pm and 6am. Please be considerate.
- Camping longer than 14 consecutive days is generally not allowed. At Corps of Engineers projects, 14 days within any 30 day period is the typical limit.
- The number of camping units per campsite varies and is set locally.

Sanitation

- Help prevent pollution by keeping garbage, litter and foreign substances out of lakes, streams and other waters.

Campfires

- Obey any restrictions on fires. Fires may be limited or prohibited at certain times.
- Within campgrounds and other recreation areas, fires may only be built in fire rings, stoves, grills or fireplaces provided for that purpose.
- Be sure your fire is completely extinguished before leaving. Do not leave your fire unattended. You are responsible for keeping fires under control.

Vehicle Operation

- Drivers must obey all traffic signs and operate their vehicles in accordance with posted regulations and applicable federal, state and local laws.
- Vehicles must be parked in designated areas only.
- Use of vehicles within campgrounds and other recreation areas is limited to entering and leaving those areas.

Pets and Animals

- Pets must be restrained or on a leash at all times while in developed recreation areas.
- Pets (except guide dogs) are not allowed in swimming areas or sanitary facilities.
- Saddle or pack animals are only allowed where authorized by posted instructions.

Fireworks

- Use of fireworks or other explosives within campgrounds and other recreation areas is prohibited.

Public Property

- Preserve and protect your Corps project areas. Leave natural areas the way you found them.
- Do not carve, chip, cut or damage any live trees.

Campsite Reservations

Recreation.gov (a private one-stop reservation service), handles all federal recreation reservations including Corps of Engineers campgrounds. Reservations may be made through this service for any of the campgrounds listed in this book (except those indicated as non-reservable.) Campgrounds or selected sites listed as non-reservable are not handled by recreation.gov; call the project office for information.

There are two ways to make campsite reservations:

- On the Internet at www.recreation.gov. You may check availability and make a reservation online anytime.

- Call toll-free 1-877-444-6777 to check availability and make reservations over the phone. Telephone hours of operation are: March 31 to October 31, 10am to midnight EST and November 1 to February 28, 10am to 10pm EST. Call Center is closed on Thanksgiving, Christmas and New Year's Day.

When making a reservation you will be asked to provide the following information:

- Campground name, project and state,
- Arrival and departure dates,
- Type of site required,
- Number of people in your party,
- Discount, if applicable, including the number on your Senior Pass or Access Pass,
- Method of payment (Visa, MasterCard, American Express, Discover).

Individual sites may be reserved up to 6 months in advance. Reserved sites will be held until checkout time on the day following your scheduled arrival. Cancellation fees will be assessed for changes, cancellations and no-shows.

Appendix C

Volunteers Are Vital

As the steward of almost 12 million acres of land and water, the U.S. Army Corps of Engineers offers many volunteer positions in recreation and natural resources management. These include:

- Campground hosting
- Visitor Center staff Park and Trail maintenance
- Presenting educational programs
- Water Safety program presenter
- Conducting interpretive tours of dam sites
- Fish and Wildlife Habitat work

Volunteers generally swap their talents and services for a free campsite and amenities. Large contingents of willing volunteers apply each year to work at Corps projects. They like the spacious and tidy campsites and the clean, well-kept appearance of the recreation areas. They enjoy being outdoors and socializing with other campers. A volunteer assignment usually lasts for a camping season, about 6 months or so, and volunteers commit to about 18-20 hours a week.

The Corps maintains a Nationwide Volunteer Clearinghouse, a toll-free hotline, and a website for individuals who are interested in offering their time and talent to the Corps. When you contact the Clearinghouse, be prepared to provide information about your interests, talents and the locations where you would like to volunteer.

The Clearinghouse is basically a matchmaker, pairing up skilled, enthusiastic workers with people at Corps projects who need their services. You can call the Clearinghouse at 1-800-865-8337 or email Volunteer.Clearinghouse@usace.army.mil to request a Point of Contact list for your area of interest. The website is www.orn.usace.army.mil/volunteer/

Appendix D

Money Saving Programs

Frequent visitors to Corps of Engineers projects can get significant savings with the America the Beautiful Senior Pass or Access Pass, recreation passes issued by the federal government. Both of these passes are honored at Corps of Engineers-managed campgrounds. The passes provide a 50 percent discount on federal use fees charged for facilities and services such as camping, swimming, parking, boat launching, and tours. In some cases where use fees are charged, only the pass signee will be given the 50 percent price reduction. It does not cover or reduce special recreation permit fees or fees charged by concessionaires.

Senior Pass

This pass is for citizens of the United States who are 62 or older. The cost for a Senior Pass is $10; proof of age must be shown. It is a lifetime entrance pass to national parks, monuments, historic sites, recreation areas, and national wildlife refuges that charge an entrance fee. The Senior Pass admits the pass signee and any accompanying passengers in a private vehicle. Senior Pass holders get 50% off camping fees at Corps-managed campgrounds.

Access Pass

This pass is for citizens of the United States who are blind or permanently disabled. The Access Pass is free; proof of

medically determined permanent disability or eligibility for receiving benefits under federal law must be shown. It is a lifetime entrance pass to national parks, monuments, historic sites, recreation areas, and national wildlife refuges that charge an entrance fee. The passport admits the pass signee and any accompanying passengers in a private vehicle. Access Pass holders get 50% off camping fees at Corps-managed campgrounds.

Where to Get A Senior Pass or Access Pass

Senior Pass or Access Pass must be obtained in person. They are available at offices of the National Park Service, Bureau of Land Management, U.S. Forest Service, U.S. Fish & Wildlife Service and Bureau of Reclamation. The Corps of Engineers honors the passes but is not authorized to issue them.

As of January 1, 2007, the America the Beautiful Senior Pass and Access Pass replaced the Golden Age and Golden Access Passports issued before 2007. However, existing Golden Age and Golden Access Passports that were issued before 2007 remain valid for the lifetime of pass holders.

Appendix E

District Offices

Albuquerque District
U.S. Army Corps of Engineers
4101 Jefferson Plaza NE
Albuquerque, NM 87109
505-342-3171
www.spa.usace.army.mil

Baltimore District
U.S. Army Corps of Engineers
P.O. Box 1715
Baltimore, MD 21203
410-962-3670
www.nab.usace.army.mil

Fort Worth District
U.S. Army Corps of Engineers
819 Taylor Street
Fort Worth, TX 76102
817-886-1326
www.swf.usace.army.mil

Huntington District
U.S. Army Corps of Engineers
502 8th Street
Huntington, WV 25701
304-399-5211
www.lrh.usace.army.mil

Jacksonville District
U.S. Army Corps of Engineers
701 San Marco Blvd
Jacksonville, FL 32207
904-232-2234
www.saj.usace.army.mil

Kansas City District
U.S. Army Corps of Engineers
700 Federal Building
601 East 12th Street
Kansas City, MO 64106
816-389-3486
www.nwk.usace.army.mil

Little Rock District
U.S. Army Corps of Engineers
Attn: PAO (CESWL-PA)
P.O. Box 867
Little Rock, AR 72203
501-324-5551
www.swl.usace.army.mil

Louisville District
U.S. Army Corps of Engineers
P.O. Box 59
Louisville, KY 40201
502-315-6766
www.lrl.usace.army.mil

Mobile District
U.S. Army Corps of Engineers
P.O. Box 2288
Mobile, AL 36628
251-690-2505
www.sam.usace.army.mil

Nashville District
U.S. Army Corps of Engineers
P.O. Box 1070
Nashville, TN 37202
615-736-7161
www.lrn.usace.army.mil

New England District

U.S. Army Corps of Engineers
696 Virginia Road
Concord, MA 01742
978-318-8238
www.nae.usace.army.mil

Omaha District
U.S. Army Corps of Engineers
106 S 15th St
Omaha, NE 68102
402-995-2417
www.nwo.usace.army.mil

Pittsburgh District
U.S. Army Corps of Engineers
William S. Moorehead Federal Bldg
1000 Liberty Avenue Room 2200
Pittsburgh, PA 15222
412-395-7500
www.lrp.usace.army.mil

Portland District
U.S. Army Corps of Engineers
P. O. Box 2946
Portland, OR 97208
503-808-4510
www.nwp.usace.army.mil

Rock Island District
U.S. Army Corps of Engineers
P.O. Box 2004
Rock Island, IL 61204
309-794-5729
www.mvr.usace.army.mil

Sacramento District
U.S. Army Corps of Engineers
1325 J Street
Sacramento, CA 95814
916-557-7461
www.spk.usace.army.mil

Saint Louis District
U.S. Army Corps of Engineers
1222 Spruce Street
St. Louis, MO 63103
314-331-8002
www.mvs.usace.army.mil

Saint Paul District
U.S. Army Corps of Engineers
190 5th Street East

St. Paul, MN 55101
651-290-5108
www.mvp.usace.army.mil

San Francisco District
U.S. Army Corps of Engineers
1455 Market St
San Francisco, CA 94103
415-503-6804
www.spn.usace.army.mil

Savannah District
U.S. Army Corps of Engineers
P.O. Box 889
Savannah, GA 31402
912-652-5279
www.sas.usace.army.mil

Seattle District
U.S. Army Corps of Engineers
P.O. Box 3755
Seattle, WA 98124
206-764-3750
www.nws.usace.army.mil

Tulsa District
U.S. Army Corps of Engineers
1645 South 101 East Ave
Tulsa, OK 74128
918-669-7342
www.swt.usace.army.mil

Vicksburg District
U.S. Army Corps of Engineers
4155 Clay Street
Vicksburg, MS 39183
601-631-5412
www.mvk.usace.army.mil

Walla Walla District
U.S. Army Corps of Engineers
201 North Third Avenue
Walla Walla, WA 99362
509-527-7020
www.nww.usace.army.mil

Wilmington District
U.S. Army Corps of Engineers
69 Darlington Ave
Wilmington, NC 28403
910-251-4000
www.saw.usace.army.mil

Index

Made in the USA
San Bernardino, CA
30 October 2017